CHOICE AND CHANCE

An Introduction to Inductive Logic

Second Edition

CHOICE

AND

CHANCE

Dickenson Publishing Company, Inc.

Encino, California and Belmont, California

An Introduction

to

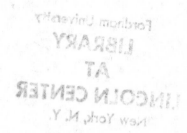

Inductive Logic

SECOND EDITION

BRIAN SKYRMS
University of Illinois, Chicago Circle

Choice and Chance:
An Introduction to Inductive Logic
Second Edition
by Brian Skyrms

ISBN-0-8221-0134-3
Library of Congress Catalog Card Number: 74-79429

Printed in the United States of America

Printing (last digit): 9 8 7 6 5 4 3 2 1

CONTENTS

IV. MILL'S METHODS OF EXPERIMENTAL INQUIRY AND THE NATURE OF CAUSALITY

V. THE PROBABILITY CALCULUS

Appendix to Chapter V: SAMPLING AND STATISTICS

VI. WHY EPISTEMIC AND INDUCTIVE PROBABILITIES ARE PROBABILITIES

VII. INTERPRETATIONS OF THE PROBABILITY CALCULUS

PREFACE TO
THE SECOND EDITION

This revised edition differs from the first edition mainly in the inclusion of a substantial amount of entirely new material (sections IV.12; IV.13; all of Chapter VI; sections VII.3 and VII.5). Almost everything in the first edition is in the second, and most of it is unchanged. Changes do occur in section I.6 and throughout Chapter II. The changes in I.6 free the exposition from reliance on the "certainty model" of knowledge and lay the groundwork for the discussion of fallibility in VI.8. Chapter II has been changed because the over-simple development of the first edition failed to give due place to the total evidence condition in the justification of induction. That is, even if we knew that inductively strong arguments gave us true conclusions from true premises most of the time, this in itself would give us no reason to prefer arguments which embody our total evidence to those which only take into account some small and possibly biased subset of it. The revised Chapter II treats the total evidence condition with more respect,* without adding much complication to the exposition. New exercises and suggested readings should show the more able student that close attention to the concerns of Chapter II leads to deep and subtle problems.

The new material fills gaps in the structure of the first edition. Section IV.12, "Sufficient Conditions and Functional Relationships," shows the relevance of Chapter IV to mathematical formulations of physical laws. Section IV.13, "Lawlike and Accidental Conditions," cautions the student that he still does not have a full analysis of causality and introduces him to the outstanding problems in this area. Sections VII.3 and VII.5, "Propensities" and "The Bayesian Interpretation," are clearly needed to complete the survey of interpretations of the probability calculus. Section VII.5 is very short, only because the whole book is more Bayesian in outlook, and the foundations for the Bayesian interpretation

---

* The need to do so was brought home to me by A. J. Ayer's "Two Notes on Probability" in *The Concept of a Person* (New York: St. Martin's Press, 1963), pp. 188-208, as was indicated in "Suggestions for Further Study," in the first edition.

have been laid in some detail, especially in Chapter VI. Chapter VI, "Why Epistemic and Inductive Probabilities *Are* Probabilities," constitutes the major addition to the book. The title of the chapter indicates a gap in the argument of the first edition—the probability calculus entered like a *deus ex machina* without any reason for believing it to be the correct representation of the intuitive probability concept. Chapter VI shows that a person who uses his probabilities to evaluate courses of action in standard ways and yet violates the rules of the probability calculus involves himself in a kind of inconsistency of appraisal—and that this inconsistency of appraisal leaves him open to a Dutch Book (a betting arrangement under which he will always sustain a net loss, no matter what the circumstances). A similar argument is given for conditionalization as a method for changing from one set of epistemic probabilities to another. The results of Chapter VI, due to Ramsey and deFinetti, form the foundation for both the Carnapian and Bayesian interpretations of the probability calculus. Although the arguments of Chapter VI may be a bit more involved than those of earlier chapters, they still require nothing more than high-school algebra and the rudiments of propositional logic developed in the first few sections of Chapter IV.

The material in the text, and the order of presentation, can be varied to suit the level and interests of the class and the taste of the instructor. Since Chapter V, "The Probability Calculus," presupposes only sections IV.1, IV.2, and IV.3, it can be attacked early in the course if desired, as in the following orders:

I, IV.1-IV.3, V, Appendix, II, III, IV

I, IV.1-IV.3, V, VI, VIII, IV, III

The sections on Mill's methods may be omitted without loss of continuity in Chapter IV.

This book can be used with collateral readings as indicated by suggestions throughout the book. The following two collections of readings are valuable for such purposes:

1. *Probabilities, Problems, and Paradoxes*, ed. Sidney Luckenbach (Belmont, Calif., Dickenson Publishing Co., 1972).
2. *Studies in Subjective Probability*, ed. Kyburg and Smokler (New York: John Wiley & Sons, Inc., 1964).

CHOICE AND CHANCE

An Introduction to Inductive Logic

Second Edition

I

PROBABILITY
AND INDUCTION

I.1 INTRODUCTION. Most people know that logic has something to do with correct reasoning and with framing compelling arguments. Many also know that there are two basic branches of logic: inductive logic and deductive logic. Fewer people know that inductive logic is somehow tied up with the concept of probability. But just what logic is, what the difference is between inductive and deductive logic, and what the relationship is between probability and induction are questions on which there is not only widespread ignorance but also widely accepted misinformation. Answers in depth to these questions can only be attained by extensive study of logic. But we can at this point give preliminary answers that will provide a perspective for the student embarking on the study of inductive logic.

I.2. ARGUMENTS. The word "argument" is used to mean several different things in the English language. We speak of two people having an argument, of one person advancing an argument, and of the value of a mathematical function as depending on the values of its arguments. One of these various senses of "argument" is selected and refined by the logician for the purposes at hand.

When we speak of a person advancing an argument, we have in mind his giving certain reasons designed to persuade us that a certain claim he is making is correct. Let us call that claim which is being argued for the *conclusion* of the argument, and the reasons advanced in support of it the *premises*. If we now abstract from the concrete situation in which one person is trying to convince others and consider the bare bones of this conception of an argument, we arrive at the following definition: An *argument* is a list of *sentences*, one of which is designated as the conclusion, and the rest of which are designated as premises.

But if we consider the matter closely, we see that this definition will not do. Questions, commands, and curses can all be expressed by sentences, but they do not make factual claims nor can they stand as reasons supporting such claims. Suppose someone said, "The Dirty Sox star

1

pitcher has just broken both his arms and legs, their catcher has glaucoma, their entire outfield has come down with bubonic plague, and their shortstop has been deported. Therefore they cannot possibly win the pennant." He would clearly be advancing an argument, to the effect that the Dirty Sox cannot win the pennant. But if someone said, "How's your sister? Stand up on the table. May you perish in unspeakable slime!" he would, whatever else he was doing, *not* be advancing an argument. That is, he would not be advancing evidence in support of a *factual claim*.

Let us call a sentence that makes a definite factual claim a *statement*. "Hannibal crossed the Alps," "Socrates was a corruptor of youth," "Every body attracts every other body with a force directly proportional to the sum of their masses and inversely proportional to the square of their distance," and "The moon is made of avocado paste" are all statements, some true, some false. We may now formulate the logician's definition of an argument:

> **Definition 1:** An argument is a list of *statements*, one of which is designated as the conclusion and the rest of which are designated as premises.

In ordinary speech we seldom come right out and say, "A, B, C are my premises and D is my conclusion." However, there are several "indicator words" that are commonly used in English to point out which statement is the conclusion and which are the premises. The word "therefore" signals that the premises have been run through, and that the conclusion is about to be presented (as in the Dirty Sox example). The words "thus," "consequently," "hence," "so," and the phrase "it follows that" function in exactly the same way.

In ordinary discourse the conclusion is sometimes stated first, followed by the premises advanced in support of it. In these cases, different indicator words are used. Consider the following argument: "Socrates is basically selfish, since after all Socrates is a man, and all men are basically selfish." Here the conclusion is stated first and the word "since" signals that reasons in support of that conclusion follow. The words "because" and "for" and the phrase "by virtue of the fact that" are often used in the same way. There is a variation on this mode of presenting an argument, where the word "since" or "because" is followed by a list of premises and then the conclusion; for example, "Since all men are basically selfish and Socrates is a man, Socrates is basically selfish."

These are the most common ways of stating arguments in English, but there are other ways, too numerous to catalog. However, you should have no trouble identifying the premises and conclusion of a given argument if you remember that:

> The conclusion states the point being argued for and the premises state the reasons being advanced in support of the conclusion.

Since in logic we are interested in clarity rather than in literary style, one simple, clear method of stating an argument (and indicating which statements are the premises and which the conclusion) is preferred to the rich variety of forms available in English. We will put an argument into standard logical form simply by listing the premises, drawing a line under them, and writing the conclusion under the line. For example, the argument "Diodorus was not an Eagle Scout, since Diodorus did not know how to tie a square knot and all Eagle Scouts know how to tie square knots" would be put into standard logical form as follows:

> Diodorus did not know how to tie a square knot.
> All Eagle Scouts know how to tie square knots.
> _____
> Diodorus was not an Eagle Scout.

Exercises:

1. Which of the following sentences are statements?
   a. Friends, Romans, countrymen, lend me your ears.
   b. The sum of the squares of the sides of a right triangle equals the square of the hypotenuse.
   c. Hast thou considered my servant Job, a perfect and an upright man?
   d. My name is Faust; in all things thy equal.
   e. $E = mc^2$.
   f. May he be boiled in his own pudding and buried with a stick of holly through his heart.
   g. Ptolemy maintained that the sun revolved around the Earth.
   h. Ouch!
   i. Did Sophocles write *Electra*?
   j. The sun never sets on the British Empire.
2. Which of the following selections advance arguments? Put all arguments in standard logical form.
   a. All professors are absent-minded, and since Dr. Wise is a professor he must be absent-minded.
   b. Since three o'clock this afternoon I have felt ill, and now I feel worse.
   c. Candidate X is certain to win the election because his backers have more money than do Candidate Y's, and furthermore Candidate X is more popular in the urban areas.

d. Iron will not float when put in water because the specific gravity of water is less than that of iron.
e. In the past, every instance of smoke has been accompanied by fire, so the next instance of smoke will also be accompanied by fire.

I.3. LOGIC. When we *evaluate* an argument, we are interested in two things:

i. Are the premises true?
ii. Supposing that the premises are true, what sort of support do they give to the conclusion?

The first consideration is obviously of great importance. The argument "All college students are highly intelligent, since all college students are insane, and all people who are insane are highly intelligent" is not very compelling, simply because it is a matter of common knowledge that the premises are false. But important as consideration (i) may be, it is not the business of a logician to judge whether the premises of an argument are true or false.[1] After all, any statements whatsoever can stand as premises to some argument, and the logician has no special access to all human knowledge. If the premises of an argument make a claim about the internal structure of the nucleus of the carbon atom, one is likely to get more reliable judgments as to their truth from a physicist than from a logician. If the premises claim that a certain mechanism is responsible for the chameleon's color changes, one would ask a biologist, not a logician, whether they are true.

Consideration (ii), however, is the logician's stock in trade. Supposing that the premises are true, does it follow that the conclusion must be true? Do the premises provide strong but not conclusive evidence for the conclusion? Do they provide any evidence at all for it? These are questions which it is the business of logic to answer.

Definition 2: *Logic* is the study of the strength of the evidential link between the premises and conclusions of arguments.

In some arguments the link between the premises and the conclusion is the strongest possible in that the truth of the premises *guarantees* the truth of the conclusion. Consider the following argument: "No Athenian ever drank to excess, and Alcibiades was an Athenian. Therefore, Alcibiades never drank to excess." Now if we suppose that the premises "No

---

[1] Except in certain very special cases which need not concern us here.

Athenian ever drank to excess" and "Alcibiades was an Athenian" are true, then we must also suppose that the conclusion "Alcibiades never drank to excess" is also true, for there is no way in which the conclusion could be false while the premises were true. Thus for this argument we say that the truth of the premises guarantees the truth of the conclusion, and the evidential link between premises and conclusion is as strong as possible. This is in no way altered by the fact that the first premise and the conclusion are false. What is important for evaluating the strength of the evidential link is that, *if* the premises were true, the conclusion would also have to be true.

In other arguments the link between the premises and the conclusion is not so strong, but the premises nevertheless provide some evidential support for the conclusion. Sometimes the premises provide strong evidence for the conclusion, sometimes weak evidence. In the following argument the truth of the premises does not guarantee the truth of the conclusion, but the evidential link between the premises and the conclusion is still quite strong:

> Black has confessed to killing White. Dr. Zed has signed a statement to the effect that he saw Black shoot White. A large number of witnesses heard White gasp with his dying breath, "Black did it." Therefore Black killed White.

But although the premises are good evidence for the conclusion, we know that the truth of the premises does not *guarantee* the truth of the conclusion, for *we can imagine circumstances in which the premises would be true and the conclusion false.*

> Suppose, for instance, that Black was insane and that he confessed to every murder he ever heard of, but that this fact was generally unknown because he had just moved into the neighborhood. This peculiarity was, however, known to Dr. Zed, who was White's psychiatrist. For his own malevolent reasons, Dr. Zed decided to eliminate White and frame Black. He convinced White under hypnosis that Black was a homocidal maniac bent on killing White. Then one day Dr. Zed shot White from behind a potted plant and fled.

Let it be granted that these circumstances are highly improbable. If they were not, the premises could not provide strong evidential support for the conclusion. Nevertheless the circumstances are not impossible and thus the truth of the premises does not guarantee the truth of the conclusion.

The following is an argument in which the premises provide some evidence for the conclusion, but in which the evidential link between the premises and the conclusion is much weaker than in the foregoing example:

> Student 777 arrived at the health center to obtain a medical excuse from his final examination. He complained of nausea and a headache. The nurse reported a temperature of 100 degrees. Therefore student 777 was really ill.

Given that the premises of this argument are true, it is not as improbable that the conclusion is false as it was in the preceding argument. Hence the argument is a weaker one, though not entirely without merit.

Thus we see that arguments may have various *degrees of strength*. When the premises present absolutely conclusive evidence for the conclusion—that is, when the truth of the premises guarantees the truth of the conclusion—then we have the strongest possible type of argument. There are cases ranging from this maximum possible strength down to arguments where the premises are irrelevant to the conclusion, which have no strength at all.

Exercises:

Arrange the following arguments in the order of the strength of the link between premises and conclusion.

1. No one who is not a member of the club will be admitted to the meeting.

    I am not a member of the club.

    I will not be admitted to the meeting.

2. The last three cars I have owned have all been sports cars. They have all performed beautifully and given me little trouble. Therefore I am sure that the next sports car I own will also perform beautifully and give me little trouble.

3. My nose itches; therefore I am going to have a fight.

4. Brutus said that Caesar was ambitious, and Brutus was an honorable man. Therefore Caesar must have been ambitious.

5. The weatherman has said that a low-pressure front is moving into the area. The sky is gray and very overcast. On the street I can see several people carrying umbrellas. The weatherman is usually accurate. Therefore it will rain.

1.4 INDUCTIVE VERSUS DEDUCTIVE LOGIC. When an argument is such that the truth of the premises guarantees the truth of the conclusion, we shall say that it is deductively valid. When an argument is not deductively valid but nevertheless the premises provide good evidence for the conclusion, the argument is said to be inductively strong. How strong it is depends on how much evidential support the premises give to the conclusion. In line with the discussion in the last section, we can define these two concepts more precisely as follows:

> **Definition 3:** An argument is *deductively valid* if and only if it is *impossible* that its conclusion is false while its premises are true.

> **Definition 4:** An argument is *inductively strong* if and only if it is *improbable* that its conclusion is false while its premises are true, and it is not deductively valid. The *degree* of inductive strength depends on how improbable it is that the conclusion is false while the premises are true.[2]

The sense of "impossible" intended in Definition 3 requires clarification. In a sense, it is impossible for me to fly around the room by flapping my arms; this sense of impossibility is called *physical impossibility*. But it is not physical impossibility that we have in mind in Definition 3. Consider the following argument:

> George is a man.
> George is 100 years old.
> George has arthritis.
> _____
> George will not run a four-minute mile tomorrow.

Although it is physically impossible for the conclusion of the argument to be false (that is, that he will indeed run a four-minute mile) while the premises are true, the argument, although a pretty good one, is *not* deductively valid.

To uncover the sense of impossibility in the definition of deductive validity, let us look at an example of a deductively valid argument:

> No gourmets enjoy banana–tuna fish soufflés with chocolate sauce.
> Antoine enjoys banana–tuna fish soufflés with chocolate sauce.
> _____
> Antoine is not a gourmet.

_____

[2] Although the "while" in Definition 3 may be read as "and" with the definition remaining correct, the "while" in Definition 4 should be read as "given that" and not "and." The reasons for this can be made precise only after some probability theory has been studied. However, the sense of Definition 4 will be explained later in this section.

In this example it is impossible in a stronger sense—we shall say *logically impossible*—for the conclusion to be false while the premises are true. What sort of impossibility is this? For the conclusion to be false Antoine would have to be a gourmet. For the second premise to be true he would also have to enjoy banana–tuna fish soufflés with chocolate sauce. But for the first premise to be true there must be no such person. Thus to suppose the conclusion is false is to contradict the factual claim made by the premises. To put the matter a different way, the factual claim made by the conclusion is already implicit in the premises. This is a feature of all deductively valid arguments.

> If an argument is deductively valid, its conclusion makes no factual claim that is not, at least implicitly, made by its premises.

Thus it is logically impossible for the conclusion of a deductively valid argument to be false while its premises are true, because to suppose that the conclusion is false is to contradict some of the factual claims made by the premises.

We can now see why the following argument is not deductively valid:

> George is a man.
> George is 100 years old.
> George has arthritis.
> _____
> George will not run a four-minute mile tomorrow.

The factual claim made by the conclusion is *not* implicit in the premises, for there is no premise stating that no 100-year-old man with arthritis can run a four-minute mile. Of course, we all believe this to be a fact, but there is nothing in the premises that claims this to be a fact; if we *added* a premise to this effect, *then* we would have a deductively valid argument.

The conclusion of an *inductively strong argument*, on the other hand, ventures beyond the factual claims made by the premises. The conclusion asserts more than the premises, since we can describe situations in which the premises would be true and the conclusion false.

> If an argument is inductively strong, its conclusion makes factual claims that go beyond the factual information given in the premises.

Thus an inductively strong argument risks more than a deductively valid one; it risks the possibility of leading from true premises to a false conclusion. But this risk is the price that must be paid for the advantage which inductively strong arguments have over deductively valid ones: the possibility of discovery and prediction of new facts on the basis of old ones.

Definition 4 stated that an argument is inductively strong if and only if it meets two conditions:

i. It is improbable that its conclusion is false, *given that* its premises true.

ii. It is not deductively valid.

Condition (ii) is required because all deductively valid arguments meet condition (i). It is *impossible* for the conclusion of a deductively valid argument to be false while its premises are true, so the probability that the conclusion is false while the premises are true is zero.

Condition (i), however, requires clarification. The "while" in this condition should be read as "given that," not as "and," so that the condition can be rephrased as:

i. It is improbable that its conclusion is false, *given that* its premises are true.

But just what do we mean by "given that"? And why is "It is improbable that its conclusion is false *and* its premises true" an incorrect formulation of condition (i)? What is the difference, in this context, between "and" and "given that"? At this stage these questions are best answered by examining several examples of arguments. The following is an inductively strong argument:

> There is intelligent life on Mercury.
> There is intelligent life on Venus.
> There is intelligent life on Earth.
> There is intelligent life on Jupiter.
> There is intelligent life on Saturn.
> There is intelligent life on Uranus.
> There is intelligent life on Neptune.
> There is intelligent life on Pluto.
> _____
> There is intelligent life on Mars.

Note that the conclusion is not by itself probable. It is, in fact, probable that the conclusion is false. But it is improbable that the conclusion is false *given that* the premises are true. That is, if the premises were true, then on the basis of that information it would be probable that the conclusion would be true (and thus improbable that it would be false). This is not affected in the least by the fact that some of the premises themselves are quite improbable. Thus although the conclusion taken by itself is improbable, and some of the premises taken by themselves are also improbable, the conclusion is probable *given the premises*. This example illustrates an important principle:

> The type of probability that grades the inductive strength of arguments—we shall call it *inductive probability*—does not depend on the premises alone or on the conclusion alone, but on the *evidential relation* between the premises and the conclusion.

Hopefully we have now gained a certain intuitive understanding of the phrase "given that." Let us now see why it is incorrect to replace it with "and" and thus incorrect to say that an argument is inductively strong if and only if it is improbable that its conclusion is false *and* its premises are true (and it is not deductively valid). Consider the following argument, which is not inductively strong:

There is a 2000-year-old man in Cleveland.
_____
There is a 2000-year-old man in Cleveland who has three heads.

Now it is quite probable that the conclusion is false *given that* the premise is true. Given that there is a 2000-year-old man in Cleveland, it is quite likely that he has only one head. Thus the argument is *not* inductively strong. But it is improbable that the conclusion is false *and* the premise is true. For the conclusion to be false and the premise true, there would have to be a non-three-headed 2000-year-old man in Cleveland, and it is quite improbable that there is *any* 2000-year-old man in Cleveland. Thus it is improbable that the conclusion is false *and* the premise is true, simply because it is improbable that the premise is true.[3]

We now see that the inductive strength of arguments cannot depend on the premises alone. Thus although it is improbable that the conclusion is false *and* the premises true, it is probable that the conclusion is false

_____

[3] A conjunction, that is, a compound sentence formed by the word "and," can be no more probable than either of its conjuncts (the simple constituent sentences), as will be shown in the section on probability. Thus if it is improbable that the premise is true, it must also be improbable that the conclusion is false *and* the premise is true.

given that the premises are true and the argument is *not* inductively strong.[4]

An argument might be such that it is improbable that the premises are true *and* the conclusion false, simply because it is improbable that the conclusion is false; that is, it is probable that the conclusion is true. It is important to note that such conditions do not guarantee that the argument is inductively strong. Consider the following example of an argument that has a probable conclusion and yet is *not* inductively strong:

> There is a man in Cleveland who is 1999 years and 11 months old and in good health.
>
> ---
>
> No man will live to be 2000 years old.

Now the conclusion itself is highly probable. Thus it is improbable that the conclusion is false and consequently improbable that the conclusion is false *and* the premise true. But if the premise were true it would be likely that the conclusion would be false. By itself the conclusion is probable, but given the premise it is not.[5]

The main points of this discussion of inductive strength can be summed up as follows:

1. The inductive probability of an argument is the probability that its conclusion is true given that its premises are true.

2. The inductive probability of an argument is determined by the evidential relation between its premises and its conclusion, not by the likelihood of the truth of its premises alone or the likelihood of the truth of its conclusion alone.

3. An argument is inductively strong if and only if:
   a. Its inductive probability is high.
   b. It is not deductively valid.

We defined logic as the study of the strength of the evidential link between the premises and conclusions of arguments. We have seen that there are two different standards against which to evaluate the strength of this link: deductive validity and inductive strength. Corresponding to

---

[4] Thus the analog of a principle of deductive logic, namely, that any statement logically follows from a contradiction, does not hold in inductive logic.

[5] Thus the analog to a principle of deductive logic, namely, that a tautology logically follows from any statement whatsoever, does not hold in inductive logic.

these two standards are two branches of logic: deductive logic and
inductive logic. *Deductive logic* is concerned with tests for deductive
validity—that is, rules for deciding whether or not a given argument is
deductively valid—and rules for constructing deductively valid arguments.
Inductive logic is concerned with tests for measuring the inductive probability, and hence the inductive strength, of arguments and with rules for
constructing inductively strong arguments.

Some books appear to suggest that there are two different types of
arguments, deductive and inductive, and that deductive logic is concerned
with deductive arguments and inductive logic with inductive arguments.
That is, they suggest the following classification, together with the assumption that every argument falls in one and only one category:

	Deductive arguments	Inductive arguments
Good	Valid	Strong
Bad	Invalid	Weak

Nothing, however, is further from the truth, for, as we have seen, all
inductively strong arguments are deductively invalid.[6]

It is more correct to picture arguments as being arranged on a scale of
descending strength, as follows:

Arguments

Deductively valid

Degrees of inductive
strength

Worthless

---

[6] One might suggest that we define a deductive argument as one that intends to
be deductively valid and an inductive argument as one that intends to be inductively strong. But this will not do, for arguments do not intend anything. People
who advance arguments intend many things. Sometimes they intend for the
argument to be deductively valid; sometimes they intend it to be inductively
strong; sometimes they intend it to be a clever sophistry; and sometimes they
don't know the difference.

Deductive and inductive logic are not distinguished by the different types of arguments with which they deal but by the different standards against which they evaluate arguments.

Exercises:

Decide whether each of the following arguments is deductively valid, inductively strong, or neither:

1. George Washington was a contemporary of Adam Smith.
   Adam Smith was a contemporary of David Hume.
   _____
   George Washington was a contemporary of David Hume.

2. Many extremely brilliant men have been extremely neurotic.
   _____
   Everyone who is slightly intelligent is slightly neurotic.

3. On all the birthdays I have ever had I have been less than 30 years old.
   _____
   On my next birthday I will be less than 30 years old.

4. Being out in the sun for long periods of time makes one highly intelligent.
   Many Californians are out in the sun for long periods of time.
   _____
   Many Californians are highly intelligent.

I.5. THE GENERAL AND THE SPECIFIC. One of the most widespread misconceptions of logic is the belief that deductive arguments proceed from the general to the specific, and inductive arguments proceed from the specific to the general. Such a view is nonsense, for, as we have seen, arguments do not fall into two categories: deductive and inductive. Perhaps then all deductively *valid* arguments proceed from the general to the specific and all inductively *strong* arguments proceed from the specific to the general. This view is not nonsense; it is simply incorrect. There are deductively valid arguments that go from general to general:

> All gorillas are apes.
> All apes are mammals.
> _____
> All gorillas are mammals.

from particular to particular:

> Ezekial is a wolf.
> Ezekial has a tail.
> _____
> Ezekial's tail is the tail of a wolf.

and from particular to general:

> Frederick is an alderman.
> Frederick is a thief.
> _____
> Anyone who knows all aldermen knows some thief.

Similarly, inductively strong arguments do not fall into the narrow category of arguments having particular premises and a general conclusion. *Arguments by analogy* proceed from particular to particular, and although such arguments are often misused, some are quite strong. The following is an example of a strong argument by analogy:

> 1. Car A is a Hotmobile 66 and car B is a Hotmobile 66.
> 2. Car A has the super-zazz engine and car B has the super-zazz engine.
> 3. Car A's engine is in perfect condition and car B's engine is in perfect condition.
> 4. Both cars have the same type of transmission and the same final drive ratio.
> 5. Car A's top speed is over 150 miles per hour.
> _____
> Car B's top speed is over 150 miles per hour.

Premises (1) through (4) are said to *set up the analogy*, that is, they describe relevant similarities between car A and car B which make it likely that their top speed is the same, and therefore license the move from premise (5) to the conclusion.

It is not difficult to find inductively strong arguments that have general premises and a general conclusion; for example:

> All students in this class are highly intelligent.
> All students in this class are strongly motivated to do well.
> No student in this class has a heavy work load.
> No student in this class has psychological difficulties that would interfere with his course work.
> _____
> All students in this class will do well.

Inductively strong arguments with general premises and general conclusions play an important role in advanced science. For example, Newton's laws of motion were confirmed because they accounted for both Galileo's laws of falling bodies and Kepler's laws of planetary motion. We can give a rough approximation of the argument supporting Newton's laws of motion as follows:

All bodies freely falling near the surface of the earth obey Galileo's
laws.
All planets obey Kepler's laws.

All material objects obey Newton's laws.

We can also give an example of an inductively strong argument with a
general premise and a particular conclusion:

All emeralds previously found have been green.

The next emerald to be found will be green.

People often use arguments of this type when they marshal generalizations about past experience in order to make a prediction about a particular impending event.

Thus the difference between inductively strong and deductively valid
arguments is not to be found in the generality or particularity of premises
and conclusion but rather in the definitions of deductive validity and
inductive strength.

I.6. EPISTEMIC PROBABILITY. We have seen that the concept
of inductive probability applies to arguments. The inductive probability
of an argument is the probability that its conclusion is true given that
its premises are true. Thus the inductive probability of an argument is a
measure of the strength of the evidence that the premises provide for the
conclusion. It is correct to speak of the inductive probability of an argument, but incorrect to speak of the inductive probability of statements.
Since the premises and conclusion of any argument are statements, it is
incorrect to speak of the inductive probability of a premise or of a
conclusion.

There is, however, some sense of probability in which it is intuitively
acceptable to speak of the probability of a premise or conclusion. When
we said that it is improbable that there is a 2000-year-old man in Cleveland, we were relying on some such intuitive sense of probability. There
must then be a type of probability, other than inductive probability, that
applies to statements rather than arguments.

Let us call this type of probability "*epistemic probability*" because the
Greek stem "*episteme*" means knowledge, and the epistemic probability
of a statement depends on just what our stock of relevant knowledge is.
Thus *the epistemic probability of a statement can vary from person to
person and from time to time,* since different people have different stocks
of knowledge at the same time and the same person has different stocks

of knowledge at different times. *For me,* the epistemic probability that there is a 2000-year-old man now living in Cleveland is quite low, since I have certain background knowledge about the current normal life span of human beings. I feel safe in using this statement as an example of a statement whose epistemic probability is low because I feel safe in assuming that your stock of background knowledge is similar in the relevant respects and thus that *for you* its epistemic probability is also low.

It is easy to imagine a situation in which the background knowledge of two people would differ in such a way as to generate a difference in the epistemic probability of a given statement. For example, the epistemic probability that Pegasus will show in the third race may be different for a fan in the grandstand than for Pegasus' jockey, owing to the difference in their knowledge of the relevant factors involved.

It is also easy to see how the epistemic probability of a given statement can change over time for a particular person. The fund of knowledge that each of us possesses is constantly in a state of flux. We are all constantly learning new things directly through experience and indirectly through information which is communicated to us. We are also, unfortunately, continually forgetting things that we once knew. This holds true for societies and cultures as well as for individuals, and human knowledge is continually in a dynamic process of simultaneous growth and decay.

It is important to see how upon the addition of new knowledge to a previous body of knowledge the epistemic probability of a given statement could either increase or decrease. Suppose we are interested in the epistemic probability of the statement that Mr. X is an Armenian and the only relevant information we have is that Mr. X is an Oriental rug dealer in Allentown, Pa., that 90 per cent of the Oriental rug dealers in the United States are Armenian, and that Allentown, Pa., is in the United States.[7] On the basis of this stock of relevant knowledge, the epistemic probability of the statement is equal to the inductive probability of the following argument:

> Mr. X is an Oriental rug dealer in Allentown, Pa.
> Allentown, Pa., is in the United States.
> Ninety per cent of the Oriental rug dealers in the United States are Armenian.
> _____
> Mr. X is an Armenian.

---

[7] All the supposed facts used in this illustration are fictitious except for the fact that Allentown, Pa., is in the United States.

The inductive probability of this argument is quite high. If we are now given the new information that although 90 per cent of the Oriental rug dealers in the United States are Armenian, only 2 per cent of the Oriental rug dealers in Allentown, Pa., are Armenian, while 98 per cent are Syrian, the epistemic probability that Mr. X is Armenian decreases drastically, for it is now equal to the inductive probability of the following argument:

> Mr. X is an Oriental rug dealer in Allentown, Pa.
> Allentown, Pa., is in the United States.
> Ninety per cent of the Oriental rug dealers in the United States are Armenian.
> Ninety-eight per cent of the Oriental rug dealers in Allentown, Pa., are Syrian.
> Two per cent of the Oriental rug dealers in Allentown, Pa., are Armenian.
> ───────────────────────────────
> Mr. X is an Armenian.

The inductive probability of this argument is quite low. Note that the decrease in the epistemic probability of the statement "Mr. X is an Armenian" results not from a change in the inductive probability of a given argument but from the fact that, upon the addition of new information, a *different* inductive argument with more premises becomes relevant in assessing its epistemic probability.

Suppose now we are given still more information, to the effect that Mr. X is a member of the Armenian Club of Allentown and that 99 per cent of the members of the Armenian Club are actually Armenians. Upon addition of this information the epistemic probability that Mr. X is an Armenian again becomes quite high, for it is now equal to the inductive probability of the following argument:

> Mr. X is an Oriental rug dealer in Allentown, Pa.
> Allentown, Pa., is in the United States.
> Ninety per cent of the Oriental rug dealers in the United States are Armenian.
> Ninety-eight per cent of the Oriental rug dealers in Allentown, Pa., are Syrian.
> Two per cent of the Oriental rug dealers in Allentown, Pa., are Armenian.
> Mr. X is a member of the Armenian Club of Allentown, Pa.
> Ninety-nine per cent of the members of the Armenian Club are Armenian.
> ───────────────────────────────
> Mr. X is an Armenian.

Notice once more that the epistemic probability of the statement changes because, with the addition of new knowledge, it became equal to the inductive probability of a new argument with additional premises.

Epistemic probabilities are *important* to us. They are the probabilities upon which we base our decisions. From a stock of knowledge we will arrive at the associated epistemic probability of a statement by the application of inductive logic. Exactly how inductive logic gets us epistemic probabilities from a stock of knowledge depends on how we characterize a stock of knowledge. Just what knowledge is; how we get it; what it is like once we have it; these are difficult epistemological questions to which we have no definitive answers. At this stage we must work within simplified models of knowing rather than attempting a full analysis of man's epistemological situation.

The Certainty Model: Suppose that our knowledge originates in observation; that observation makes particular sentences (observation reports) certain and that the probability of other sentences is attributable to the certainty of these. In such a situation we can identify our stock of knowledge with a *list of sentences,* those observation reports that have been rendered certain by observational experience. It is then natural to evaluate the probability of a statement by looking at an argument with all our stock of knowledge as premises and the statement in question as the conclusion. The inductive strength of that argument will determine the probability of the statement in question. In the certainty model, the relation between epistemic probability and inductive probability is quite simple:

> **Definition 5:** In the *certainty model* the *epistemic* probability of a statement is the *inductive* probability of that argument which has the statement in question as its conclusion and whose premises consist of all of the observation reports which comprise our stock of knowledge.

The certainty model lives up to its name in assigning epistemic probability of one to each observation report in our stock of knowledge. If an observation report is part of our stock of knowledge, the argument relevant to its epistemic probability contains it both as conclusion and premise and is thus trivially deductively valid.

The simplicity of the certainty model is attractive, and some philosophers have argued that it really mirrors the actual human situation. The weight of current opinion, however, is that certainty is not so easy to come by and that while we like to pretend that we have it, we rarely (if ever) do. Such a view leads to a different kind of model.

Fallability Models: Suppose that our knowledge originates in observation and that observation makes the appropriate observation report likely, but not certain. For instance, I see a bird that looks like a black swan at the zoo. I am fairly confident in my ability to identify black swans, but not so confident as to think I could not make a mistake. My act of observation might thus confer Probability .99 on the observation report: "The bird in cage 31 of the zoo is a black swan," leaving a 1 per cent chance that I goofed.

In a fallibility model, our stock of knowledge can no longer be represented as simply a list of observation reports. Now we need observation reports paired with the probabilities that observation has conferred upon them:

$$Pr\,(0_1) = .99$$
$$Pr\,(0_2) = .87$$
$$Pr\,(0_3) = .95$$

And calculating the epistemic probability of a sentence, S, on such a stock of knowledge will not be such a simple proposition. Certainly the inductive probability of

$$\frac{\begin{array}{c}0_1\\0_2\\0_3\end{array}}{S}$$

is relevant. But we stand a 13 per cent chance of having been mistaken about 0_2! We shall have to take into account the inductive probability of:

$$\frac{\begin{array}{c}0_1\\\text{not-}0_2\\0_3\end{array}}{S}$$

and similarly for all other mistakes and combinations of mistakes we might have made. Then we will have to put together the inductive probabilities of these arguments in exactly the right way to get the epistemic probability of S.

Fallibility models are too complicated for us to discuss at this point. Now that you know they exist, we can forget about them until you know a little more about probabilities. Until then, let us always think about epistemic probabilities as in the certainty model.

Exercises:

1. Construct several new examples in which the epistemic probability of a statement is increased or decreased by the addition of new information to a previous stock of knowledge.

For the advanced student:

2. An incorrigible statement is one which can never be corrected. Does the certainty model render any statements incorrigible?

Suggested readings

William Kneale, *Probability and Induction* (London: Oxford University Press, 1952), "The Relation of Probability to Evidence," pp. 9–13.

For the advanced student:

Israel Scheffler, *Science and Subjectivity* (Indianapolis: Bobbs-Merrill, 1967).

I.7. PROBABILITY AND THE PROBLEMS OF INDUCTIVE LOGIC. Deductive logic, at least in its basic branches, is well developed. The definitions of its basic concepts are precise, its rules are rigorously formulated, and the interrelations between the two are well understood. Such is not the case, however, with inductive logic. There are no universally accepted rules for constructing inductively strong arguments; no general agreement on a way of measuring the inductive strength of arguments; no precise, uncontroversial definition of inductive probability. Thus inductive logic cannot be learned in the sense in which one learns algebra or the basic branches of deductive logic. This is not to say that inductive logicians are wallowing in a sea of total ignorance; many things are known about inductive logic, but many problems still remain to be solved. We shall try to get an idea of just what the problems are, as well as what progress has been made toward their solution.

Some of the main problems of inductive logic can be framed in terms of the concept of inductive probability. I said that there is no precise, uncontroversial definition of inductive probability. I did give a definition of inductive probability. Was it controversial? I think not, but, if you will remember, it was imprecise. I said that the inductive probability of an argument is the probability that its conclusion is true, given that its premises are true. But at that point I could not give an exact definition of "the probability that an argument's conclusion is true, given that its premises are true." I was, instead, reduced to giving examples so that you could get an intuitive feeling for the meaning of this phrase. The logician, however, is not satisfied with an intuitive feeling for the meaning of key words and phrases. He wishes to analyze the concepts involved and arrive at precise, unambiguous definitions. Thus one of the problems of inductive logic which remains outstanding is, what, exactly, is inductive probability?

This problem is intimately connected with two other problems: How is the inductive probability of an argument measured? And, what are the rules for constructing inductively strong arguments? Obviously we cannot develop an exact measure of inductive probability if we do not know precisely what it is. And before we can devise rules for constructing inductively strong arguments, we must have ways of telling which arguments measure up to the required degree of inductive strength. Thus the solution to the problem of providing a precise definition of inductive probability determines what solutions are available for the problems of determining the inductive probabilities of arguments and constructing systematic rules for generating inductively strong arguments.

Let us call a precise definition of inductive probability, together with the associated method of determining the inductive probability of arguments and rules for constructing inductively strong arguments, an *inductive logic*. Thus different definitions of inductive probability give rise to different inductive logics. Now we are not interested in finding just any system of inductive logic. We want a system that accords well with common sense and scientific practice. We want a system that gives the result that most of the cases that we would intuitively classify as inductively strong arguments do indeed have a high inductive probability. We want a system that accords with scientific practice and common sense, but that is more precise, more clearly formulated, and more rigorous than they are; a system that codifies, explains, and refines our intuitive judgments. We shall call such a system of inductive logic a *scientific inductive logic*. The problem that we have been discussing can now be reformulated as *the problem of constructing a scientific inductive logic*.

The second major problem of inductive logic, and the one that has been more widely discussed in the history of philosophy, is *the problem of rationally justifying the use of a system of scientific inductive logic* rather than some other system of inductive logic. After all, there are many different possible inductive logics. Some might give the result that arguments that we think are inductively strong are, in fact, inductively weak, and arguments that we think inductively weak are, in fact, inductively strong. That is, there are possible inductive logics which are diametrically opposed to scientific inductive logic, which are in total disagreement with scientific practice and common sense. Why should we not employ one of these systems rather than scientific induction?

Any adequate answer to this question must take into account the uses to which we put inductive logic (or, at present, the vague intuitions we use in place of a precise system of inductive logic). One of the most important uses of inductive logic is to frame our expectations of the future on the basis of our knowledge of the past and present. We must use our knowledge of the past and present as a guide to our expectations of the future; it is the only guide we have. But it is impossible to have a *deductively valid* argument whose premises contain factual information solely about the past and present and whose conclusion makes factual claims about the future. For the conclusion of a deductively valid argument makes no factual claim that is not already made by the premises. Thus the gap separating the past and present from the future cannot be bridged in this way by deductively valid arguments, and if the arguments we use to bridge that gap are to have any strength whatsoever they must be inductively strong.[8]

Let us look a little more closely, then, at the way in which inductive logic would be used to frame our expectations of the future. Suppose our plans depend critically on whether it will rain tomorrow. Then the reasonable thing to do, before we decide what course of action to take, is to ascertain the epistemic probability of the statement "It will rain tomorrow." This we do by putting all the relevant information we now have into the premises of an argument whose conclusion is "It will rain tomorrow" and ascertaining the inductive probability of that argument. If the probability is high, we will have a strong expectation of rain and will

---

[8] The inference from the past and present to the future is not, of course, the only type of inference that cannot be accomplished by a deductively valid argument. Whenever the conclusion must make a factual claim that is not made by the premises, a deductively valid argument is out of the question. For instance, if we wished to conclude something about the distant past from premises that embody current geological data, a deductively valid argument could not do the job.

make our plans on that basis. If the probability is near zero, we will be reasonably sure that it will not rain and act accordingly.[9]

Now although it is doubtful that anyone carries out the formal process outlined above when he plans for the future, it is hard to deny that, if we were to make our reasoning explicit, it would fall into this pattern. Thus the making of rational decisions is dependent, via the concept of epistemic probability, on our inductive logic. The second main problem of inductive logic, then, leads us to the following question: How can we rationally justify the use of scientific inductive logic, rather than some other inductive logic, as an instrument for shaping our expectations of the future?

The two main problems of inductive logic are:

1. The construction of a system of scientific inductive logic.
2. The rational justification of the use of that system rather than some other system of inductive logic.

It would seem that the first problem must be solved before the second, since we can hardly justify the use of a system of inductive logic before we know what it is. Nevertheless I shall discuss the second problem first. It makes sense to do this because we can see why the second problem is *such* a problem without having to know all the details of scientific inductive logic. Furthermore, philosophers historically came to appreciate the difficulty of the second problem much earlier than they realized the full force of the first problem. This second problem, the traditional problem of induction, is discussed in the next chapter.

Suggested readings

Rudolf Carnap, *Logical Foundations of Probability* (2nd ed.), (Chicago: University of Chicago Press, 1962), pp. 1–15). (Advanced students may also wish to see pp. 252–64.)

Irwin D. Bross, Design for Decision (New York: The Macmillan Company, 1953), chaps. 1 and 2.

---

[9] The account of decision-making under uncertainty sketched above is, of necessity, drastically oversimplified. The theory of how epistemic probabilities are to be used to make decisions under conditions of uncertainty is a quite complex matter, dealt with by the branch of statistics called statistical decision theory. For an easy introduction to this theory, see Irwin D. Bross, *Design for Decision* (New York: The Macmillan Company, 1953). For a more detailed and rigorous treatment, see Herman Chernoff and Lincoln E. Moses, *Elementary Decision Theory* (New York: John Wiley & Sons, Inc., 1959).

II

THE TRADITIONAL PROBLEM
OF INDUCTION

II.1. INTRODUCTION. In Chapter I we saw that inductive logic is used to shape our expectations of that which is as yet unknown on the basis of those facts that are already known; for instance, to shape our expectations of the future on the basis of our knowledge of the past and present. Our problem is the rational justification of the use of a system of scientific inductive logic, rather than some other system of inductive logic, for this task.

The Scottish philosopher David Hume first raised this problem, which we shall call the *traditional problem of induction*, in full force.[1] Hume gave the problem a cutting edge, for he advanced arguments designed to show that no such rational justification of inductive logic is possible, no matter what the details of a system of scientific inductive logic turn out to be. The history of philosophical discussion of inductive logic since Hume has been in large measure occupied with attempts to circumvent the difficulties he raised. This chapter examines these difficulties and the various attempts to overcome them.

II.2. HUME'S ARGUMENT. Before we can meaningfully discuss arguments which purport to show that it is impossible to rationally justify scientific induction, we must be clear on what would be required to rationally justify a system of inductive logic. Presumably we could rationally justify such a system if we could show that it is well suited for the uses to which it is put. One of the most important uses of inductive logic is in setting up our predictions of the future.[2] Inductive logic figures in these predictions by way of *epistemic probabilities*. If a claim about the future has high epistemic probability, we predict that it will prove

---

[1] I have taken some liberties with Hume and have given the traditional problem of induction a new twist for reasons that will become apparent. For Hume's own statement of the problem, see David Hume, *An Inquiry Concerning Human Understanding*, section IV, reprinted in *A Modern Introduction to Philosophy* (rev. ed.), Paul Edwards and Arthur Pap, eds. (Glencoe, Ill.: The Free Press, 1965), pp. 123–32.

[2] Its other uses do not differ in ways essential to the argument.

24

true. And, more generally, we expect something more or less strongly as its epistemic probability is higher or lower. The epistemic probability of a statement is just the inductive probability of the argument which embodies all available information in its premises.[3] Thus the epistemic probability of a statement depends on two things: (i) the stock of knowledge and (ii) the inductive logic used to grade the strength of the argument from that stock of knowledge to the conclusion.

Now obviously what we want is for our predictions to be correct. If we could get by with deductively valid arguments we could be assured of true predictions all the time. Deductively valid arguments lead from true premises always to true conclusions and the statements comprising our stock of knowledge are known to be true. But deductively valid arguments are too conservative to leap from the past and present to the future. For this sort of daring behavior we will have to rely on inductively strong arguments—and we will have to give up the comfortable assurance that we will be right all the time.

How about most of the time? Let us call the sort of argument used to set up an epistemic probability an e-argument. That is, an *e-argument* is an argument which has, as its premises, some stock of knowledge. We might hope, then, that inductively strong e-arguments will give us *true conclusions most of the time*. Remember that there are *degrees* of inductive strength and that, on the basis of our present knowledge, we do not always simply predict or not-predict that an event will occur, but anticipate it with various *degrees of confidence*. We might hope further that inductively *stronger* e-arguments have true conclusions *more often* than inductively *weaker* ones. Finally, since we think that it is useful to gather evidence to enlarge our stock of knowledge, we might hope that inductively strong e-arguments give us true conclusions more often when the stock of knowledge embodied in the premises is great than when it is small.

The last consideration really has to do with justifying epistemic probabilities as tools for prediction. The epistemic probability is the inductive probability of an argument embodying *all* our stock of knowledge in its premises. The requirement that it embody *all* our knowledge, and not just some part of it, is known as the Total Evidence Condition.[4] If we

---

[3] In the certainty model.

[4] Sometimes the Total Evidence Condition is stated as the requirement that an e-argument embody only all our *relevant* knowledge. This comes to the same thing, however, since by definition, the remainder of our stock of knowledge is irrelevant just in case its addition or deletion from the premises makes no difference to the probability.

could show that basing our predictions on more knowledge gives us better success ratios, we would have justified the total evidence condition.

The other considerations have to do with justifying the other determinant of epistemic probability—the inductive logic which assigns inductive probabilities to arguments.

We are now ready to suggest what is required to rationally justify a system of inductive logic:

> **Rational Justification**
>
> *Suggestion I:* A system of inductive logic is rationally justified if and only if it is shown that the arguments to which it assigns high inductive probability yield true conclusions from true premises most of the time, and the e-arguments to which it assigns higher inductive probability yield true conclusions from true premises more often than the arguments to which it assigns lower inductive probability.

It is this sense of rational justification, or something quite close to it, that Hume has in mind when he advances his arguments to prove that a rational justification of scientific induction is impossible.

If scientific induction is to be rationally justified in the sense of Suggestion I, we must establish that the arguments to which it assigns high inductive probability yield true conclusions from true premises most of the time. By what sort of reasoning, asks Hume, could we establish such a conclusion? If the argument that we must use is to have any force whatsoever, it must be either deductively valid or inductively strong. Hume proceeds to show that neither sort of argument could do the job.

Suppose we try to rationally justify scientific inductive logic by means of a deductively valid argument. The only premises we are entitled to use in this argument are those that state things we know. Since we do not know what the future will be like (if we did, we would have no need of an inductive logic on which to base our predictions), the premises can contain knowledge of only the past and present. But if the argument is deductively valid, then the conclusion can make no factual claims that are not already made by the premises. Thus the conclusion of the argument can only refer to the past and present, not to the future, for the premises made no factual claims about the future. Such a conclusion cannot, however, be adequate to rationally justify scientific induction.

To rationally justify scientific induction we must show that e-arguments to which it assigns high inductive probability yield true conclusions from true premises most of the time. And "most of the time" does not mean most of the time in only the past and present; it means most of the time, *past, present, and future.* It is conceivable that a certain type of argument might have given us true conclusions from true premises in the past and might cease to do so in the future. Since our conclusion cannot tell us how successful arguments will be in the future, it cannot establish that the e-arguments to which scientific induction assigns high probability will give us true conclusions from true premises *most of the time.* Thus we cannot use a deductively valid argument to rationally justify induction.

Suppose we try to rationally justify scientific induction by means of an inductively strong argument. We construct our argument, whatever it may be, and present it as an inductively strong argument. "Why do you think that this is an inductively strong argument?" Hume might ask. "Because it has a high inductive probability," we would reply. "And what system of inductive logic assigns it a high probability?" "Scientific induction, of course." What Hume has pointed out is that if we attempt to rationally justify scientific induction by use of an inductively strong argument, we are in the position of having to *assume* that scientific induction is reliable in order to prove that scientific induction is reliable; we are reduced to begging the question. Thus we cannot use an inductively strong argument to rationally justify scientific induction.

A common argument is that scientific induction is justified because it has been quite successful in the past. On reflection, however, we see that this argument is really an attempt to justify induction by means of an inductively strong argument, and thus begs the question. More explicitly, the argument reads something like this:

> Arguments that are judged by scientific inductive logic to have high inductive probability have given us true conclusions from true premises most of the time in the past.
>
> ---
>
> Such arguments will give us true conclusions from true premises most of the time, past, present, and future.

It should be obvious that this argument is not deductively valid. At best it is assigned high inductive probability by a system of scientific inductive logic. But the point at issue is whether we should put our faith in such a system.

We can view the traditional problem of induction from a different perspective by discussing it in terms of the *principle of the uniformity of nature.* Athough we do not have the details of a system of scientific induction in hand, we do know that it must accord well with common sense and scientific practice, and we are reasonably familiar with both. A few examples will illustrate a general principle which appears to underlie both scientific and common-sense judgments of inductive strength.

If you were to order fillet mignon in a restaurant, and a friend were to object that fillet mignon would corrode your vitals and lead to quick and violent death, it would seem quite sufficient to respond that you had often eaten fillet mignon without any of the dire consequences he predicted. That is, you would intuitively judge the following argument to be inductively strong:

I have eaten fillet mignon many times and it has never corroded my vitals.

Fillet mignon will not now corrode my vitals.

Suppose a scientist is asked whether a rocket would work in reaches of space beyond the range of our telescopes. He replies that it would, and to back up his answer appeals to certain principles of theoretical physics. When asked what evidence he has for these principles, he can refer to a great mass of observed phenomena that corroborate them. The scientist is then judging the following argument to be inductively strong:

Principles A, B, and C correctly describe the behavior of material bodies in all of the many situations we have observed.

Principles A, B, and C correctly describe the behavior of material bodies in those reaches of space that we have not as yet observed.

There appears to be a common assumption underlying the judgments that these arguments are inductively strong. As a steak eater you assume that the future will be like the past, that types of food that proved healthful in the past will continue to prove so in the future. The scientist assumes that the distant reaches of space are like the nearer ones, that material bodies obey the same general laws in all areas of space. Thus it seems that underlying our judgments of inductive strength in both common sense and science is the presupposition that nature is uniform or, as it is sometimes put, that like causes produce like effects throughout all regions of space and time. Thus we can say that a system of scientific induction will base its judgments of inductive strength on the presupposition that *nature is uniform* (and in particular that the future will resemble the past).

We ought to realize at this point that we have only a vague, intuitive understanding of the principle of the uniformity of nature, gleaned from examples rather than specified by precise definitions. This rough understanding is sufficient for the purposes at hand. But we should bear in mind that the task of giving an *exact* definition of the principle, a definition of the sort that would be presupposed by a system of scientific inductive logic, is as difficult as the construction of such a system itself. One of the problems is that nature is simply not uniform in all respects, the future does not resemble the past in all respects. Bertrand Russell once speculated that the chicken on slaughter-day might reason that whenever the humans came it had been fed, so when the humans would come today it would also be fed. The chicken thought that the future would resemble the past, but it was dead wrong.

The future may resemble the past, but it does not do so in all respects. And we do not know beforehand what those respects are nor to what degree the future resembles the past. Our ignorance of what these respects are is a deep reason behind the total evidence condition. Looking at more and more evidence helps us reject spurious patterns which we might otherwise project into the future. Trying to say exactly *what* about nature we believe is uniform thus turns out to be a surprisingly delicate task.[5]

But suppose that a subtle and sophisticated version of the principle of the uniformity of nature can be formulated which adequately explains the judgments of inductive strength rendered by scientific inductive logic. Then if nature is indeed uniform in the required sense (past, present, and future), e-arguments judged strong by scientific induction will indeed give us true conclusions most of the time. Therefore the problem of rationally justifying scientific induction could be reduced to the problem of establishing that nature is uniform.

But by what reasoning could we establish such a conclusion? If an argument is to have any force whatsoever it must be either deductively valid or inductively strong. A deductively valid argument could not be adequate, for if the information in the premises consists solely of our knowledge of the past and present, then the conclusion cannot tell us that nature will be uniform in the future. The conclusion of a deductively valid argument can make no factual claims that are not already made by the premises, and factual claims about the future are not factual claims about the past and present. But if we claim to have established the principle of the uniformity of nature by an argument that is rated inductively strong by scientific inductive logic, we are open to a challenge as to why we should place our faith in such arguments. But we cannot reply

---

[5] About which we will have more to say in Chapter III.

"Because nature is uniform," for that is precisely what we are trying to establish.

Let us summarize the traditional problem of induction. It appears that to rationally justify a system of scientific inductive logic we would have to establish that the e-arguments it judges to be inductively strong give us true conclusions most of the time. If we try to prove that this is the case by means of a deductively valid argument whose premises state things we already know, then the conclusion must fall short of the desired goal. But to try to rationally justify scientific induction by means of an argument that scientific induction judges to be inductively strong is to beg the question. The same difficulties arise if we attempt to justify scientific inductive logic by establishing that nature is uniform.

Exercise:

What problems are there in trying to justify the total evidence condition?

Suggested readings

David Hume, *An Inquiry Concerning Human Understanding*, sec. IV, reprinted in *A Modern Introduction to Philosophy* (rev. ed), ed. Paul Edwards and Arthur Pap (Glencoe, Ill.: The Free Press, 1965), pp. 123–32, and in *Probabilities, Problems and Paradoxes*, ed. Sidney Luckenbach (Belmont, Calif.: Dickenson Publishing Co., 1972), pp. 14–21.

II.3 THE INDUCTIVE JUSTIFICATION OF INDUCTION.

Hume has presented us with a dilemma. If we try to justify scientific inductive logic by means of a deductively valid argument with premises known to be true, our conclusion will be too weak. If we try to use an inductively strong argument, we are reduced to begging the question. The proponent of the inductive justification of induction tackles the second horn of the dilemma. He maintains that we can justify scientific induction by an inductively strong argument without begging the question. Although his attempt is not altogether successful, there is a great deal to be learned from it.

The answer to the question "Why should we believe that scientific induction is a reliable guide for our expectations?" that immediately occurs to everyone is "Because it has worked well so far." Hume's objection to this answer was that it begs the question, that it assumes scientific induction is reliable in order to prove that scientific induction is reliable.

The proponents of the inductive justification of induction, however, claim that the answer only *appears* to beg the question, because of a mistaken conception of scientific induction. They claim that if we properly distinguish *levels* of scientific induction, rather than lumping all arguments that scientific induction judges to be strong in one category, we will see that the inductive justification of induction does not beg the question.

Just what then are these levels of scientific induction? And what is their relevance to the inductive justification of induction? We can distinguish different *levels of argument*, in terms of the things they talk about. Arguments on level 1 will talk about individual things or events; for instance:

> Many jub-jub birds have been observed, and they have all been purple.

> The next jub-jub bird to be observed will be purple.

Level 1 of scientific inductive logic would consist of rules for assigning inductive probabilities to arguments of level 1. Presumably the rules of level 1 of scientific induction would assign high inductive probability to the preceding argument. Arguments on level 2 will talk about arguments on level 1; for instance:

> Some deductively valid arguments on level 1 have true premises. All deductively valid arguments on level 1 which have true premises have true conclusions.

> Some deductively valid arguments on level 1 have true conclusions.

This is a deductively valid argument on level 2 which talks about deductively valid arguments on level 1. The following is also an argument on level 2 which talks about arguments on level 1:

> Some arguments on level 1 which the rules of level 1 of scientific inductive logic say are inductively strong have true premises. The denial of a true statement is a false statement.

> Some arguments on level 1 which the rules of level 1 of scientific inductive logic say are inductively strong have premises whose denial is false.

This is a deductively valid argument on level 2 which talks about arguments on level 1, which the rules of level 1 of scientific inductive logic classify as inductively strong.

There are, of course, arguments on level 2 which are not deductively valid, and there is a corresponding second level of scientific inductive logic which consists of rules that assign degrees of inductive strength to *these* arguments. There are arguments on level 3 which talk about arguments on level 2, arguments on level 4 which talk about arguments on level 3, etc. For each level of argument, scientific inductive logic has a corresponding level of rules.

This characterization of the levels of argument, and the corresponding levels of scientific induction, is summarized in Table 1. As the table shows,

Table 1

Levels of argument	Levels of scientific inductive logic
k: Arguments about arguments on level $k - 1$.	k: Rules for assigning inductive probabilities to arguments on level k.
⋮	⋮
2: Arguments about arguments on level 1.	2: Rules for assigning inductive probabilities to arguments on level 2.
1: Arguments about individuals.	1: Rules for assigning inductive probabilities to arguments on level 1.

scientific inductive logic is seen not as a simple, homogeneous system but rather as a complex structure composed of an infinite number of strata of distinct sets of rules. The sets of rules on different levels are not, however, totally unrelated. The rules on each level presuppose, in some sense, that nature is uniform and that the future will resemble the past. If this were not the case, we would have no reason for calling the whole system of levels a system of *scientific* inductive logic.

We are now in a position to see how the system of levels of scientific induction is to be employed in the inductive justification of induction. In answer to the question, "Why should we place our faith in the rules of level 1 of scientific inductive logic?" the proponent of the inductive justification of induction will advance an argument on level 2:

> Among arguments used to make predictions in the past, e-arguments on level 1 (which according to level 1 of scientific inductive logic are inductively strong) have given true conclusions most of the time.
>
> ---
>
> With regard to the next prediction, an e-argument judged inductively strong by the rules of scientific inductive logic will yield a true conclusion.

The proponent will maintain that the premise of this argument is true, and if we ask why he thinks that this is an inductively strong argument, he will reply that *the rules of level 2 of scientific inductive logic* assign it a high inductive probability. If we now ask why we should put our faith in *these* rules, he will advance a similar argument on level 3, justify that argument by appeal to the rules of scientific inductive logic on level 3, justify those rules by an argument on level 4, etc.

The inductive justification of induction is summarized in Table 2. The arrows in the table show the order of justification. Thus the rules of level 1 are justified by an argument on level 2, which is justified by the rules on level 2, which are justified by an argument on level 3, etc.

Let us now see how it is that the proponent of the inductive justification of induction can plead not guilty to Hume's charge of begging the question, that is, of presupposing exactly what one is trying to prove. In justifying the rules of level 1, the proponent of the inductive justification of induction does not presuppose that *these* rules will work the next time; in fact, he advances an argument (on level 2) to show that they will work next time. Now it is true that the use of this argument presupposes that the rules of level 2 will work next time. But there is another argument waiting on level 3 to show that the rules of level 2 will work. The use of that argument does not presuppose what it is trying to establish; it presupposes that the rules on level 3 will work. Thus none of the arguments used in the inductive justification of induction presuppose what they are trying to prove, and the inductive justification of induction does not technically beg the question.

Perhaps how these levels work can be made clearer by looking at a simple example. Suppose our only observations of the world have been of 100 jub-jub birds and they have all been purple. After observing 99 jub-jub birds, we advanced argument jj-99:

> We have seen 99 jub-jub birds and they were all purple.
>
> ---
>
> The next jub-jub bird we see will be purple.

Table 2

Levels of argument	Levels of scientific inductive logic
⋮	⋮
3: Rules of level 2 of sci- ⟶ entific inductive logic have worked well in the past.	3: Rules for assigning inductive probabilities to arguments on level 3.
They will work well next time.	
2: Rules of level 1 of sci- ⟶ entific inductive logic have worked well in the past.*	2: Rules for assigning inductive probabilities to arguments on level 2.
They will work well next time.	
1:	1: Rules for assigning inductive probabilities to arguments on level 1.

* The statement "rules of level 1 of scientific inductive logic have worked well in the past," is to be taken as shorthand for "arguments on level 1, which according to the rules of level 1 of scientific inductive logic are inductively strong and which have been used to make predictions in the past, have given us true conclusions, when the premises were true, most of the time." Thus the argument on level 2 used to justify the rules of level 1 is exactly the same one as put forth in the second paragraph on page 33.

This argument was given high inductive probability by rules of level 1 of scientific inductive logic. We know its premises to be true, and we took its conclusion as a prediction. The 100th jub-jub bird can thus be correctly described as purple—or as the color that makes the conclusion of argument jj-99 true—or as the color that results in a successful prediction by the rules of level 1 of scientific inductive logic. Let us also suppose that similar arguments had been advanced in the past: jj-98, jj-97, etc. Each of these arguments was an e-argument to which the rules of level 1 assigned high inductive probability. Thus the observations of jub-jub birds 98 and 99, etc., are also observations of successful outcomes to predictions based on assignments of probabilities to e-arguments by rules of level 1. This gives rise to an argument on level 2:

e-arguments on level 1, which are assigned high inductive probability by rules of level 1, have had their conclusions predicted 98 times and all those predictions were successful.

Predicting the conclusion of the next e-argument on level 1 which is assigned high inductive probability will also lead to success.

This argument is assigned high inductive probability by rules of level 2. If the next jub-jub bird to be observed is purple, it makes this level 2 argument successful in addition to making the appropriate level 1 argument successful. A string of such successes gives rise to a similar argument on level 3 and so on, up the ladder, as indicated in Table 2.[6]

If someone were to object that what is wanted is a justification of scientific induction as a whole and that this has not been given, the proponent of the inductive justification of induction would reply that, for every level of rules of scientific inductive logic, he has a justification (on a higher level), and that certainly if every level of rules is justified, then the whole system is justified. He would maintain that it makes no sense to ask for a justification for the system *over and above* a justification for each of its parts. This position, it must be admitted, has a good deal of plausibility; a final evaluation of its merits, however, must await some further developments.

The position held by the proponent of the inductive justification of induction contrasts with the position held by Hume in that it sets different requirements for the rational justification of a system of inductive logic. The following is implicit in the inductive justification of induction:

Rational Justification

Suggestion II: A system of inductive logic is rationally justified if, for every level (k) of rules of that system, there is an e-argument on the next highest level ($k + 1$) which:

i. Is adjudged inductively strong by its own system's rules (these will be rules of level $k + 1$).

ii. Has as its conclusion the statement that the system's rules on the original level (k) will work well next time.

It is important to see that *whether a system of induction meets these conditions depends not only on the system of induction itself but also on*

---

[6] In Table 2, "works well" is used as shorthand for "assigns high inductive probability to an e-argument whose conclusion turns out to be true."

the facts, on the way that the world is. We can imagine a situation in which scientific induction would indeed not meet these conditions. Imagine a world which has been so chaotic that scientific induction on level 1 has not worked well; that is, suppose that the e-arguments on level 1, which according to the rules of level 1 of scientific inductive logic are inductively strong and which have been used to make predictions in the past, have given us *false* conclusions from true premises most of the time. In such a situation the inductive justification of induction could not be carried through. For although the argument on level 2 used to justify the rules of level 1 of scientific induction, that is:

> Rules of level 1 of scientific inductive logic have worked well in the past.
> _____
> They will work well next time.

would still be adjudged inductively strong by the rules of level 2 of scientific inductive logic, its premise would not be true. Indeed in the situation under consideration the following argument on level 2 *would* have a premise that was known to be true and would also be adjudged inductively strong by the rules of level 2 of scientific inductive logic:

> Rules of level 1 of scientific inductive logic have not worked well in the past.
> _____
> They will not work well next time.

Thus we can conceive of situations in which level 2 of scientific induction, instead of justifying level 1 of scientific induction, would tell us that level 1 is unreliable.

We are not, in fact, in such a situation. Level 1 of scientific induction has served us quite well,[7] and it is upon this fact that the inductive justification of induction capitalizes. This is indeed an important fact, but it remains to be seen whether it is sufficient to rationally justify a system of scientific inductive logic.

The proponent of the inductive justification of scientific inductive logic has done us a service in distinguishing the various levels of induction. He has also made an important contribution by pointing out that there are possible situations in which the higher levels of scientific induction do not always support the lower levels and that we are, in fact, not in

_____

[7] Considering the history of science, this statement is an oversimplification whose status deserves serious consideration.

such a situation. But as a justification of the system of scientific induction his reasoning is not totally satisfactory. While he has not technically begged the question, he has come very close to it. Although he has an argument to justify every level of scientific induction, and although none of his arguments presuppose exactly what they are trying to prove, the justification of each level presupposes the correctness of the level above it. Lower levels are justified by higher levels, but always higher levels of scientific induction. No matter how far we go in the justifying process, we are always within the system of scientific induction. Now, isn't this loading the dice? Couldn't someone with a completely different system of inductive logic execute the same maneuver? Couldn't he justify each level of *his* logic by appeal to higher levels of *his* logic? Indeed he could. Given the same factual situation in which the inductive justification of scientific induction is carried out, an entirely different system of inductive logic could also meet the conditions laid down under Rational Justification, Suggestion II. Let us take a closer look at such a contrasting system of inductive logic.

We said that scientific induction assumes that, in some sense, nature is uniform and the future will be like the past. Some such assumption is to be found backing the rules on each level of scientific inductive logic. The assumptions are not exactly the same on each level; they must be different because we can imagine a situation in which scientific induction on level 2 would tell us that scientific induction on level 1 will not work well. Thus different principles of the uniformity of nature are presupposed on different levels of scientific inductive logic. But although they are not exactly the same, they are similar; they are all principles of the uniformity of nature. Thus each level of scientific inductive logic presupposes that, in some sense, nature is uniform and the future will be like the past. A system of inductive logic that would be *diametrically opposed* to scientific inductive logic would be one which presupposed on all levels that the future will not be like the past. We shall call this system a system of *counterinductive logic*.

Let us see how counterinductive logic would work on level 1. Scientific inductive logic, which assumes that the future will be like the past, would assign the following argument a high inductive probability:

> Many jub-jub birds have been observed and they have all been purple.
> _____
> The next jub-jub bird to be observed will be purple.

Counterinductive logic, which assumes that the future will *not* be like the past, would assign it a low inductive probability and would instead assign a high inductive probability to the following argument:

> Many jub-jub birds have been observed and they have all been purple.
> _____
> The next jub-jub bird to be observed will not be purple.

In general, counterinductive logic assigns low inductive probabilities to arguments that are assigned high inductive probabilities by scientific inductive logic, and high inductive probabilities to arguments that are assigned low inductive probabilities by scientific inductive logic.

Now suppose that a counterinductivist decided to give an inductive justification of counterinductive logic. The scientific inductivist would justify his rules of level 1 by the following level 2 argument:

> Rules of level 1 of counterinductive logic have *not* worked well in the past.
> _____
> They will work well next time.

The counterinductivist, on the other hand, would justify his rules of level 1 by another kind of level 2 argument:

> Rules of level 1 of counterinductive logic have *not* worked well in the past.
> _____
> They will work well next time.

By the counterinductivist's rules, this is an inductively strong argument, for on level 2 he also assumes that the future will be unlike the past. Thus the counterinductivist is not at all bothered by the fact that his level 1 rules have been failures; indeed he takes this as evidence that they will be successful in the future. Granted his argument appears absurd to us, for we are all at heart scientific inductivists. But if the scientific inductivist is allowed to use his own rules on level 2 to justify his rules on level 1, how can we deny the same right to the counterinductivist? If asked to justify his rules on level 2, the counterinductivist will advance a similar argument on level 3, etc. If an inductive justification of scientific inductive logic can be carried through, then a parallel inductive justification of counterinductive logic can be carried through. Table 3 summarizes how this would be done.

Table 3

Level of argument	Justifying arguments of the scientific inductivist	Justifying arguments of the counterconductivist
⋮	⋮	⋮
3:	Rules of level 2 of scientific inductive logic have worked well in the past.	Rules of level 2 of counter-inductive logic have not worked well in the past.
	They will work well next time.	They will work well next time.
2:	Rules of level 1 of scientific inductive logic worked well in the past.	Rules of level 1 of counter-inductive logic have not worked well in the past.
	They will work well next time.	They will work well next time.

The counterinductivist is, of course a fictitious character. No one goes through life consistently adhering to the canons of counterinductive logic, although some of us do occasionally slip into counterinductive reasoning. The poor poker player who thinks that his luck is due to change because he has been losing so heavily is a prime example. But aside from a description of gamblers' rationalizations, counterinductive logic has little practical significance.

It does, however, have great theoretical significance. For what we have shown is that if scientific inductive logic meets the conditions laid down under Rational Justification, Suggestion II so does counterinductive logic. This is sufficient to show that Suggestion II is inadequate as a definition for rational justification. A rational justification of a system of inductive logic must provide reasons for using that system rather than any other. Thus if two inconsistent systems, scientific induction and counterinduction, can meet the conditions of Suggestion II, then Suggestion II cannot be an adequate definition of rational justification. The arguments examined in this section do show that scientific inductive logic meets the conditions of Suggestion II, but these arguments do not rationally justify scientific induction.

This is not to say that what has been pointed out is not both important and interesting. Let us say that any system of inductive logic that meets the conditions of Suggestion II is *inductively coherent with the facts.* It may be true that for a system of inductive logic to be rationally justified it must be inductively coherent with the facts; that is, that inductive coherence with the facts may be a necessary condition for rational justification. But the example of the counterinductivist shows conclusively that inductive coherence with the facts is not by itself sufficient to rationally justify a system of inductive logic. Consequently the inductive justification of scientific inductive logic fails.

We may summarize our discussion of the inductive justification of induction as follows:

1. The proponent of the inductive justification of scientific induction points out that scientific inductive logic is inductively coherent with the facts.

2. He claims that this is sufficient to rationally justify scientific inductive logic.

3. But it is not sufficient since counterinductive logic is also inductively coherent with the facts.

4. Nevertheless it is important and informative since we can imagine circumstances in which scientific inductive logic would not be inductively coherent with the facts.

5. The proponent of the inductive justification of scientific induction has also succeeded in calling to our attention the fact that there are various levels of induction.

Exercises for the advanced student:

1. The discussion in this section is all carried on in terms of *instance prediction*, e.g.:

> The next jub-jub bird will be purple.
>
> The next e-argument assigned high inductive probability by rules of level 2 will have a conclusion that turns out to be true.

rather than *generality prediction:*

> All jub-jub birds are purple.

or

> Most jub-jub birds are purple.
>
> Most e-arguments assigned high inductive probabilities by rules of level 2 will have true conclusions.

Show that if we change the account to generality prediction, the inductivist cannot have the premises of his higher-level arguments as part of his stock of knowledge.

2. Show that if we change the account to generality prediction, the conclusions of the counterinductivist on different levels are inconsistent with one another.

3. The proponent of the inductive justification of induction tacitly assumes that an infinite number of observations and corresponding arguments on level 1 have already taken place. What happens to his argument if he is forced to admit that the number is really finite?

4. Can you imagine a world in which the counterinductive strategy in level 1 would be successful all the time? Most of the time?

Can you imagine a world in which the counterinductive strategy on all levels would be successful all of the time? Most of the time? Some of the time?

5. Does "works well" mean the same thing in the premises and conclusion of the inductivist's arguments? If not, can you find a common meaning which will serve his purposes?

Suggested readings

John Stuart Mill, "The Ground of Induction," reprinted in *A Modern Introduction to Philosophy* (rev. ed), Paul Edwards and Arthur Pap, eds. (Glencoe, Ill.: The Free Press, 1965), pp. 133–41.

F. L. Will, "Will the Future Be Like the Past?", reprinted in *A Modern Introduction to Philosophy* (rev. ed.), Paul Edwards and Arthur Pap, eds. (Glencoe, Ill.: The Free Press, 1965), pp. 148–58.

Max Black, "Inductive Support of Inductive Rules," *Problems of Analysis* (Ithaca, N.Y.: Cornell University Press, 1954), pp. 191-208.

All of these authors are arguing for some type of inductive justification of induction, although none of them holds the exact position outlined in this section, which is a synthesis of several viewpoints. The student cannot only broaden his knowledge of attempts to justify scientific induction inductively, but also test his knowledge of the major points of this section, by critically examining the positions taken by these authors.

II.4. THE PRAGMATIC JUSTIFICATION OF INDUCTION.

Remember that the traditional problem of induction can be formulated as a dilemma: If the reasoning we use to rationally justify scientific inductive logic is to have any strength at all it must be either deductively valid or inductively strong. But if we try to justify scientific inductive logic by means of a deductively valid argument with premises that are known to be true, our conclusion will be too weak. And if we try to use an inductively strong argument, we are reduced to begging the question. Whereas the proponent of the *inductive* justification of scientific induction attempts to go over the second horn of the dilemma, the proponent of the *pragmatic* justification of induction attacks the first horn; he attempts to justify scientific inductive logic by means of a deductively valid argument.

The pragmatic justification of induction was proposed by Herbert Feigl and elaborated by Hans Reichenbach, both founders of the logical empiricist movement.[8] Reichenbach's pragmatic justification of induction is quite complicated, for it depends on what he believes are the details (at least the basic details) of scientific inductive logic. Thus no one can fully understand Reichenbach's arguments until he has studied Reichenbach's definition of probability and the method he prescribes for discovering probabilities. We shall return to these questions later; at this point we will discuss a simplified version of the pragmatic justification of induction. This version is correct as far as it goes. Only bear in mind that there is more to be learned.

Reichenbach wishes to justify scientific inductive logic by a deductively valid argument. Yet he agrees with Hume that no deductive valid argument with premises that are known to be true can give us the conclusion that scientific induction will give us true conclusions most of the time. He agrees with Hume that the conditions of Rational Justification, Suggestion I, cannot be met. Since he fully intends to rationally justify scientific inductive logic, the only path open to him is to argue that the conditions of Rational Justification, Suggestion I, need not be met in order to justify a system of inductive logic. He proceeds to advance his own suggestion as to what is required for rational justification and to attempt to justify scientific inductive logic in these terms.

If Hume's arguments are correct, there is no way of showing that scientific induction will give us true conclusions from true premises most of the time. But since Hume's arguments apply equally well to any system of inductive logic there is no way of showing that any competing system of inductive logic will give us true conclusions from true premises most of the time either. Thus scientific inductive logic has the same status as all other systems of inductive logic in this matter. No other system of inductive logic can be demonstrated to be superior to scientific inductive logic in the sense of showing that it gives true conclusions from true premises more often than scientific inductive logic.

---

[8] However, the intellectual ancestry of the pragmatic justification can be traced back to Charles Saunders Peirce, the founder of American pragmatism and, in the opinion of many, the greatest philosopher that America has produced.

Reichenbach claims that although it is impossible to show that any inductive method will be successful, it can be shown that scientific induction will be successful, if any method of induction will be successful. In other words, it is possible that no inductive logic will guide us to e-arguments that give us true conclusions most of the time, but if any method will then scientific inductive logic will also. If this can be shown, then it would seem fair to say that scientific induction has been rationally justified. After all we must make some sort of judgments, conscious or unconscious, as to the inductive strength of arguments if we are to live at all. We must base our decisions on our expectations of the future, and we base our expectations of the future on our knowledge of the past and present. We are all gamblers, with the stakes being the success or failure of our plans of action. Life is an exploration of the unknown, and every human action presumes a wager with nature.

But if our decisions are a gamble and if no method is guaranteed to be successful, then it would seem rational to bet on that method which will be successful, if any method will. Suppose that you were forcibly taken into a locked room and told that whether or not you will be allowed to live depends on whether you win or lose a wager. The object of the wager is a box with red, blue, yellow, and orange lights on it. You know nothing about the construction of the box but are told that either all of the lights, some of them, or none of them will come on. You are to bet on one of the colors. If the colored light you choose comes on, you live; if not, you die. But before you make your choice you are also told that neither the blue, nor the yellow, nor the orange light can come on without the red light also coming on. If this is the only information you have, then you will surely bet on red. For although you have no guarantee that your bet on red will be successful (after all, all the lights might remain dark) you know that, if any bet will be successful, a bet on red will be successful. Reichenbach claims that scientific inductive logic is in the same privileged position vis-à-vis other systems of inductive logic as is the red light vis-à-vis the other lights.

This leads us to a new proposal as to what is required to rationally justify a system of inductive logic:

Rational Justification

Suggestion III: A system of inductive logic is rationally justified if we can show that the e-arguments that it adjudges inductively strong will give us true conclusions most of the time, if e-arguments adjudged inductively strong by any method will.

Reichenbach attempts to show that scientific inductive logic meets the conditions of Rational Justification, Suggestion III, by a deductively valid argument. The argument goes roughly like this:

.   Either nature is uniform or it is not.
If nature is uniform, scientific induction will be successful.
If nature is not uniform, then no method will be successful.

If any method of induction will be successful, then scientific induction will be successful.

There is no question that this argument is deductively valid, and the first and second premises are surely known to be true. But how do we know that the third premise is true? Couldn't there be some strange inductive method that would be successful even if nature were not uniform? How do we know that for any method to be successful nature must be uniform?

Reichenbach has a response ready for this challenge. Suppose that in a completely chaotic universe, some method, call it method X, were successful. Then there is still at least one outstanding uniformity in nature: the uniformity of method X's success. And scientific induction would discover *that* uniformity. That is, if method X is successful on the whole, if it gives us true predictions most of the time, then sooner or later the statement "Method X has been reliable in the past" will be true, and the following argument would be adjudged inductively strong by scientific inductive logic:

Method X has been reliable in the past.

Method X will be reliable[9] in the future.

Thus if method X is successful, scientific induction will also be successful in that it will discover method X's reliability, and, so to speak, license method X as a subsidiary method of prediction. This completes the proof that scientific induction will be successful if any method will.

The job may appear to be done, but in fact there is a great deal more to be said. In order to analyze just what has been proved and what has not, we shall use the idea of levels of inductive logic, which was developed in the last section. When we talk about a method, we are really talking about a system of inductive logic, while glossing over the fact that a system of inductive logic is composed of distinct levels of rules. Let us now pay attention to this fact. Since a system of inductive logic is composed of distinct

---

[9] Note that we are here using generality, rather than instance prediction. See exercise 1, p. 40.

levels of rules, in order to justify that system we would have to justify each level of its rules. Thus to justify scientific inductive logic we would have to justify level 1 rules of scientific inductive logic, level 2 rules of scientific inductive logic, level 3 rules of scientific inductive logic, etc. If each of these levels of rules is to be justified in accordance with the principle "It is rational to rely on a method that is successful if any method is successful," then the pragmatic justification of induction must establish the following:

1: Level 1 rules of scientific induction will be successful if level 1 rules of any system of inductive logic will be successful.

2: Level 2 rules of scientific induction will be successful if level 2 rules of any system of inductive logic will be successful.

⋮ ⋮

k: Level k rules of scientific induction will be successful if level k rules of any system of inductive logic will be successful.

But if we look closely at the pragmatic justification of induction, we see that it does not establish this but rather something quite different.

Suppose that system X of inductive logic is successful on level 1. That is, the arguments that it adjudges to be inductively strong give us true conclusions from true premises most of the time. Then sooner or later an argument on level 2 which is adjudged inductively strong by scientific inductive logic, that is:

Rules of level 1 of system X have been reliable in the past.

Rules of level 1 of system X will be reliable in the future.

will come to have a premise that is known to be true. If the rules on level 1 of system X give true predictions most of the time, then sooner or later it will be true that they have given us true predictions most of the time *in the past*. And once we have this premise, scientific induction on level 2 leads us to the conclusion that they will be reliable in the future.

Thus what has been shown is that if any system of inductive logic has successful rules on level 1, then scientific induction provides a justifying argument for these rules on level 2. Indeed we can generalize this principle and say that if a system of inductive logic has successful rules on a given level, then scientific induction provides a justifying argument on the next highest level. More precisely, the pragmatist has demonstrated the following: If system X of inductive logic has rules on level k which pick out, as inductively strong arguments of level k, those which give true predictions most of the time, then there is an argument on level

$k + 1$, which is adjudged inductively strong by the rules of level $k + 1$ of scientific inductive logic, which has as its conclusion the statement that the rules of system X on level k are reliable, and which has a premise that will sooner or later be known to be true.

Now this is quite different from showing that if any method works on any level then scientific induction will also work on *that* level, or even from showing that if any method works on level 1 then scientific induction will work on level 1. Instead what has been shown is that if any other method is generally successful on level 1 then scientific induction will have at least one notable success on level 2: it will eventually predict the continued success of that other method on level 1.

Although this is an interesting and important conclusion, it is not sufficient for the task at hand. Suppose we wish to choose a set of rules for level 1. In order to be in a position analogous to the wager about the box with the colored lights, we would have to know that scientific induction would be successful on level 1 if any method were successful on level 1. But we do not know this. For all we know, scientific induction might fail on level 1 and another method might be quite successful. If this were the case, scientific induction on level 2 would eventually tell us so, but this is quite a different matter.

In summary, the attempt at a pragmatic justification of induction has made us realize that a deductive justification of induction would be acceptable if it could establish that: if any system of inductive logic has successful rules on a given level, then scientific inductive logic will have successful rules on that level. But the arguments advanced in the pragmatic justification fail to establish this conclusion. Instead they show that if any system of inductive logic has successful rules on a given level, then scientific inductive logic will license a justifying argument for those rules on the next higher level.

Both the attempt at a pragmatic justification and the attempt at an inductive justification have failed to justify scientific induction. Nevertheless, both of them have brought forth useful facts about scientific induction, and we should try to utilize these facts. For instance, we might try to combine the pragmatic and inductive justifications of induction. That is, we might argue that the facts that were established in the pragmatic justification of induction provide a rationale for using scientific induction on higher levels to justify rules of induction on lower levels, and that the inductive justification of induction shows that, by this process, scientific induction is rationally justified on all levels. After all, the chief thorn in the side of the inductive justification of induction was the counterinductivist. And the pragmatic justification of induction shows one clear advantage of scientific induction over counterinduction. The counterinductivist cannot prove that if any method is successful on level 1, counterinduction on level 2 will eventually·predict its continued success.

I am not advancing this view as *the* answer to the traditional problem of induction; it has several difficulties, one of which involves the word "eventually." What I am emphasizing is that there is still room for constructive thought on the problem, and that we can learn much from previous failures to solve it.

Exercise:

Try combining the pragmatic and inductive justifications and see what you get.

Further exercises for the advanced student

1. Is a world in which *no* method of induction will work possible?

2. Is it possible that scientific induction works on level 3, but not on levels 1 or 2? Is the following true: For any *n*, it is possible that scientific induction works on level *n*, but does not work on any level less than *n*?

3. Is the following true: For any *n*, it is possible that scientific induction does not work on level *n*, but another method does?

Suggested readings

Wesley Salmon, "Should We Attempt to Justify Induction?" *Philosophical Studies*, April 1957, pp. 38–48.

Hans Reichenbach, "The Logical Foundations of the Theory of Probability," in *Readings in Philosophical Analysis*, ed. Herbert Feigl and Wilfred Sallers (New York: Appleton-Century-Crofts, Inc., 1949), pp. 305–23.

Hans Reichenbach, "On the Justification of Induction," in *Readings in Philosophical Analysis*, ed. Herbert Feigl and Wilfred Sallers (New York: Appleton-Century-Crofts, Inc., 1949), pp. 324–29.

The following are recommended for the advanced student:

On pragmatic justification:
Hacking, "Salmon's Vindication of Induction," *Journal of Philosophy*, 1965, pp. 260–266.

Skyrms, "On Failing to Vindicate Induction," *Philosophy of Science*, 1965, pp. 253–68.

On levels:
Tarski, "The Semantic Conception of Truth," in *Readings in Philosophical Analysis*, ed. Feigl and Sellars (N.Y.: Appleton-Century-Crofts, Inc., 1949), pp. 52–84.

On chaotic and orderly worlds (in sequences):
Russell, "On the Notion of Cause," in *Mysticism and Logic* (London: Longmans Green and Company, 1921), pp. 180–208.

Van Mises, *Probability Statistics and Truth*, 2nd ed. (N.Y.: The Macmillan Company, 1957).

Church, "On the Concept of a Random Sequence," *Bulletin of the American Mathematical Society*, Vol. 44 (1938): 130–35.

Martin-Löf, "The Definition of Random Sequences," *Information and Control*, Vol. 9 (1966): 602–19.

II.5. AN ATTEMPTED DISSOLUTION OF THE TRADITIONAL PROBLEM OF INDUCTION.

The inductive justification of induction attacked one horn of Hume's dilemma by attempting to rationally justify induction by means of inductively strong arguments. The pragmatic justification of induction attacked the other horn by attempting to rationally justify induction by means of a deductively valid argument. Those who attempt to dissolve the problem of induction take the third alternative. They attempt to go between the horns of the dilemma by claiming that no argument whatsoever is necessary to justify induction.

There are many variations on the philosophical theme of dissolving the traditional problem of induction. We shall not try to survey every nuance of every possible variation, but rather examine those considerations which are at present most frequently advanced to show that no argument whatsoever is necessary to justify scientific inductive logic.

Those who wish to dissolve the traditional problem of induction say that the question that generates this problem, that is, "Why is it rational to accept scientific inductive logic?" is a silly question, a question born of confusion. There are three main contentions as to why it is a silly question: (1) It asks us to turn induction into deduction. (2) Someone who doubts the rationality of accepting scientific inductive logic simply does not understand the words he is using. (3) It asks for a justification beyond the limits where justification makes sense. Let us survey these contentions and the considerations adduced in their favor.

1. It is a silly question because it asks us to turn induction into deduction: The problem of justifying scientific inductive logic arises because it is logically possible for an argument adjudged inductively strong by scientific

inductive logic to lead us from true premises to a false conclusion. Now if one is accustomed to thinking of deductive validity as the only standard against which the strength of arguments can be measured, he will be unsatisfied with this situation and wish to provide some logical guarantee that inductively strong arguments will give true conclusions from true premises. He will demand certainty where certainty cannot be had. And when he asks why it is rational to accept scientific inductive logic he is demanding a proof that arguments adjudged strong by scientific inductive logic will give us true conclusions from true premises all the time. Of course, there is no such proof because certainty that the conclusion will be true if the premises are true is the hallmark of deductive validity, not inductive strength. Thus he is demanding that the arguments adjudged strong by scientific inductive logic should really be deductively valid, which is impossible. Once we realize that deductive validity is not the only standard against which the strength of arguments can be measured and that inductive strength is a legitimate standard in its own right; once we realize that arguments that give high probability rather than certainty are still good arguments: we see that this demand is ridiculous. The request for a justification of scientific inductive logic arises from the mistaken opinion that deductive validity is the only standard against which the strength of arguments can be measured, and from an adolescent desire for certainty in a world of chance.

2. It is a silly question because someone who doubts that it is rational to accept scientific inductive logic simply does not understand the words he is using: Suppose someone asked you why he should believe that the father of Genghis Khan was male. You would probably be at a loss to know what was troubling him. There is no question of gathering evidence for the assertion that the father of Genghis Khan was male. There is no question of advancing arguments in its favor. Being male is simply part of what we mean by being a father. Someone who grants that there was such a person as the father of Genghis Khan and yet protests that he is not sure that that person was male simply does not understand the words he is using.

We have a parallel case with the traditional problem of induction, for part of what we mean by being *rational* is accepting scientific inductive logic. Suppose that a person does not form his expectations of the future roughly in accordance with scientific inductive logic, but rather in accordance with counterinductive logic. Would we not, *on this basis*, judge him to be irrational? Suppose that another person based all his major decisions on visions of the future he has when asleep. Furthermore, he has always been wrong. When we point out this fact to him, he replies that he does not care because he has just had a vision that assured him that all his future visions will be accurate. Would we not, *on this basis*, judge him to be irrational? Examples could be multiplied to show that the use of scientific inductive logic is a standard of rationality, that part of what we mean by being rational is accepting scientific inductive logic. Thus the question "Why is it rational to accept scientific inductive logic?" is as silly as the question "Why was Genghis Khan's father male?" Someone who doubts that it is rational to accept scientific inductive logic simply does not understand the words he is using.

3. It is a silly question because it asks for a justification beyond the limits where justification makes sense: Suppose some unredeemable skeptic were to ask why it is rational to accept any argument at all. One could not advance any argument to convince him without begging the question, for he has called into doubt the acceptability of all arguments. Clearly there is no possibility of rational discussion with such an individual, for he has called into doubt all the machinery of rational discussion. He has asked for justification beyond the limits where justification makes sense. For justification to make sense there must be some machinery left for that justification, and scientific inductive logic is an essential part of the machinery for rational discussion. To call it into question is also to ask for a justification beyond the limits where rational justification makes sense. For if inductively strong arguments are called into question, then the only machinery left for rational discussion consists in deductively valid arguments, and, as Hume has shown, these are particularly unsuitable for the task of rationally justifying induction. The request for rational justification does not make sense when it is directed at the machinery of rational justification itself. Thus the question "Why is it rational to accept scientific inductive logic?" is as silly as the question "Why is it rational to accept any argument at all?"

The foregoing contentions are a sample of the considerations advanced by those who wish to dissolve the traditional problem of induction. If they are correct in stating that no argument whatsoever is necessary to justify scientific inductive logic, then Hume's dilemma is a paper tiger and the proponents of the inductive and pragmatic justifications of induction have been tilting at windmills. The considerations so far advanced in favor of the dissolution of the traditional problem of induction do have a certain amount of weight. But it is doubtful that they are sufficient to pull the teeth out of Hume's problem. Let us examine the three main objections to the question "Why is it rational to accept scientific inductive logic?"

1. It is a silly question because it asks us to turn induction into deduction: This is the most popular and the most unsophisticated objection to the

traditional problem of induction; it simply misrepresents the problem. Suggestion I for rational justification did *not* demand that e-arguments adjudged inductively strong by scientific inductive logic should *always* give us true conclusions. What it required for rational justification is that it be shown that these arguments give true conclusions most of the time. Thus those who ask for a rational justification in the sense of Suggestion I are not asking us to turn induction into deduction and they are not asking that the link between premises and conclusion in inductively strong arguments be one of certainty rather than high probability. They realize that inductively strong arguments can, on occasion, lead us from true premises to a false conclusion, and that this is simply the nature of the beast. What they want is some sort of guarantee that with respect to our e-arguments, this will prove the exception rather than the rule. Thus the problem of justification arises not simply because it is logically possible for an inductively strong argument to lead us from true premises to a false conclusion some of the time, but because it is logically possible for inductively strong e-arguments to lead us to false conclusions most of the time.

Although this objection is easily disposed of, it does have a point. Some philosophers have been so awed by the traditional problem of induction that they have come to the conclusion that if there is any strength at all to those arguments we think are inductively strong, then those arguments must really be deductively valid arguments in disguise.[10] The objection we have been considering is a reply to those philosophers, although it should not be directed at the traditional problem of induction itself.

One can still feel the force of the traditional problem of induction even if one realizes that deductive validity is not the only standard against which the strength of arguments can be measured, and that inductively strong arguments give us high probability rather than certainty. For the traditional problem of induction is generated by a request for assurance that inductive probability is a useful tool for its ultimate purpose: prediction of the future. The desire is not to change inductive probability into deductive certainty; it is to justify the use of inductive probability as a guide to rational decision making.

2. It is a silly question because someone who doubts that it is rational to accept scientific inductive logic simply does not understand the words he is using: Those who advance this objection against the traditional problem of induction would contend that part of what we mean by rational decision making is the use of scientific inductive logic and that that is the end of the

---

[10] That is, deductively valid arguments with a missing premise.

question. In a sense they are right, although this is not the end of the question. They are correct in claiming that if a person consistently based his expectations of the future on methods that conflict with scientific inductive logic, then he would be judged, on that basis, as acting irrationally. So it seems that acceptance of scientific induction is part of what we mean by rationality.

But, to pursue this example a little further, suppose we came upon a whole culture that based its expectations of the future on methods that conflicted with scientific induction. Let us call the members of this culture "Omegas." Whenever the Omegas have a particularly important decision to make, they base their predictions of relevant future happenings on the pronouncements of a witch doctor rather than on scientific induction. Unfortunately for the Omegas the witch doctors are usually wrong, although they have occasionally made successful predictions; nevertheless the Omegas continue to place faith in their witch doctors. Now we would indeed judge the Omegas' reliance on the witch doctor to be irrational.

Suppose, having learned their language and wishing to speed the "progress of civilization," we decide to convert the Omegas to scientific induction. We point out that the witch doctors have not been very successful in the past and they reply that they have indeed had a very long period of bad luck but that they are sure that witch doctors will be successful in the future. Suppose then we ask them to justify this faith. They reply that this is a silly question, that relying on the witch doctor is part of what they mean by being rational; if we doubt that it is rational, we must simply not understand the words we are using.

What are we now to say to them? Perhaps we *did not* understand the words we used, since the discussion took place in their language, not ours. Perhaps their conception of rationality is different from ours, and their word which we thought was an exact translation of the English word "rational" is not. Suppose their word is "brational." Then part of the meaning of "brational" is to rely on the witch doctor, and part of the meaning of "rational" is to accept scientific inductive logic. They proudly call themselves brational and we proudly call ourselves rational. Once this is understood, the Omegas will even agree that they are irrational, but will maintain that what is important is that they are brational and we are unbrational. In this situation, what sort of considerations could we advance to convince them that they should accept scientific induction? In other words, *how could we convince them that rationality is superior to brationality?*

We could convince them if we could show them that scientific induction is better suited to the task of predicting the future than reliance on the witch doctor, for they too are interested in correctly predicting the future. We could certainly convince them if we could show that scientific induction would be right more often than the witch doctor. Thus we are back to the traditional problem of induction.

The point is that if we simply say that the acceptance of scientific inductive logic is part of the meaning of rationality and refuse to pursue its justification any further, then we are holding scientific induction as a dogma built into our language, just as the Omegas are holding reliance on the witch doctor as a dogma built into theirs. Thus even if we agree that part of the meaning of rationality is accepting scientific inductive logic, the traditional problem of induction reappears to haunt us as the question "Why is rationality superior to brationality?"

3. It is a silly question because it asks for a justification beyond the limits where justification makes sense: Those who wish to raise this objection against the traditional problem of induction have an answer ready concerning our difficulties with the Omegas. The Omegas, they will contend, are in a position parallel to the hypothetical person who would not accept any argument whatsoever. There is really no possibility of fruitful discussion with Omegas on this matter since they refuse to accept the machinery necessary for fruitful discussion. There is no way to convince *them* that rationality is superior to brationality, but the ultimate answer for *us* must simply be that it is rational to be rational and irrational to be brational. This does not mean that our acceptance of scientific inductive logic is a *dogma*, for what we mean by dogma is an irrationally held belief. If one refuses to test his beliefs by scientific inductive logic, these beliefs are said to be dogmatically held. If one is willing to test his beliefs by scientific inductive logic, then he is not dogmatic. Thus the acceptance of scientific inductive logic is not a dogma; it is one of the ultimate principles of reason.

Notice that someone who argues in this way is really suggesting another type of rational justification; he is claiming that his type of rational justification is the only type possible and the only type that makes sense. This type of rational justification is embodied in the following suggestion:

Rational Justification

Suggestion IV: A system of inductive logic is rationally justified if it can be shown to be an embodiment of those inductive rules of science and common sense that we take to be a standard of rationality.

Since what we mean by scientific inductive logic is a system that accords well with common sense and scientific practice, scientific inductive logic is automatically justified in the sense of Suggestion IV.

But let us remember that it has nowhere been demonstrated that rational justification in the sense of Suggestion IV is the best that we can do. Hume may have shown that rational justification in the sense of Suggestion I is impossible, but there may be a sense of rational justification that is weaker than Suggestion I but stronger than Suggestion IV in which rational justification is possible. After all, when we attempt to justify scientific inductive logic without begging the question, we are not deprived of all machinery for rational discussion (as we would be if we attempted to answer the question "Why should one accept any argument at all?"). The discussion of the attempts at inductive and pragmatic justifications of induction showed that we could still do quite a bit without begging the question.

Suppose that we could somehow show that scientific inductive logic is better suited for accomplishing the purposes of inductive logic than any other system. We would then have a stronger justification than Suggestion IV, and rather than merely condemning the Omegas as irrational we could give them reasons why our way of thinking is superior to theirs. We would not have to be satisfied simply with commitment to scientific inductive logic as an integral part of the machinery of reason; we could explain why it is and ought to be an integral part of that machinery. Thus a rational justification that is stronger than that proposed by Suggestion IV will make sense if we can discover one.

We can summarize the main conclusions of this section as follows:

1. Those who wish to dissolve the traditional problem of induction claim that scientific inductive logic is rationally justified simply because acceptance of scientific inductive logic is part of what we mean by being rational, and that it does not make sense to look for a different kind of rational justification.

2. There is a sense of rational justification in which they are correct in saying that scientific inductive logic is justified because it is an essential part of the machinery of rational thought.

3. But they are incorrect in saying that it does not make sense to look for a stronger type of rational justification because:

    a. A stronger type of justification would be valuable if we could find one.

    b. No one has demonstrated that a stronger type of justification is impossible.

Before we leave the attempted dissolution of the traditional problem of induction, one final point should be noted. Even if we are satisfied with Suggestion IV, a problem remains. Once we have a system of scientific inductive logic we can say that, in terms of Suggestion IV, it is automatically justified. But constructing a system of scientific inductive logic is an immensely difficult task in itself. We shall see in the next chapter that the job of making explicit and systemizing "those inductive rules of science and common sense that we take to be a standard of rationality" is a complex and delicate enterprise. To justify a system of inductive logic in terms of Suggestion IV we must complete this enterprise, for we must show that it *is* a system of scientific inductive logic. Thus even if the traditional problem of induction is dissolved, the new riddle of induction, which we will encounter in the next chapter, will remain.

Suggested readings

Peter Strawson, *Introduction to Logical Theory* (New York: John Wiley & Sons, Inc., 1952), pp. 248–63.

Paul Edwards, "Bertrand Russell's Doubts about Induction," in *Logic and Language*, Anthony Flew, ed. (Garden City, N.Y.: Anchor Books, 1965), pp. 59–85.

II.6. SUMMARY. We have developed the traditional problem of induction and discussed several answers to it. We found that each position we discussed had a different set of standards for rational justification of a system of inductive logic.

I. *Position:* The original presentation of the traditional problem of induction. *Standard for Rational Justification:* A system of inductive logic is rationally justified if and only if it is shown that the e-arguments that it adjudges inductively strong yield true conclusions most of the time.

II. *Position:* The inductive justification of induction. *Standard for Rational Justification:* A system of inductive logic is rationally justified if for every level (k) of rules of that system there is an e-argument on the next highest level ($k+1$) which:

    i. Is adjudged inductively strong by its own system's rules.

    ii. Has as its conclusion the statement that the system's rules on the original level (k) will work well next time.

III. *Position:* The pragmatic justification of induction.

Standard for Rational Justification: A system of inductive logic is rationally justified if it is shown that the e-arguments that it adjudges inductively strong yield true conclusions most of the time, if e-arguments adjudged inductively strong by any method will.

IV. *Position:* The dissolution of the traditional problem of induction.

Standard for Rational Justification: A system of inductive logic is rationally justified if it is shown to be an embodiment of those inductive rules of science and common sense which we take to be a standard of rationality.

The attempt at an inductive justification of scientific inductive logic taught us to recognize different levels of arguments and corresponding levels of inductive rules. It also showed that scientific inductive logic meets the standards for Rational Justification, Suggestion II. However, we saw that Suggestion II is really not a sense of rational justification at all, for both scientific inductive logic and counterinductive logic can meet its conditions. Thus it cannot justify the choice of one over the other.

The attempt at a pragmatic justification of scientific inductive logic showed us that Suggestion III, properly interpreted in terms of levels of induction, would be an acceptable sense of rational justification, although it would be a weaker sense than that proposed in Suggestion I. However, the pragmatic justification fails to demonstrate that scientific induction meets the conditions of Suggestion III.

The attempt at a dissolution of the traditional problem of induction shows that Suggestion IV is a sense of rational justification, although a very weak one. Furthermore, it shows that scientific inductive logic meets the conditions of Suggestion IV. However, it fails to show that it is senseless to look for a stronger justification than Suggestion IV.

The remaining problem is to construct a detailed system of inductive logic which meets the conditions of Suggestion IV, that is, which is a system of scientific inductive logic, and to find a stronger justification of this system if one is possible.

III

THE GOODMAN PARADOX
AND THE NEW RIDDLE
OF INDUCTION

III.1. INTRODUCTION. In Chapter II we presented some general specifications for a system of scientific inductive logic. We said it should be a system of rules for assigning inductive probabilities to arguments, with different levels of rules corresponding to the different levels of arguments. This system must accord fairly well with common sense and scientific practice. It must on each level presuppose, in some sense, that nature is uniform and that the future will resemble the past. These general specifications were sufficient to give us a foundation for surveying the traditional problem of induction and the major attempts to solve or dissolve it.

However, to be able to apply scientific inductive logic, as a rigorous discipline, we must know precisely what its rules are. Unfortunately no one has yet produced an adequate formulation of the rules of scientific inductive logic. In fact, inductive logic is in much the same state as deductive logic was before Aristotle. This unhappy state of affairs is not due to a scarcity of brainpower in the field of inductive logic. Some of the great minds of history have attacked its problems. The distance by which they have fallen short of their goals is a measure of the difficulty of the subject. Formulating the rules of inductive logic, in fact, appears to be a more difficult enterprise than doing the same for deductive logic. Deductive logic is a "yes or no" affair; an argument is either deductively valid or it is not. But inductive strength is a matter of degree. Thus while deductive logic must *classify* arguments as valid or not, inductive logic must *measure* the inductive strength of arguments.

Setting up such rules of measurement is not an easy task. It is in fact beset with so many problems that some philosophers have been convinced it is impossible. They maintain that a system of scientific induction cannot be constructed; that prediction of the future is an art, not a science; and that we must rely on the intuitions of experts, rather than on scientific inductive logic, to predict the future. We can only hope that this gloomy doctrine is as mistaken as the view of those early Greeks who believed deductive logic could never be reducd to a precise system of rules and must forever remain the domain of professional experts on reasoning.

If constructing a system of scientific inductive logic were totally impossible, we would be left with an intellectual vacuum, which could not be filled by appeal to "experts." For, to decide whether someone is an expert predictor or a charlatan, we must assess the evidence that his predictions will be correct. And to assess this evidence, we must appeal to the second level of scientific inductive logic.

Fortunately there are grounds for hope. Those who have tried to construct a system of scientific inductive logic have made some solid advances. Although the intellectual jigsaw puzzle has not been put together, we at least know what some of the pieces look like. Later we shall examine some of these "building blocks" of inductive logic, but first we shall try to put the problem of constructing a system of scientific induction in perspective by examining one of the main obstacles to this goal.

III.2. REGULARITIES AND PROJECTION. At this point you may be puzzled as to why the construction of a system of scientific inductive logic is so difficult. After all, we know that scientific induction assumes that nature is uniform and that the future will be like the past, so if, for example, all observed emeralds have been green, the premise embodying this information confers high probability on the conclusion that the next emerald to be observed will be green. We say that scientific inductive logic *projects an observed regularity* into the future because it assigns high inductive probability to the argument:

All observed emeralds have been green.
_____
The next emerald to be observed will be green.

In contrast, counterinduction would assume that the observed regular connection between being an emerald and being green would not hold in the future, and thus would assign high inductive probability to the argument:

All observed emeralds have been green.
_____
The next emerald to be observed will not be green.

So it seems that scientific induction, in a quite straightforward manner, takes observed patterns or regularities in nature and assumes that they will hold in the future. Along these same lines, the premise that 99 per cent of the observed emeralds have been green would confer a slightly lower probability on the conclusion that the next emerald to be observed would be green. Why can we not simply say, then, that arguments of the form

> All observed X's have been Y's.
> _____
> The next observed X will be a Y.

have an inductive probability of 1, and that all arguments of the form

> Ninety-nine per cent of the observed X's have been Y's.
> _____
> The next observed X will be a Y.

have an inductive probability of 99/100?

That is, why can we not simply construct a system of scientific induction by giving the following rule on each level?

> **Rule S:** An argument of the form
>
> > N per cent of the observed X's have been Y's.
> > _____
> > The next observed X will be a Y.
>
> is to be assigned the inductive probability $N/100$.

Rule S does project observed regularities into the future. But there are several reasons why it cannot constitute a system of scientific inductive logic.

The most obvious inadequacy of Rule S is that it only applies to arguments of a specific form, and we are interested in assessing the inductive strength of arguments of different forms. Consider arguments which, in addition to a premise stating the percentage of observed X's that have been Y's, have another premise stating how many X's have been observed. Here the rule does not apply, for the arguments are not of the required form. For example, Rule S does not tell us how to assign inductive probabilities to the following arguments:

I	II
Ten emeralds have been observed.	One million emeralds have been observed.
Ninety per cent of the observed emeralds have been green.	Ninety per cent of the observed emeralds have been green.
The next emerald to be observed will be green.	The next emerald to be observed will be green.

Obviously scientific inductive logic should tell us how to assign inductive probabilities to these arguments, and in assigning these probabilities it should take into account that the premises of Argument II bring a much greater amount of evidence to bear than the premises of Argument I.

Another type of argument that Rule S does not tell us how to evaluate is one that includes a premise stating in what variety of circumstances the regularity has been found to hold. That is, Rule S does not tell us how to assign inductive probabilities to the following arguments:

III	IV
Every person who has taken drug X has exhibited no adverse side reactions.	Every person who has taken drug X has exhibited no adverse side reactions.
Drug X has only been administered to persons between 20 and 25 years of age who are in good health.	Drug X has been administered to persons of all ages and varying degrees of health.
The next person to take drug X will have no adverse side reactions.	The next person to take drug X will have no adverse side reactions.

Again scientific inductive logic should tell us how to assign inductive probabilities to these arguments, and in doing so it should take into account the fact that the premises of Argument IV tell us that the regularity has been found to hold in a great variety of circumstances, whereas the premises of Argument III inform us that the regularity has been found to hold in only a limited area.

There are many other types of argument that Rule S does not tell us how to evaluate, including most of the arguments advanced as examples in Chapter I. We can now appreciate why an adequate system of rules for scientific inductive logic must be a fairly complex structure. But there is another shortcoming of Rule S which has to do with arguments to which it does apply, that is, arguments of the form:

N per cent of the observed X's have been Y's.

The next observed X will be a Y.

The following two arguments are of that form, so we can apply Rule S to evaluate them:

V

One hundred per cent of the observed samples of pure water have had a freezing point of +32 degrees Fahrenheit.

The next observed sample of pure water will have a freezing point of +32 degrees Fahrenheit.

VI

One hundred per cent of the recorded economic depressions have occurred at the same time as large sunspots.

The next economic depression will occur at the same time as a large sunspot.

If we apply Rule S we find that it assigns an inductive probability of 1 to each of these arguments. But surely Argument V has a much higher degree of inductive strength than Argument VI! We feel perfectly justified in projecting into the future the observed regular connection between a certain type of chemical compound and its freezing point. But we feel that the observed regular connection between economic cycles and sunspots is a coincidence, an accidental regularity or spurious correlation, which should not be projected into the future. We shall say that the observed regularity reported in the premise of Argument V is *projectible*, while the regularity reported in the premise of Argument VI is not. We must now sophisticate our conception of scientific inductive logic still further. Scientific inductive logic does project observed regularities into the future, but only projectible regularities. It does assume that nature is uniform and that the future will resemble the past, but only in certain respects. It does assume that observed patterns in nature will be repeated, but only certain types of patterns. Thus Rule S is not adequate for scientific inductive logic because it is incapable of taking into account differences in projectibility of regularities.

Exercises:

1. Construct five inductively strong arguments to which Rule S does not apply.

2. Give two new examples of projectible regularities and two new examples of unprojectible regularities.

3. For each of the following arguments, state whether Rule S is applicable. If it is applicable, what inductive probability does it assign to the argument?

a. One hundred per cent of the crows observed have been black.

The next crow to be observed will be black.

b. One hundred per cent of the crows observed have been black.

All crows are black.

c. Every time I have looked at a calendar, the date has been before January 1, 1984.

The next time I look at a calendar the date will be before January 1, 1984.

d. Every time fire has been observed, it has continued to burn according to the laws of nature until extinguished.

All unobserved fires continue to burn according to the laws of nature until extinguished.

e. Eighty-five per cent of the time when I have dropped a piece of silverware, company has subsequently arrived.

The next time I drop a piece of silverware company will subsequently arrive.

III.3. THE GOODMAN PARADOX. If one tries to construct various examples of projectible and unprojectible regularities, he will soon come to the conclusion that projectibility is not simply a "yes or no" affair but rather a matter of degree. Some regularities are highly projectible, some have a middling degree of projectibility, and some are quite unprojectible. Just how unprojectible a regularity can be has been demonstrated by Nelson Goodman in his famous "grue-bleen" paradox.

Goodman invites us to consider a new color word, "grue." It is to have the general logical features of our old color words such as "green," "blue," and "red." That is, we can speak of things being a certain color at a certain time —for example, "John's face is red now"—and we can speak of things either remaining the same color or changing colors. The new color word "grue" is defined in terms of the familiar color words "green" and "blue" as follows:

Definition 6: A certain thing X is said to be *grue* at a certain time t if and only if:

X is green at t *and* t is before the year 2000
or
X is blue at t *and* t is during or after the year 2000.

Let us see how this definition works. If you see a green grasshopper today, you can correctly maintain that you have seen a grue grasshopper today. Today is before the year 2000, and before the year 2000 something is grue just when it is green. But if you or one of your descendants sees a green grasshopper during or after the year 2000, it would then be incorrect to maintain that a grue grasshopper had been seen. During and after the year

2000, something is grue just when it is blue. Thus after the year 2000, a blue sky would also be a grue sky.

Suppose now that a chameleon were kept on a green cloth until the beginning of the year 2000 and then transferred to a blue cloth. In terms of green and blue we would say that the chameleon changed color from green to blue. But in terms of the new color word "grue" we would say that it remained the same color: "grue." The other side of the coin is that when something remains the same color in terms of the old color words, it will change color in terms of the new one. Suppose we have a piece of glass that is green now and that will remain green during and after the year 2000. Then we would have to say that it was a grue before the year 2000 but was not grue during and after the year 2000. At the beginning of the year 2000 it changed color from grue to some other color. To name the color that it changed to we introduce the new color word "bleen." "Bleen" is defined in terms of "green" and "blue" as follows:

> **Definition 7:** A certain thing X is said to be *bleen* at a certain time t if and only if:
> X is blue at t *and* t is before the year 2000
> *or*
> X is green at t *and* t is during or after the year 2000.

Thus before the year 2000 something is grue just when it is green and bleen just when it is blue. After the year 2000 something is grue just when it is blue and bleen just when it is green. In terms of the old color words the piece of glass remains the same color (green), but in terms of the new color words the piece of glass changes color (from grue to bleen).

Imagine a tribe of people speaking a language that had "grue" and "bleen" as basic color words rather than the more familiar ones that we use. Suppose we describe a situation in our language—for example, the piece of glass being green before the year 2000 and remaining green afterward— in which we would say that there is no change in color. But if they correctly describe the same situation in their language, then, *in their terms*, there is a change. This leads to the important and rather startling conclusion that whether a certain situation involves change or not may depend on the descriptive machinery of the language used to discuss that situation.

One might object that "grue" and "bleen" are not acceptable color words because they have reference to a specific date in their definitions. It is quite true that *in our language*, in which blue and green are the basic color words, grue and bleen must be defined not only in terms of blue and green but also in terms of the date "2000 A.D." But a speaker of the grue-bleen language could maintain that definitions of our color words in his language must also have reference to a specific date. In the grue-bleen language, "grue" and "bleen" are basic, and "blue" and "green" are defined as follows:

> **Definition 8:** A certain thing X is said to be *green* at a certain time t if and only if:
> X is grue at t *and* t is before the year 2000
> *or*
> X is bleen at t *and* t is during or after the year 2000.

> **Definition 9:** A certain thing X is said to be *blue* at a certain time t if and only if:
> X is bleen at t *and* t is before the year 2000
> *or*
> X is grue at t *and* t is during or after the year 2000.

Defining the old color words in terms of the new requires reference to a specific date as much as defining the new words in terms of the old. So the formal structure of their definitions gives no reason to believe that "grue" and "bleen" are not legitimate, although unfamiliar, color words.

Let us see what can be learned about regularities and projectibility from these new color words. We have already shown that whether there is change in a given situation may depend on what linguistic machinery is used to describe that situation. We shall now show that what regularities we find in a given situation also may depend on our descriptive machinery. Suppose that at one minute to midnight on December 31, 1999, a gem expert is asked to predict what the color of a certain emerald will be after midnight. He knows that all observed emeralds have been green. He projects this regularity into the future and predicts that the emerald will remain green. Notice that this is in accordance with Rule S, which assigns an inductive probability of 1 to the argument:

> One hundred per cent of the times that emeralds have been observed they have been green.
> _____
> The next time that an emerald is observed it will be green.

But if the gem expert were a speaker of the grue-bleen language, he would find a different regularity in the color of observed emeralds. He would notice that every time an emerald had been observed it had been grue. (Remember that before the year 2000 everything that is green is also grue.) Now if he followed Rule S he would project *this* regularity into the future, for Rule S also assigns an inductive probability of 1 to the argument:

> One hundred per cent of the times emeralds have been observed they have been "grue."
>
> ---
>
> The next time an emerald is observed it will be "grue."

And if he projected the regularity that all observed emeralds have been grue into the future he would predict that the emerald will remain grue. But during the year 2000 a thing is "grue" only if it is blue. So by projecting this regularity he is in effect predicting that the emerald will change from green to blue.

Now, we will all agree that this is a ridiculous prediction to make on the basis of the evidence. And no one is really claiming that it should be made. But it cannot be denied that this prediction results from the projection into the future of an observed regularity in accordance with Rule S. The point is that the regularity of every observed emerald having been grue is a totally unprojectable regularity. And the prediction of our hypothetical grue-bleen-speaking gem expert is an extreme case of the trouble we get into when we try to project, via some rule such as Rule S, regularities that are in fact unprojectible.

The trouble we get into is indeed deep, for the prediction so arrived at will conflict with the prediction arrived at by projecting a projectible regularity. If we project the projectible regularity that every time an emerald has been observed it has been green, then we arrive at the prediction that the emerald will remain green. If we project the unprojectible regularity that every time an emerald has been observed, it has been grue, then we arrive at the prediction that the emerald will change from green to blue. These two predictions clearly are in conflict.[1]

Thus the mistake of projecting an unprojectible regularity may not only lead to a ridiculous prediction. It may, furthermore, lead to a prediction that conflicts with a legitimate prediction which results from projecting a projectible regularity discovered in *the same set of data.* An acceptable system of scientific inductive logic must provide some means to escape this conflict. It must incorporate rules that tell us which regularities are projectible. From the discussion of accidental regularities and the sunspot theory of economic cycles, we already know that scientific inductive logic must have rules for determining projectibility. But the Goodman paradox gives

---

[1] Actually they are inconsistent only under the assumption that the emerald will not be destroyed before 2000 A.D., but presumably we will have independent inductive evidence for this assumption.

this point new urgency by demonstrating how unprojectible a regularity can be and how serious are the consequences of projecting a totally unprojectible regularity.

Let us summarize what is to be learned from the discussion of "grue" and "bleen":

1. Whether we find change or not in a certain situation may depend on the linguistic machinery we use to describe that situation.

2. What regularities we find in a sequence of occurrences may depend on the linguistic machinery used to describe that sequence.

3. We may find two regularities in a sequence of occurrences, one projectible and one unprojectible, such that the predictions that arise from projecting them both are in conflict.

Exercises:

1. Translate the following descriptions in terms of "blue" and "green" into equivalent descriptions in terms of "grue" and "bleen":
   a. Ten million years from now the grass will be green and the sea blue.
   b. In 50 years from now the following songs will be very popular: "Green Eyes" and "My Blue Heaven."
   c. In the 1950's these songs were very popular: "She Wore Blue Velvet," "The Wearing of the Green," and "Birth of the Blues."
   d. There will be a miracle at the beginning of the year 2000: the color of the sky will change from blue to green.

2. Define "grue" in terms of "blue," "green," and "bleen" without mentioning the year 2000.

III.4. THE GOODMAN PARADOX, REGULARITY, AND THE PRINCIPLE OF THE UNIFORMITY OF NATURE.

We saw, in the last section, that projecting observed regularities into the future is not as simple as it first appears. The regularities found in a certain sequence of events may depend on the language used to describe that sequence of events. The Goodman paradox showed that if we try to project all regularities that can be found by using any language, our predictions may conflict with one another. This is a startling result, and it dramatizes the need for rules for determining projectibility in scientific induction. (This might be accomplished through the specification of the most fruitful language for scientific description of events.)

This need is further dramatized by the following, even more startling result: For any prediction whatsoever, we can find a regularity whose projection licenses that prediction. Of course, most of these regularities will be unprojectible. The point is that we need rules to eliminate those predictions based on unprojectible regularities. I shall illustrate this principle in three ways: (1) in an example that closely resembles Goodman's "grue-bleen" paradox, (2) with reference to the extrapolation of curves on graphs, (3) with reference to the problem, often encountered on intelligence tests, of continuing a sequence of numbers. The knowledge gained from this discussion will then be applied to a reëxamination of the principle of the uniformity of nature.

Example 1

Suppose you are presented with four boxes, each labeled "Excelsior!" In the first box you discover a green insect; in the second, a yellow ball of wax; in the third, a purple feather. You are now told that the fourth box contains a mask and are asked to predict its color. You must look for a regularity in this sequence of discoveries, whose projection will license a prediction as to the color of the mask. Although on the face of it, this seems impossible, with a little ingenuity a regularity can be found. What is more, for any prediction you wish to make, there is a regularity whose projection will license that prediction. Suppose you want to predict that the mask will be red. The regularity is found in the following manner.

Let us define a new word, "snarf." A snarf is something presented to you in a box labeled "Excelsior!" and is either an insect, a ball of wax, a feather, or a mask. Now you have observed three snarfs and are about to observe a fourth. This is a step toward regularity, but there is still the problem that the three observed snarfs have been different colors. One more definition is required in order to find regularity in apparent chaos. A thing X is said to be "murkle" just when:

> X is an insect *and* X is green
> *or*
> X is a ball of wax *and* X is yellow
> *or*
> X is a feather *and* X is purple
> *or*
> X is some other type of thing *and* X is red.

Now we have found the regularity: all observed snarfs have been murkle. If we project this regularity into the future, assuming that the next snarf to be observed will be murkle, we obtain the required prediction.[2] The next snarf to be observed will be a mask, and for a mask to be murkle it must be red. Needless to say, this regularity is quite unprojectible. But it is important to see that we could discover an unprojectible regularity that, if it were projected, would lead to the prediction that the mask is red. And it is easy to see that, if we wanted to discover a regularity that would lead to a prediction that the mask will be a different color, a few alterations to the definition of "murkle" would accomplish this aim. This sort of thing can always be done and, as we shall see, in some areas we need not even resort to such exotic words as "snarf," "murkle," "grue," and "bleen."

Example 2

When basing predictions on statistical data, we often make use of graphs, which help summarize the evidence and guide us in making our predictions. To illustrate, suppose a certain small country takes a census every 10

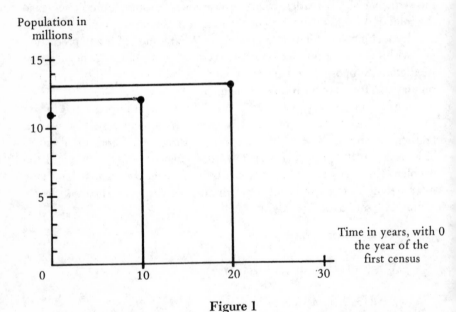

Figure 1

---

[2] This projection is in accordance with Rule S, which assigns an inductive probability of 1 to the argument:

> All observed snarfs have been murkle.
> _____
> The next snarf to be observed will be murkle.

years, and has taken three so far. The population was 11 million at the time of the first census, 12 million at the second census, and 13 million at the third. This information is represented on a graph in Figure 1. Each dot represents the information as to population size gained from one census. For example, the middle dot represents the second census, taken in the year 10, and showing a population of 12 million. Thus it is placed at the intersection of the vertical line drawn from the year 10 and the horizontal line drawn from the population of 12 million.

Suppose now you are asked to predict the population of this country at the time of the fourth census, that is, in the year 30. You would have to look for a regularity that could be projected into the future. In the absence of any further information, you would probably proceed as follows: First you would notice that the points representing the first three census all fall on the straight line labeled A in Figure 2, and would then project this regularity into the future. This is in accordance with Rule S, which assigns an inductive probability of 1 to the following argument:

> All points representing census so far taken have fallen on line A.
> _____
> The point representing the next census to be taken will fall on line A.

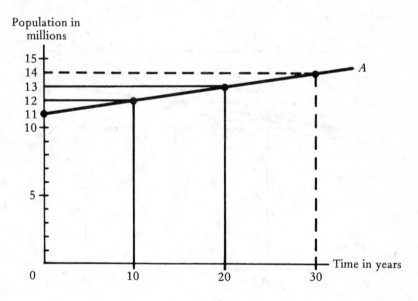

Figure 2

This projection would lead you to the prediction that the population at the time of the fourth census will be 14 million, as shown by the dotted lines in Figure 2. The process by which you would arrive at your prediction is called *extrapolation*. If you had used similar reasoning to estimate the population during the year 15 at 12½ million, the process would be called *interpolation*. Interpolation is estimating the position of a point that lies *between* the points representing the data. Extrapolation is estimating the position of a point that lies *outside* the points representing the data. So your prediction would be obtained by extrapolation, and your extrapolation would be a projection of the regularity that all the points plotted so far fell on line *A*.

But it is obvious that there are quite a few other regularities to be found in the data which you did not choose to project. As shown in Figure 3 there is the regularity that all the points plotted so far fall on curve *B*, and the regularity that all the points plotted so far fall on curve *C*. The projection of one of these regularities will lead to a different prediction.

If you extrapolate along curve *B*, you can predict that the population in the year 30 will be back to 11 million. If you extrapolate along curve *C*, you can predict that the population will leap to 17 million. There are

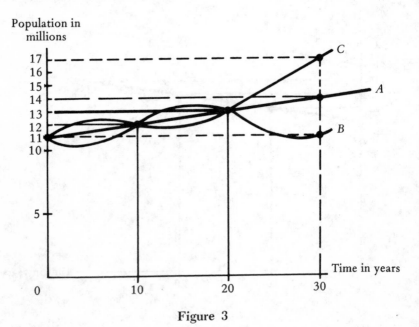

Figure 3

indeed an infinite number of curves that pass through all the points and thus an infinite number of regularities in the data. Whatever prediction you wish to make, a regularity can be found whose projection will license that prediction.

Example 3

Often intelligence and aptitude tests contain problems where one is given a sequence of numbers and asked to continue the sequence; for example:

    i. $1, 2, 3, 4, 5, \ldots$;
   ii. $2, 4, 6, 8, 10, \ldots$;
  iii. $1, 3, 5, 7, 9, \ldots$.

The natural way in which to continue sequence (i) is to add 6 to the end, for sequence (ii) to add 12, and for sequence (iii) to add 11. These problems are really problems of inductive logic on the intuitive level; one is asked to discover a regularity in the segment of the series given and to project that regularity in order to find the next number of the series.

Let us make this reasoning explicit for the three series given. In example (i) the first member of the series is 1, the second member is 2, the third member is 3, and, in general, for all the members given, the kth member is k. If we project this regularity to find the next member of the series, we will reason that the sixth member is 6, which is the answer intuitively arrived at before. In example (ii) the first member is twice 1, the second is twice 2, and, in general, for all the members given, the kth member is twice k. If we project this regularity, we will reason that the sixth member is twice 6, or 12, which is the answer intuitively arrived at before. In example (iii) the first member is twice 1 less 1, the second member is twice 2 less 1, and the third member is twice 3 less 1. In general, for all the members given, the kth member is twice k less 1. If we project this regularity, we will reason that the sixth member of the series is twice 6 less 1, or 11, which is the result intuitively arrived at. We say that k is a *generating function* for the first series, $2k$ a generating function for the second series, and $2k-1$ a generating function for the third series. Although "generating function" may sound like a very technical term, its meaning is quite simple. It is a formula with k in it, such that if 1 is substituted for k it gives the first member of the series, if 2 is substituted for k it gives the second member, etc.

Thus the regularity we found in each of these series is that a certain generating function yielded all the given members of the series. This regularity was projected by assuming that the same generating function would yield the next member of the series, and so we were able to fill in the ends of the series. For example, the prediction that the sixth member of series (iii) is 11 implicitly rests on the following argument:

> For every given member of series (iii) the kth member of that series was $2k-1$.
>
> ---
>
> For the next member of series (iii) the kth member will be $2k-1$.

But, as you may expect, there is a fly in the ointment. If we look more closely at these examples, we can find *other* regularities in the given members of the various series. And the projection of these other regularities conflicts with the projection of the regularities we have already noted. The generating function $(k-1)(k-2)(k-3)(k-4)(k-5)+k$ also yields the five given members of series (i). (This can be checked by substituting 1 for k, which gives 1; 2 for k, which gives 2; and so on, up through 5.) But if we project this regularity, the result is that the sixth member of the series is 126!

Indeed whatever number we wish to predict for the sixth member of the series, there is a generating function that will fit the given members of the series and that will yield the prediction we want. It is a mathematical fact that in general this is true. For any finite string of numbers which begins a series, there are generating functions that fit that string of given numbers and yield whatever next member is desired. Whatever prediction we wish to make, we can find a regularity whose projection will license that prediction.

Thus if the intelligence tests were simply looking for the projection of a regularity, any number at the end of the series would be correct. What they are looking for is not simply the projection of a regularity but the projection of an intuitively projectible regularity.

If we have perhaps belabored the point in Examples (1), (2), and (3) we have done so because the principle they illustrate is so hard to accept. Any prediction whatsoever can be obtained by projecting regularities. As Goodman puts it, "To say that valid predictions are those based on past regularities, without being able to say *which* regularities, is thus quite pointless. Regularities are where you find them, and you can find them anywhere."[3] An acceptable scientific inductive logic must have rules for determining the projectibility of regularities.

---

[3] Nelson Goodman, *Fact, Fiction and Forecast* (Cambridge, Mass.: Harvard University Press, 1955), p. 82.

It remains to be shown how this discussion of regularities and projectibility bears on the principle of the uniformity of nature. Just as we saw that the naïve characterization of scientific inductive logic as a system that projects observed regularities into the future was pointless unless we can say which regularities it projects, so we shall see that the statement that scientific inductive logic presupposes the uniformity of nature is equally pointless unless we are able to say *in what respects* nature is presupposed to be uniform. For it is self-contradictory to say that nature is uniform in all respects, and trivial to say it is uniform in some respects.

In the original statement of the Goodman paradox, the gem expert, who spoke our ordinary language, assumed nature to be uniform with respect to the blueness or greenness of emeralds. Since observed emeralds had always been green, and since he was assuming that nature is uniform and that the future would resemble the past in this respect, he predicted that the emerald would remain green. But the hypothetical gem expert who spoke the grue-bleen language assumed nature to be uniform *with respect to the grueness or bleenness of emeralds.* Since observed emeralds had always been grue and since he was assuming that nature is uniform and that the future would resemble the past in this respect, he predicted that the emerald would remain grue. But we saw that these two predictions were in conflict. The future cannot resemble the past in both these ways. As we have seen, such conflicts can be multiplied *ad infinitum.* The future cannot resemble the past in all respects. It is self-contradictory to say that nature is uniform in all respects.

We might try to retreat to the claim that scientific induction presupposes that nature is uniform in some respects. But this claim is so weak as to be no claim at all. To say that nature is uniform in some respects is to say that it exhibits some patterns, that there are some regularities in nature taken as a whole (in both the observed and unobserved parts of nature). But as we have seen in this section, in any sequence of observations, no matter how chaotic the data may seem, there are always regularities. This holds not only for sequences of observations but also for nature as a whole. No matter how chaotic nature might be, it would always exhibit some patterns; it would always be uniform in some respects. These uniformities might seem highly artificial, such as a uniformity in terms of grue and bleen or snarf and murkle. They might be fiendishly complex. But no matter how nature might behave, there would always be some uniformity, "natural" or "artificial," simple or complex. It is therefore trivial to say that nature is uniform in some respects. Thus if the statement that scientific induction presupposes that nature is uniform is to convey any information at all, it must specify in what respects scientific induction presupposes that nature is uniform.

The points about regularities and projectibility and the uniformity of nature are really two sides of the same coin. There are so many regularities in any sequence of observations and so many ways for nature to be uniform that the statements "Scientific induction projects observed regularities into the future" and "Scientific induction presupposes the uniformity of nature" lose all meaning. They can, however, be reinvested with meaning if we can formulate *rules of projectibility* for scientific inductive logic. Then we could say that scientific inductive logic projects regularities that meet these standards. And that would be saying something informative. We could reformulate the principle of the uniformity of nature to mean: Nature is such that projecting regularities that meet these standards will lead to correct predictions most of the time. Thus the whole concept of scientific inductive logic rests on the idea of projectibility. The problem of formulating precise rules for determining projectibility is the new riddle of induction.

Exercise:

In the example of the four boxes labeled "Excelsior!" find a regularity in the observations whose projection would lead to the prediction that the mask will be blue.

III.5. SUMMARY. This chapter described the scope of the problem of constructing a system of scientific inductive logic. We began with the supposition that scientific inductive logic could be simply characterized as the projection of observed regularities into the future in accordance with some rule such as Rule S. We saw that this characterization of scientific inductive logic is inadequate for several reasons, the most important being that too many regularities are to be found in any given set of data. In one set of data we can find regularities whose projection leads to conflicting predictions. In fact, for any prediction we choose, there will be a regularity whose projection licenses that prediction.

Scientific inductive logic must select from the multitude of regularities present in any sequence of observations, for indiscriminate projection leads to paradox. Thus in order to characterize scientific inductive logic we must specify the rules used to determine which regularities it considers to be projectible. The problem of formulating these rules is called the new riddle of induction.

Essentially the same problem reappears if we try to characterize scientific inductive logic as a system that presupposes that nature is uniform. To say that nature is uniform in *some* respects is trivial. To say that nature is uniform in *all* respects is not only false but self-contradictory. Thus if we are to characterize scientific inductive logic in terms of some principle of the uniformity of nature which it presupposes, we must say in what respects nature is presupposed to be uniform, which in turn determines what regularities scientific inductive logic takes to be projectible. So the problem about the uniformity of nature is just a different facet of the new riddle of induction.

The problem of constructing a system of scientific inductive logic will not be solved until the new riddle of induction and other problems have been solved. Although these solutions have not yet been found, there have been developments in the history of inductive logic which constitute progress towards a system.

In the next chapter we shall pursue an analysis of causality which casts some light on well-known features of the experimental method. Then we will discuss the major achievement of the field, the probability calculus.

Suggested readings

Nelson Goodman, *Fact, Fiction and Forecast* (Cambridge, Mass.: Harvard University Press, 1955), chap. 3, "The New Riddle of Induction."

Bertrand Russell, "On the Notion of Cause," in *Mysticism and Logic* (New York: Anchor Books, 1957), pp. 174–201.

IV

MILL'S METHODS OF
EXPERIMENTAL INQUIRY
AND THE NATURE OF
CAUSALITY

IV.1. INTRODUCTION. One of the purposes of scientific inductive logic is, presumably, to assess the evidential warrant for statements of cause and effect. But what exactly do statements claiming causal connection *mean*, and what is their relation to statements describing *de facto* regularities? These are old and deep questions and at best we can give only partial answers to them.

Yet even partial answers can be illuminating. In his *System of Logic*, published in 1853, John Stuart Mill discussed five "methods of experimental inquiry" aimed at discovering causes. Although not original with Mill, these methods have become famous as *Mill's methods*. It so happens that a relatively simple distinction between different types of causal relationships will allow a complete analysis of the logic of Mill's methods.

But before this elementary analysis can be made to pay its dividends, and before more profound problems can be raised, it is necessary to introduce the basic logical machinery of simple and complex statements and properties.

IV.2. THE STRUCTURE OF SIMPLE STATEMENTS. A *statement* is a sentence that makes a definite factual claim. A straightforward way of making a factual claim is to (1) identify what you are talking about and (2) make a claim about it. Thus in the simple statement "Socrates is bald," the proper name "Socrates" identifies who we are talking about and the predicate "is bald" makes our claim about him. In general, expressions that identify what we are talking about are called *referring expressions* and the expressions used to make factual claims about the things we are talking about are called *characterizing expressions*. Thus the name "Socrates" refers to a certain individual, and the predicate "is bald" characterizes that individual.

Although proper names are an important type of referring expression, there are others. Pronouns such as "I," "you," "he," and "it" are referring expressions often used in ordinary speech, where context is relied upon to make clear what is being talked about. Sometimes whole phrases are used as referring expressions. In the statement "The first President of the United States had wooden false teeth," the phrase "The first President of the United States" is used to refer to George Washington. He is then characterized as having wooden false teeth (as in fact he did).

Although statements are often constructed out of one referring expression, as in the examples above, sometimes they are constructed out of more than one referring expression, plus an expression that characterizes the relationship between the things referred to. For instance, the statement "Mercury is hotter than Pluto" contains two referring expressions—"Mercury" and "Pluto"—and one characterizing expression—"is hotter than." Characterizing expressions that characterize an individual thing are called *property expressions* or *one-place predicates*. "Is bald," "is red," "conducts electricity" are examples of property expressions. Characterizing expressions that characterize the relationship between two or more individual things are called *relational expressions* or *many-place predicates*. "Is hotter than," "is a brother of," "is to the north of," "is between" are examples of relational expressions.

The basic way to construct a simple statement is to combine referring and characterizing expressions to make the appropriate factual claim. In the next section it will be seen how these simple statements can be combined with logical connectives to form complex statements.

Exercises:

Pick out the referring and characterizing expressions in the following statements. State whether each chacterizing expression is a property expression or a relational expression.

1. It is the East and Juliet is the sun.

2. Mozart is far superior to Chopin.

3. The Pyrenees are located between Spain and France.

4. All the points along the circumference of a circle are equidistant from the center.

5. I'm back.

6. $3 + 2 = 5$.

IV.3. THE STRUCTURE OF COMPLEX STATEMENTS. Consider the two simple statements "Socrates is bald" and "Socrates is wise." Each of these statements is composed of one referring expression and one characterizing expression. From these statements, together with the words "not," "and," and "or," we can construct a variety of complex statements:

> Socrates is *not* bald.
> Socrates is bald *and* Socrates is wise.
> Socrates is bald *or* Socrates is wise.
> Socrates is *not* bald *or* Socrates is wise.
> Socrates is bald *and* Socrates is wise *or* Socrates is *not* bald *and* Socrates is *not* wise.

The words "not," "and," and "or" are neither referring nor characterizing expressions. They are called *logical connectives* and are used together with referring and characterizing expressions to make complex factual claims.

We can see how the logical connectives are used in the making of complex factual claims by investigating how the truth or falsity of a complex statement depends on the truth or falsity of its simple constituent statements. A simple statement is true just when its characterizing expression correctly characterizes the thing or things it refers to. For instance, the statement "Socrates is bald" is true if and only if Socrates is in fact bald; otherwise it is false. Whether a complex statement is true or not depends on the truth or falsity of its simple constituent statements *and* the way that they are put together with the logical connectives. Let us see how this process works for each of the connectives.

Not. We *deny* or *negate* a simple statement by placing the word "not" at the appropriate place within it. For instance, the denial or negation of the simple statement "Socrates is bald" is the complex statement "Socrates is not bald." Often we abbreviate a statement by using a single letter; for example, we may let the letter "*s*" stand for "Socrates is bald." And we may deny a statement by placing a sign for negation, "$\sim$," in front of the letter that abbreviates that statement. Thus "$\sim s$" stands for "Socrates is not bald." Now it is obvious that when a statement is true its denial is false, and when a statement is false its denial is true. Using the shorthand introduced above, we can symbolize this information in the following *truth table*, where T stands for true and F for false:

p	$\sim p$
T	F
F	T

What this table tells us is that if the statement "p" is true, then its denial, "$\sim p$," is false. If the statement "p" is false, then its denial, "$\sim p$," is true. The truth table is a summary of the way in which the truth or falsity of the complex statement depends on the truth or falsity of its constituent statements.

And. We form the *conjunction* of two statements by putting the word "and" between them. Each of the original statements is then called a *conjunct.* A conjunction is true just when both of the conjuncts are true. Using the symbol "&" to abbreviate the word "and" we can represent this in the following truth table:

p	q	$p\&q$
T	T	T
T	F	F
F	T	F
F	F	F

Here we have four possible combinations of truth and falsity that the constituent statements "p" and "q" might have, and corresponding to each combination we have an entry telling us whether the complex statement "$p\&q$" is true or false for that combination. Thus in the case where "p" is true and "q" is true, "$p\&q$" is also true. Where "p" is true and "q" is false, "$p\&q$" is false. Where "p" is false and "q" is true, "$p\&q$" is again false. And where both "p" and "q" are false, "$p\&q$" remains false.

Or. The word "or" has two distinct uses in English. Sometimes "p or q" means "either p or q, *but not both,*" as in "I will go to the movies or I will stay home and study." This is called the *exclusive* sense of "or." Sometimes "p or q" means "p or q *or both,*" as in "Club members or their wives may attend." This is called the *inclusive* use of "or." We are especially interested in the inclusive sense of "or," which we shall represent by the symbol "v." "pvq" is called a *disjunction* (or alternation), with "p" and "q" being the *disjuncts.* The truth table for disjunction is:

p	q	pvq
T	T	T
T	F	T
F	T	T
F	F	F

By reference to the truth tables for "~," "&" and "v" we can construct a truth table for any complex statement. Consider the complex statement "Socrates is not bald or Socrates is wise." This complex statement contains two simple constituent statements: "Socrates is bald" and "Socrates is wise." We may abbreviate the first statement as "s" and the second as "w." We can then symbolize the complex statement as "~svw." We may use the following procedure to construct a truth table for this complex statement:

>Step 1: List all the possible combination of truth and falsity for the simple constituent statements, "s," "w."
>Step 2: For each of these combinations, find whether "~s" is true or false from the truth table for negation.
>Step 3: For each of the combinations, find whether "~svw" is true or false from step 2 and the truth table for disjunction.

The result is the following truth table for "~svw":

	Step 1		Step 2	Step 3
	s	w	~s	~svw
Case 1:	T	T	F	T
Case 2:	T	F	F	F
Case 3:	F	T	T	T
Case 4:	F	F	T	T

This truth table tells us exactly what factual claim the complex statement makes, for it shows us in which cases that statement is true and in which it is false.

Since a truth table tells us what factual claim is made by a complex statement, it can tell us when two statements make the same factual claim. Let us examine the truth table for "(s&w)v(~s&w)":

	s	w	~s	s&w	~s&w	(s&w)v(~s&w)
Case 1:	T	T	F	T	F	T
Case 2:	T	F	F	F	F	F
Case 3:	F	T	T	F	T	T
Case 4:	F	F	T	F	F	F

Note that in reading across the truth table we start with the simple constituent statements, proceed to the next largest complex statements, until we finally arrive at the complex statement that is the goal. The truth table shows that the final complex statement is true in cases 1 and 3 and false in cases 2 and 4. But notice that the simple statement "w" is also true in cases 1 and 3 and false in cases 2 and 4. This shows that the simple statement "w" and the complex statement "$(s\&w)$ v $(\sim s\&w)$" make the same factual claim. To claim that Socrates is either bald and wise or not bald and wise is just a complicated way of claiming that Socrates is wise. When two statements make the same factual claim, they are logically *equivalent*.

Truth tables may also be used to show that two complex statements make conflicting factual claims. For example, the claim made by the statement "$\sim s\&\sim w$" obviously conflicts with the claim made by the statement "$s\&w$." Socrates cannot both be bald and wise and be not bald and not wise. This conflict is reflected in a truth table for both statements:

	s	w	$\sim s$	$\sim w$	$s\&w$	$\sim s\&\sim w$
Case 1:	T	T	F	F	T	F
Case 2:	T	F	F	T	F	F
Case 3:	F	T	T	F	F	F
Case 4:	F	F	T	T	F	T

The statement "$s\&w$" is true only in case 1, while the statement "$\sim s\&\sim w$" is true only in case 4. There is no case in which both statements are true. Thus the two statements make conflicting factual claims. When two statements make conflicting factual claims, they are *inconsistent* with each other, or *mutually exclusive*.

There are some peculiar complex statements that make no factual claim whatsoever. If we say "Either Socrates is bald or Socrates is not bald" we have really not said anything at all about Socrates. Let us see how this situation is reflected in the truth table for "$sv\sim s$":

	s	$\sim s$	$sv\sim s$
Case 1:	T	F	T
Case 2:	F	T	T

The reason why the statement "$sv\sim s$" makes no factual claim is that it is true no matter what the facts are. This is illustrated in the truth table by the statement being true in all cases. When a complex statement is true no matter what the truth values of its constituent statements are, that statement is called a *tautology*.

At the opposite end of the scale from a tautology is the type of statement that makes an impossible claim. For instance, the statement "Socrates is bald and Socrates is not bald" must be false no matter what the state of Socrates' head. This is reflected in the truth table by the statement being false in all cases:

	s	$\sim s$	$s \& \sim s$
Case 1:	T	F	F
Case 2:	F	T	F

Such a statement is called a *self-contradiction*. Self-contradictions are false no matter what the facts are, in contrast to tautologies, which are true no matter what the facts are. Statements that are neither tautologies nor self-contradictions are called *contingent statements* because whether they are true or not is contingent on what the facts are. A contingent statement is true in some cases and false in others.

The purpose of this section has been to convey an understanding of the basic ideas behind truth tables and the logical connectives. We shall apply these ideas in our discussion of Mill's methods and the theory of probability.

The main points of this section are:

1. Complex statements are constructed from simple statements and the logical connectives "$\sim$," "$\&$," "v."

2. The truth tables for "$\sim$," "$\&$," "v" show how the truth or falsity of complex statements depends on the truth or falsity of their simple constituent statements.

3. With the aid of the truth tables for "$\sim$," "$\&$," "v," a truth table may be constructed for any complex statement.

4. The truth table for a complex statement will have a case for each possible combination of truth or falsity of its simple constituent statements. It will show in each case whether the complex statement is true or false.

5. The factual claim made by a complex statement can be discovered by examining the cases in which it is true and those in which it is false.

6. If two statements are true in exactly the same cases, they make the same factual claim and are said to be logically equivalent.

7. If two statements are such that there is no case in which they are both true, they make conflicting factual claims and are said to be inconsistent with each other, or mutually exclusive.

8. If a statement is true in all cases, it is a tautology; if it is false in all cases, it is a self-contradiction; otherwise it is a contingent statement.

Exercises:

1. Using truth tables, find which of the following pairs of statements are logically equivalent, which are mutually exclusive, and which are neither:

    a. p, $\sim\sim p$.

    b. $\sim p \vee \sim q$, $p \& q$.

    c. $p \& \sim q$, $\sim(p \& q)$.

    d. $\sim p \vee q$, $p \& \sim q$.

    e. $(p \vee p) \& q$, $p \& (q \vee q)$.

    f. $\sim p \vee q$, $p \& \sim q$.

2. Using truth tables, find which of the following statements are tautologies, which are self-contradictions, and which are contingent statements:

    a. $\sim\sim p \vee \sim p$.

    b. $p \vee q \vee r$.

    c. $(p \vee p) \& \sim(p \vee p)$.

    d. $(p \vee \sim q) \vee \sim(p \vee \sim q)$.

    e. $p \& q \& r$.

    f. $\sim\sim(p \vee \sim p)$.

    g. $\sim p \vee p \vee q$.

IV.4. SIMPLE AND COMPLEX PROPERTIES.[1] Just as complex statements may be constructed out of simple ones with the logical connectives, so complex properties may be constructed out of simple ones. From the simple properties "is red," "is black," "is fat," "is short," and the logical connectives, we can construct the complex properties "is not red," "is red or black," "is fat and short," "is not fat and is short," etc. We shall use capital letters to abbreviate properties; for example, "R" stands for "is red."

We can use a method to examine complex properties which is quite similar to the method of truth tables used to examine complex statements. Whether a complex property is present or absent in a given thing or event depends on whether its constituent simple properties are present or absent, just as the truth or falsity of a complex statement depends on the truth or falsity of its simple constituent statements. When the logical connectives are used to construct complex properties, we can refer to the following

---

[1] In this and the following section the word "property" is used ambiguously to mean "property" or "property expression," but there should be no difficulty resolving any instance of the ambiguity. Things *exhibit properties*; that is, properties are *present* in things. *Property expressions*, on the other hand, *describe* things. A property expression correctly describes a thing or event just when the corresponding property is in fact present in that thing or event.

presence tables, where "*F*" and "*G*" stand for simple properties and where "*P*" stands for "present" and "*A*" for "absent":

Table I		Table II			Table III		
F	~*F*	*F*	*G*	*F&G*	*F*	*G*	*FvG*
P	A	P	P	P	P	P	P
A	P	P	A	A	P	A	P
		A	P	A	A	P	P
		A	A	A	A	A	A

Note that these tables are exactly the same as the truth tables for the logical connectives except that "present" is substituted for "true" and "absent" is substituted for "false." With the aid of these presence tables for the logical connectives, we can construct a presence table for any complex property in exactly the same way as we constructed truth tables for complex statements. The presence table for a complex property will have a case for each possible combination of presence or absence of its simple constituent properties. For each case, it will tell whether the complex property is present or absent. As an illustration, we may construct a presence table for "~*FvG*":

	F	*G*	~*F*	~*FvG*
Case 1:	P	P	A	P
Case 2:	P	A	A	A
Case 3:	A	P	P	P
Case 4:	A	A	P	P

There are other parallels between the treatment of complex statements and the treatment of complex properties. Two complex properties are logically equivalent if they are present in exactly the same cases; two properties are mutually exclusive if there is no case in which they are both present. When a property is present in all cases (such as "*Fv~F*") it is called a *universal* property. A universal property is analogous to a tautology. When a property is absent in all cases, it is called a *null* property. A null property is analogous to a self-contradiction. The properties in which we are most interested in inductive logic are those which are neither universal nor null. These are called *contingent* properties. Mill's methods of experimental inquiry are directed toward discovering causal relations between contingent properties. These causal relations are discussed further in the next section.

Exercises:

1. Using presence tables, find which of the following pairs of properties are logically equivalent, which are mutually exclusive, and which are neither:
   a. $\sim F v G$, $\sim\sim G v \sim F$.
   b. $\sim F v \sim G$, $\sim (F\&G)$.
   c. $\sim F v G$, $F\&\sim G$.
   d. $F v \sim (F\&G)$, $\sim (F\&G)\&F$.
   e. $\sim F\&\sim G$, $\sim (F v G)$.
   f. $\sim (F v G v H)$, $F v G v H$.
   g. $F\&\sim G$, $\sim (F\&G)$.

2. Using presence tables, find out which of the following properties are universal, which are null, and which are contingent:
   a. $\sim F v G v F$.
   b. $(F v F)\&\sim (F v F)$.
   c. $\sim (F v \sim F)$.
   d. $(F v \sim G)\&(G v \sim F)$.
   e. $F v G v H$.
   f. $\sim (F\&\sim G) v \sim (G v \sim F)$.

IV.5. CAUSALITY AND NECESSARY AND SUFFICIENT CONDITIONS. Many of the inquiries of both scientific research and practical affairs may be characterized as the search for the causes of certain effects. The practical application of knowledge of causes consists either in producing the cause in order to produce the effect or in removing the cause in order to prevent the effect. Knowledge of causes is the key to control of effects. Thus physicians search for the cause of certain diseases so that they may remove the cause and prevent the effect. On the other hand, advertising men engage in motivational research into the causes of consumer demand so that they can produce the cause and thus produce the effect of consumer demand for their products.

However, the word "cause" is used in English to mean several different things. For this reason, it is more useful to talk about *necessary conditions* and *sufficient conditions* rather than about causes.

> **Definition 10:** A property F is a *sufficient condition* for a property G if and only if *whenever F is present, G is present.*
> **Definition 11:** A property H is a *necessary condition* for a property I if and only if *whenever I is present, H is present.*

Being run over by a steamroller is a sufficient condition for death, but it is not a necessary condition. Whenever someone has been run over by a steamroller, he is dead. But it is not the case that anyone who is dead has been run over by a steamroller. On the other hand, the presence of oxygen is a necessary condition, but not a sufficient condition for combustion. Whenever combustion takes place, oxygen is present. But happily it is not true that whenever oxygen is present, combustion takes place. When we say that A causes B we sometimes mean that A is a sufficient condition for B, sometimes that A is a necessary condition for B, sometimes that A is both necessary and sufficient for B, and sometimes none of these things.

If we are looking for causes in order to produce an effect, it is reasonable to look for sufficient conditions for that effect. If we can manipulate circumstances so that the sufficient condition is present, the effect will also be present. If we are looking for causes in order to prevent an effect, it is reasonable to look for necessary conditions for that effect. If we prevent a necessary condition from materializing, we can prevent the effect. The eradication of yellow fever is a striking illustration of this strategy. Doctors discovered that being bitten by a certain type of mosquito was a necessary condition for contracting yellow fever. It was not a sufficient condition, for some people who were bitten by these mosquitos did not contract yellow fever. Consequently a campaign was instituted to destroy these mosquitos through the widespread use of insecticide and thus to prevent yellow fever.

From the definitions of necessary and sufficient conditions, we can prove several important principles. It follows immediately from the definitions that:

> 1. If A is a sufficient condition for B, then B is a necessary condition for A.
> 2. If C is a necessary condition for D, then D is a sufficient condition for C.

To say that A is a sufficient condition for B is, by definition, to say that whenever A is present, B is present. But to say that B is a necessary condition for A is, by definition, to say the same thing.

Let us look at some illustrations of these principles. Since the presence of oxygen is a *necessary* condition for combustion, then by principle 2 combustion is *sufficient* to ensure the presence of oxygen. Thus suppose someone lowers a burning candle into a deep mine shaft he proposes to explore. If the candle continues to burn, he will know that the shaft contains sufficient oxygen to breathe. To illustrate principle 1, let us suppose that a professor has constructed a test such that a high grade on the test is *sufficient* to guarantee that the student has studied the material. Then studying the material is a *necessary* condition for doing well on the test.

Two additional principles require a little more thought:

3. If A is a sufficient condition for B, then $\sim B$ is a sufficient condition for $\sim A$.

4. If C is a necessary condition for D, then $\sim D$ is a necessary condition for $\sim C$.

Using the definition of sufficient condition, principle 3 becomes:

3′. If whenever A is present B is present, then whenever $\sim B$ is present $\sim A$ is present.

Now remember from the presence table for negation that $\sim B$ is present just when B is absent and $\sim A$ is present just when A is absent. So principle 3 can be rewritten again as:

3″. If whenever A is present B is present, then whenever B is absent A is absent.

We can now see why this principle is correct. Suppose that whenever A is present, B is present. Suppose further that B is absent in a certain case. Then A must also be absent, for if A were present, B would be present, and it is not. Let us see how this works in a concrete case. Suppose that a certain infection is a sufficient condition for a high fever; that is, everyone who suffers from this infection runs a high fever. Then the absence of a high fever is sufficient to guarantee that a person is not suffering from this infection.

That principle 4 is correct can be demonstrated in the same way. Using the definition of necessary condition, we can rewrite principle 4 as:

4′. If whenever D is present C is present, then whenever $\sim C$ is present $\sim D$ is present.

And using the presence table for negation, we can rewrite it again as:

4″. If whenever D is present C is present, then whenever C is absent D is absent.

And this is simply a restatement of principle 3″ using different letters.

We can use the same example to illustrate principle 4. Since suffering from the infection is a sufficient condition for running a high fever, running the fever is a necessary condition for having the infection (principle 1). By principle 4, since running the fever is a necessary condition for having the infection, not having the infection is a necessary condition for not running a fever. (It is not a sufficient condition since other diseases might result in a fever.)

Two more principles will complete this survey of the basic principles governing necessary and sufficient conditions:

5. If A is a sufficient condition for B, then $\sim A$ is a necessary condition for $\sim B$.
6. If C is a necessary condition for D, then $\sim C$ is a sufficient condition for $\sim D$.

Using the definitions and the presence table for negation we can rewrite principle 5 as:

5′. If whenever A is present B is present, then whenever B is absent A is absent.

But this is exactly what we established in 3″. In the same manner, we can rewrite 6 as:

6′. If whenever D is present C is present, then whenever C is absent, D is absent.

But this is exactly what we established in principle 4″. A concrete illustration of principle 5 is that, since being run over by a steamroller is a sufficient condition for death, not being run over by a steamroller is a necessary condition for staying alive. And principle 6 can be illustrated by the observation that, if studying is a necessary condition for passing a test, not studying is a sufficient condition for failing it.

When we speak of the cause of an effect in ordinary language, we sometimes mean a sufficient condition, as when we say that the infection was the cause of the fever or that being run over by a steamroller was the cause of death. Sometimes we mean a necessary condition, as when we say that yellow fever was caused by the bite of the mosquito or a high score on the test was due to diligent study. On the other hand, necessary and sufficient conditions are sometimes not causes at all but rather *symptoms* or *signs*. The continued burning of the candle was a sign of the presence of oxygen. The high fever was a *symptom* of the infection. When we analyze Mill's methods, it will be seen that the precise language of necessary and sufficient conditions is much more useful than the vague language of cause and effect, sign and symptom.

Exercises:

Show that the following principles are correct and give a concrete illustration of each:

1. If $\sim B$ is a sufficient condition for $\sim A$, then A is a sufficient condition for B.

2. If $\sim D$ is a necessary condition for $\sim C$, then C is a necessary condition for D.

3. If $\sim A$ is a necessary condition for $\sim B$, then A is a sufficient condition for B.

4. If $\sim C$ is a sufficient condition for $\sim D$, then C is a necessary condition for D.

5. If A is a necessary condition for E and B is a necessary condition for E, then $A\&B$ is a necessary condition for E.

6. If $A\&B$ is a necessary condition for E, then A is a necessary condition for E and B is a necessary condition for E.

7. If A is a sufficient condition for E and B is a sufficient condition for E, then AvB is a sufficient condition for E.

8. If AvB is a sufficient condition for E, then A is a sufficient condition for E and B is a sufficient condition for E.

9. If A is a necessary condition for E, then whatever the property F, AvF is a necessary condition for E.

10. If A is a sufficient condition for E, then whatever the property F, $A\&F$ is a sufficient condition for E.

Suggested reading

Israel Scheffler, *The Anatomy of Inquiry* (New York: Alfred A. Knopf, 1963), pp. 19–25.

IV.6. MILL'S METHODS. Mill presented five methods designed to guide the experimenter in his search for causes. They are the *method of agreement,* the *method of difference,* the *joint method,* the *method of concomitant variation,* and the *method of residues.* However, Mill did not actually originate these methods, nor did he fully understand them.

The theoretical basis of Mill's methods has only recently been fully explored by the philosopher G. H. Von Wright.[2] Following Von Wright, we will present Mill's methods a little differently than Mill did. We will be able to uncover the theoretical basis of Mill's methods in a discussion of the method of agreement, the method of difference, and the joint method. Since there is nothing essentially new in the method of concomitant variation and

---

[2] Georg Henrik Von Wright, *A Treatise on Induction and Probability* (Patterson, N.J.: Littlefield, Adams & Co., 1960).

the method of residues, we shall not discuss them. However, we shall still be left with five methods, for there are two variations of the method of agreement and two variations of the joint method.

These methods are to be viewed as methods of finding the necessary or sufficient conditions of a given property. The property whose necessary or sufficient conditions are being sought is called the *conditioned property*. A conditioned property may have more than one sufficient condition. If the conditioned property is death, being run over by a steamroller is one sufficient condition for it, but there are many others. A conditioned property may also have more than one necessary condition. If the conditioned property is the occurrence of combustion, the presence of oxygen is a necessary condition for it, but so is the presence of an oxidizable substance. Those properties suspected of being necessary or sufficient conditions for a given conditioned property are called *possible conditioning properties*. The general problem is, "How is the information gained from observing various occurrences used to pick out the necessary and sufficient conditions from the possible conditioning properties?" The following methods are attempts to answer this question.

IV.7. THE DIRECT METHOD OF AGREEMENT. Suppose that one of the possible conditioning properties A, B, C, or D is suspected of being a necessary condition for the conditioned property E, but which one is not known. Suppose further that, either by experimental manipulation or simply by studious observation, a wide variety of occurrences are observed in which E is present, and that the only possible conditioning property that is present on all these occasions is C. The set of observations shown in

Example 1

	Possible conditioning properties				Conditioned property
	A	B	C	D	E
Occurrence 1:	P	P	P	A	P
Occurrence 2:	P	A	P	P	P
Occurrence 3:	A	P	P	A	P

Example 1 corresponds to this description. Occurrence 1 shows that D cannot be a necessary condition for E. The definition of necessary condition tells us that a necessary condition for E must be present whenever E

is present. But in 1, E is present while D is absent. Thus occurrence 1 eliminates D from the list of possible necessary conditions. In the same manner, occurrence 2 shows that B cannot be a necessary condition for E, since E is present while B is absent. Occurrence 3 eliminates A and eliminates D once more. The only candidate left for the office of necessary condition for E is C. The observations show that if one of the possible conditioning properties is in fact a necessary condition for E, then C must be that necessary condition.

In Example 1 three occurrences were required before A, B, and D could be eliminated as possible necessary conditions for E. Actually we might have done without occurrence 1 since occurrence 3 also eliminated D. However, in the occurrence shown in Example 2 all could be eliminated at one stroke. The principle of elimination is the same: Any property that is absent when E is present cannot be a necessary condition for E.

Suppose someone were to object that the absence of D might be necessary for the presence of E, that is, that $\sim D$ might be a necessary condition for E, and that the data in Example 2 have not eliminated that possibility. This is correct, but it shows no defect in the argument. Only the simple properties A, B, C, and D were included in the possible conditioning prop-

Example 2

	Possible conditioning properties				Conditioned property
	A	B	C	D	E
Occurrence 1:	A	A	P	A	P

Example 3

	Possible conditioning properties								Conditioned property
	Simple				Complex				
	A	B	C	D	$\sim A$	$\sim B$	$\sim C$	$\sim D$	E
Occurrence 1:	A	A	P	A	P	P	A	P	P

erties; the complex property $\sim D$ was not. And all that was claimed was that *if* one of the possible conditioning properties is a necessary condition for E, *then* C is that necessary condition. But if we were to add the negations of A, B, C, and D to our list of possible conditioning properties, then occurrence 1 of Example 2 would not suffice to eliminate all the alternatives but C. This is readily shown in Example 3.

We can tell whether a complex property is present or absent in a given occurrence from the information as to whether its constituent simple properties are present or absent. This information will be found in the presence table for that complex property. Here it need only be remembered, from the presence table for negation, that the negation of a property is absent when that property is present, and present when that property is absent. Now in Example 3, occurrence 1 shows that A, B, D, and $\smallsmile C$ cannot be necessary conditions for E. This leaves C, $\smallsmile A$, $\smallsmile B$, and $\smallsmile D$ as likely candidates. If the field is to be narrowed down, some more occurrences must be observed. These might give the results shown in Example 4. Again occurrence 1 eliminates A, B, D, and $\smallsmile C$. Occurrence 2 further eliminates $\smallsmile A$, occurrence 3 eliminates $\smallsmile B$, and occurrence 4 eliminates $\smallsmile D$. Thus the only possible conditioning property left is C. If any one of the possible conditioning properties is a necessary condition for E, then C is that necessary condition.

Example 4

	Possible conditioning properties							Conditioned property
	Simple				Complex			
	A	B	C	D	$\smallsmile A$	$\smallsmile B$	$\sim C$	$\sim D$	E
Occurrence 1:	A	A	P	A	P	P	A	P	P
Occurrence 2:	P	A	P	A	A	P	A	P	P
Occurrence 3:	A	P	P	A	P	A	A	P	P
Occurrence 4:	A	A	P	P	P	P	A	A	P

Example 5

	Possible conditioning properties							Conditioned property
	Simple				Complex			
	A	B	C	D	$\smallsmile A$	$\smallsmile B$	$\smallsmile C$	$\smallsmile D$	E
Occurrence 1:	A	P	P	P	P	A	A	A	P
Occurrence 2:	P	A	P	A	A	P	A	P	P

In Example 4 it took four occurrences to eliminate all the possible conditioning properties but one. However, the two occurrences observed in Example 5 would have done the job. Occurrence 1 shows that A, $\sim B$, $\sim C$, and $\sim D$ cannot be necessary conditions for E since they are absent when E is present. Occurrence 2 further eliminates B, D, $\sim A$, and $\sim C$, leaving only C. Thus in this example if one of the possible conditioning properties is a necessary condition for E, then C is that necessary condition. It is true, in general, that if we admit both simple properties and their negation as possible conditioning properties, then the minimum number of occurrences that can eliminate all but one of the possible conditioning properties is 2. As we saw before, when only simple properties are admitted as possible conditioning properties, the minimum number of occurrences that can eliminate all but one of them is 1. But the basic principle of elimination remains the same in both cases: A property that is absent when E is present cannot be a necessary condition for E.

We were able to extend Mill's method of agreement to cover negative possible conditioning properties, and this makes sense, for negative properties are quite often necessary conditions. Not being run over by a steamroller is a necessary condition for remaining alive and not letting one's grade average fall below a certain point may be a necessary condition for remaining in college. We are interested in negative necessary conditions because they tell us what we must avoid in order to attain our goals. But negations of simple properties are not the only complex properties that may be important necessary conditions.

Let us consider disjunctions of simple properties as necessary conditions. Either having high grades in high school *or* scoring well on the entrance examination might be a necessary condition for getting into college. It might not be a sufficient condition since someone who meets this qualification might still be rejected on the grounds that he is criminally insane. To take another example, in football either making a touchdown *or* a field goal

Example 6

		Possible conditioning properties				Conditioned property
		Simple			Complex	
	A	B	C	D	BvC	E
Occurrence 1:	A	P	A	A	P	P
Occurrence 2:	A	A	P	A	P	P

or a conversion *or* a safety is a necessary condition for scoring. In this case
the necessary condition is also a sufficient condition. We are interested in
disjunctive necessary conditions because they lay out a field of alternatives,
one of which must be realized if we are to achieve certain ends.

The question of what happens when disjunctions (alternations) of simple
properties are allowed into a set of possible conditioning properties is too
involved to be treated fully here. But the principle of elimination remains
the same. We can see how this principle operates in two simplified examples
that allow only simple properties and one disjunction as possible conditioning properties. In Example 6 the complex property BvC is the only property
that is always present when E is present. Occurrences 1 and 2 eliminate all
the simple properties as necessary conditions. Thus if one of the possible
conditioning properties is a necessary condition for E, BvC is that necessary condition.

In Example 6 the disjunction was the property left after all the others had
been eliminated. Let us now look at Example 7, where the disjunction itself
is eliminated. Occurrence 1 eliminates A and C as necessary conditions, and

Example 7

	Possible conditioning properties					Conditioned property
	Simple				Complex	
	A	B	C	D	BvC	E
Occurrence 1:	A	P	A	P	P	P
Occurrence 2:	P	A	A	P	A	P

occurrence 2 shows that neither B nor C nor BvC can be a necessary condition for E. This leaves only D, so if one of the possible conditioning properties is a necessary condition for E, then D is that necessary condition. We
shall not explore further the treatment of complex possible conditioning
properties by the direct method of agreement.[3] But you cannot go wrong if

---

[3] The direct method of agreement can be expanded to include simple properties,
negations of simple properties, and disjunctions of simple properties and their
negations as possible conditioning properties. There is no need to worry about
conjunctions since a conjunction, that is, *F&G*, is a necessary condition for *E* if
and only if F is a necessary condition for *E* and *G* is a necessary condition for *E*.
Thus if we can discover all the individual necessary conditions, we automatically
have all the conjunctive necessary conditions.

you remember that the principle of elimination in the direct method of agreement is: A property that is absent when E is present cannot be a necessary condition for E.

Use of the direct method of agreement requires looking for occurrences of the conditioned property in circumstances as varied as possible. If these circumstances are so varied that only one of the possible conditioning properties is present whenever the conditioned property is present, it may be suspected that that property is a necessary condition for the conditioned property. It has been shown that the logic behind this method is the same as the logic behind the method of the master detective who eliminates suspects one by one in order to find the murderer. If only one of the possible conditioning properties is present whenever the conditioned property is present, then all the other possible conditioning properties are eliminated as necessary conditions since they are each absent in at least one occurrence in which the conditioned property is present.

But the method of agreement resembles the method of the master detective in two further ways. When starting on a murder case, the detective cannot be sure that he will be able to eliminate all the suspects but one. After all, the murder might have been done by two people working together. The same is true of the method of agreement, for a conditioned property can have more than one necessary condition. Moreover the master detective may not have the murderer or murderers in his initial list of suspects and may end up eliminating all the possibilities. In this case he will have to go back and look for more suspects to include in a more comprehensive list. In a similar manner the scientist may not have included the necessary condition or conditions for a conditioned property in his initial list of possible conditioning properties. Thus his observations might eliminate all his possible conditioning properties.

Exercises:

1. In Example 1 which of the following complex properties are eliminated as necessary conditions for E by occurrences 1, 2, and 3?

a. $\sim A$.	d. $\sim D$.
b. $\sim B$.	e. $A \lor D$.
c. $\sim C$.	f. $B \lor C$.

2. In the following example, for each occurrence find whether the complex properties are present or absent and which of the possible conditioning properties are eliminated as necessary conditions for E:

	Possible conditioning properties							Conditioned property
	Simple				Complex			
	A	B	C	$\sim A$	$\sim B$	$\sim C$	$A v C$	$B v C$	E
Occurrence 1:	P	P	P						P
Occurrence 2:	P	P	A						P
Occurrence 3:	P	A	P						P
Occurrence 4:	P	P	A						P
Occurrence 5:	A	A	P						P
Occurrence 6:	A	A	P						P

3. In Exercise 2 one of the possible conditioning properties was not eliminated. Describe an occurrence which would eliminate it.

IV.8. THE INVERSE METHOD OF AGREEMENT. The inverse method of agreement is a method for finding sufficient conditions. To find a sufficient condition for a given property, E, we look for a property that is absent whenever E is absent. This is illustrated in Example 8. D is the only possible conditioning property that is absent whenever the conditioned

Example 8

	Possible conditioning properties				Conditioned property
	A	B	C	D	E
Occurrence 1:	P	A	A	A	A
Occurrence 2:	A	P	A	A	A
Occurrence 3:	P	A	P	A	A

property is absent. Thus by the inverse method of agreement, if one of the possible conditioning properties is a sufficient condition for E, then D is that sufficient condition.

The inverse method of agreement operates in the following manner: We know from the definition of sufficient condition that a sufficient condition for E cannot be present when E is absent. To say that a certain property is a sufficient condition for E means that whenever that property is present, E is also present. Thus in Example 8 occurrence 1 shows that A cannot be a sufficient condition for E since it is present when E is absent. Occurrence 2 shows that B cannot be a sufficient condition for E for the same reason, and occurrence 3 does the same for C and A once again. D is therefore the only property left that can be a sufficient condition for E. In this way the inverse method of agreement, like the direct method, works by eliminating possible candidates one by one.

Example 9

	Possible sufficient conditions for E				Possible necessary conditions for $\sim E$					
	A	B	C	D	$\sim A$	$\sim B$	$\sim C$	$\sim D$	E	$\sim E$
Occurrence 1:	A	A	A	A	P	P	P	P	A	P
Occurrence 2:	A	P	P	A	P	A	A	P	A	P
Occurrence 3:	P	A	P	A	A	P	A	P	A	P

The inverse method of agreement may be viewed as an application of the direct method to negative properties. This is possible in light of the principle: if $\sim A$ is a necessary condition for $\sim E$, then A is a sufficient condition E.[4] Example 9 illustrates this method in action. The only possible necessary condition for $\sim E$ that is present whenever $\sim E$ is present is $\sim D$. Notice that this comes to the same thing as saying that the only one of the possible sufficient conditions for E that is absent whenever E is absent is D. Thus by the direct method of agreement, if one of the possible necessary conditions for $\sim E$ is actually a necessary condition for $\sim E$, then $\sim D$ is that necessary condition. But by the principle connecting negative necessary conditions for $\sim E$ and positive sufficient conditions for E, this is the same as saying if one of the possible sufficient conditions for E is actually a sufficient condition for E, then D is that sufficient condition. Thus we arrive at the inverse method of agreement.

At this point it may be useful to compare the direct and inverse methods of agreement. The direct method is a method of finding *necessary conditions*. To find a necessary condition for E, we look for a property that is present whenever E is present. The direct method depends on the following principle of elimination: A property that is absent when E is present cannot be a necessary condition for E. The inverse method is a method for finding sufficient conditions. To find a sufficient condition for E, we look for a

---

4 This principle can be easily proved with the aid of the preceding principles governing necessary and sufficient conditions. If $\sim A$ is a necessary condition for $\sim E$, then E is a necessary condition for A. And if E is a necessary condition for A, then A is a sufficient condition for E. If we find by the direct method of agreement that $\sim A$ is a necessary condition for $\sim E$, we may conclude that A is a sufficient condition for E.

property that is absent whenever E is absent. The inverse method depends on the following principle of elimination: A property that is present when E is absent cannot be a sufficient condition for E.

In Example 8 it required three occurrences to narrow down the field to D. However, the occurrence shown in Example 10 would alone eliminate A, B, and C. In the inverse method of agreement, as in the direct method, if we only admit simple properties as possible conditioning properties, then the least number of occurrences that can eliminate all but one of the possible conditioning properties is 1.

Example 10

	\multicolumn{4}{c}{Possible conditioning properties}	Conditioned property
	A	B	C	D	E
Occurrence 1:	P	P	P	A	A

Suppose, however, we wish to admit negative properties as possible conditioning properties. This is a reasonable step to take, for negative sufficient conditions can be quite important. Not staying awake while driving may be a sufficient condition for having an accident. Not being able to see may be a sufficient condition for not being called for military service. (By the principle that if $\sim F$ is sufficient for $\sim G$, then F is necessary for G, this would mean that being able to see would be a necessary condition for being called for military service.) We will introduce negative possible conditioning properties as in the section on the direct method of agreement. But this time we will rely on the principle of elimination of the inverse method of agreement: A property that is present when E is absent cannot be a sufficient condition for E. In Example 11 the only possible conditioning

Example 11

	\multicolumn{7}{c}{Possible conditioning properties}	Conditioned property
	\multicolumn{4}{c}{Simple}	\multicolumn{3}{c}{Complex}	
	A	B	C	D	$\sim A$	$\sim B$	$\sim C$	$\sim D$	E
Occurrence 1:	A	P	A	P	P	A	P	A	A
Occurrence 2:	A	P	A	A	P	A	P	P	A
Occurrence 3:	P	P	A	A	A	A	P	P	A
Occurrence 4:	A	P	P	A	P	A	A	P	A

property that is not eliminated is a negative one. $\sim B$ is the only possible conditioning property that is absent in every occurrence in which E is absent, so if one of the possible conditioning properties is a sufficient condition for E, then $\sim B$ is that sufficient condition.

It need not take as many occurrences as in Example 11 to eliminate all the possible conditioning properties but one. Two occurrences of the right kind could do the job, as shown in Example 12. In this example, if one of the

Example 12

	Possible conditioning properties							Conditioned property
	Simple				Complex			
	A	B	C	D	$\sim A$	$\sim B$	$\sim C$	$\sim D$	E
Occurrence 1:	P	P	P	A	A	A	A	P	A
Occurrence 2:	A	P	A	P	P	A	P	A	A

possible conditioning properties is a sufficient condition for E, then $\sim B$ is that sufficient condition. In the inverse method of agreement, as in the direct method, if only simple properties and their negations are admitted as possible conditioning properties, then the least number of occurrences that can eliminate all but one of the possible conditioning properties is 2.

We may further extend the inverse method of agreement to allow conjunctions of simple properties as possible conditioning properties. For example, suppose we are told that eating good food *and* getting plenty of rest *and* getting a moderate amount of exercise is a sufficient condition for good health. The inverse method of agreement would *support* this contention if we found that whenever good health was absent, this complex condition was also absent (that is, if everyone who was in poor health had not eaten good food *or* had not gotten enough rest *or* had not exercised). The inverse method of agreement would *disprove* this contention if an occurrence was found where good health was absent and the complex condition was present (that is, if someone was found in poor health who had eaten good food, and gotten plenty of rest, and gotten a moderate amount of exercise).

Let us look at two examples of the inverse method of agreement where a conjunction is admitted as a possible conditioning property. In Example 13 all the possible conditioning properties except the conjunction are eliminated. The only possible conditioning property that is absent whenever E is absent is the complex property $C\&D$. If one of the possible conditioning

Example 13

	Possible conditioning properties					Conditioned property
		Simple			Complex	
	A	B	C	D	C&D	E
Occurrence 1:	P	P	A	P	A	A
Occurrence 2:	P	A	P	A	A	A

properties is a sufficient condition for E, C&D is that sufficient condition.

In Example 14 the conjunction itself is eliminated. If one of the possible conditioning properties is a sufficient condition for E, then D is that sufficient condition. We shall not explore further the treatment of complex possible conditioning properties by the inverse method of agreement.[5] But you cannot go wrong if you remember that the principle of elimination in

Example 14

	Possible conditioning properties					Conditioned property
		Simple			Complex	
	A	B	C	D	B&C	E
Occurrence 1:	P	P	A	A	A	A
Occurrence 2:	A	P	P	A	P	A

the inverse method of agreement is: A property that is present when E is absent cannot be a sufficient condition for E.

The parallels drawn between the method of the master detective and the direct method of agreement hold also for the inverse method of agreement. It should not be thought that the field of possible sufficient conditions can always be narrowed down to one, for a property can have several sufficient conditions. We should also be prepared for the eventuality that the observed occurrences will eliminate all possible conditioning properties in the

---

[5] The inverse method of agreement can be expanded to include simple properties, negations of simple properties, and conjunctions of simple properties and their negations as possible conditioning properties. There is no need to worry about disjunctions, since a disjunction, FvG, is a sufficient condition for E if *and only if* F is a sufficient condition for E and G is a sufficient condition for E. For this reason if one can discover all the sufficient conditions that are not disjunctions, he will automatically have all the sufficient conditions that are disjunctions.

list. After all, a sufficient condition may not have been included in the list of possible conditioning properties. In such a case we would have to construct a more comprehensive list of possible conditioning properties. In some cases this more comprehensive list might be constructed by considering complex properties that were not included in the original list.

In Example 15 the five occurrences show that none of the possible conditioning properties can be a sufficient condition for E. But they suggest that the complex property $B\&C$ might be added to the list of possible conditioning properties. This property is always absent when E is absent.

The situation, however, might be more problematic. The observed

Example 15

	Possible conditioning properties $A \quad B \quad C \quad D$	Conditioned property E
Occurrence 1:	A P A P	A
Occurrence 2:	P A P P	A
Occurrence 3:	P A A P	A
Occurrence 4:	A A A P	A
Occurrence 5:	P P A A	A

occurrences might not only eliminate all the simple properties in the list but also all the (contingent) complex properties that can be constructed out of them. Such is the case in Example 16. It is impossible to discover in this list

Example 16

	Possible conditioning properties $A \quad B \quad C$	Conditioned property E
Occurrence 1:	P P P	A
Occurrence 2:	P P A	A
Occurrence 3:	P A P	A
Occurrence 4:	P A A	A
Occurrence 5:	A P P	A
Occurrence 6:	A P A	A
Occurrence 7:	A A P	A
Occurrence 8:	A A A	A

any (contingent) complex property constructed out of A, B, and C which is not eliminated as a sufficient condition for E by these eight occurrences. In such a case some new simple properties would have to be added to the list of possible conditioning properties.

   Exercises:

   1. In Example 9 which of the following complex properties are eliminated as sufficient conditions for E by occurrences 1, 2, and 3?

    a. *A.*   e. *A&B.*
    b. *B.*   f. *B&C.*
    c. *C.*   g. *A&D.*
    d. *D.*

   2. In Example 10 which of the following complex properties are eliminated by occurrence 1?

    a. *A.*   e. *A&C.*
    b. *B.*   f. *B&C.*
    c. *C.*   g. *A&C.*
    d. *D.*   h. *A&D.*

   3. In Example 11 which of the following complex properties are eliminated by the four occurrences?

    a. *A&B.*   d. *A&D.*
    b. *B&C.*   e. *A&C.*
    c. *B&D.*   f. *C&D.*

   4. In Example 13 are there any conjunctions of the simple properties listed other than *C&D* which are not eliminated by occurrences 1 and 2?

   IV.9. THE METHOD OF DIFFERENCE. The direct method of agreement was a method for finding the necessary conditions of a given property. The inverse method of agreement was a method for finding the sufficient conditions of a given property. Suppose, however, that our inquiry had a more restricted goal. Suppose that we wanted to find out which of the properties present in a certain occurrence of the conditioned property are sufficient conditions for it. To illustrate, let us suppose we find a dead man with no marks of violence on his body. In trying to determine the cause of death, we are looking for a sufficient condition for death. But we are not looking for *any* sufficient condition for death. Being run over by a steamroller is a sufficient condition for death, but that fact is irrelevant to our inquiry since this particular man was not run over by a steamroller. The conditioning property "being run over by a steamroller" is absent in this particular occurrence. What we are looking for is a sufficient condition for death among the properties that are present in this particular occurrence in which death is present. It is this sort of inquiry for which the method of difference is designed.

It is important to note why no analogous question can be raised for necessary conditions. It follows from the definition of necessary condition that all the necessary conditions for a given property must be present whenever that property is present. If loss of consciousness is a necessary condition for death, it will be present in every case of death. The questions "What properties are necessary conditions for E?" and "Which of the properties that are present in this particular occurrence of E are necessary conditions for E?" have exactly the same answer. In contrast, when a given property is present, some of its sufficient conditions may be absent. Many people who die have not been run over by a steamroller nor been decapitated on the guillotine. The question "Which of the properties that are present in this particular occurrence of E are sufficient conditions for E?" will, in general, have a shorter list of properties as its answer than the question "Which properties are sufficient conditions for E?"

In Example 17 occurrence * does not eliminate any of the possible conditioning properties as sufficient conditions for E. But if the question of interest is "Which of the properties that are present in occurrence * are

Example 17

	Possible conditioning properties				Conditioned property
	A	B	C	D	E
Occurrence *:	P	A	P	P	P

sufficient conditions for E?" then the candidates are limited to A, C, and D. Let us now look for other occurrences that will narrow down the field. The principle of elimination is the same as that employed in the inverse method of agreement: A property that is present when E is absent cannot be a sufficient condition for E. Therefore let us look for additional occurrences when E is absent. Suppose that the results of our investigation are as shown in Example 18. In this example occurrences 1 and 2 eliminate A and D as sufficient conditions for E. Of the possible conditioning properties that were present in occurrence *, only C is left. Thus if one of the possible conditioning properties that was present in occurrence * is a sufficient condition for E, then C is that sufficient condition. Note that B might also be a sufficient condition for E, but it is not one we would be

Example 18

	Possible conditioning properties				Conditioned property
	A	B	C	D	E
Occurrence *:	P	A	P	P	P
Occurrence 1:	P	A	A	A	A
Occurrence 2:	A	A	A	P	A

interested in, since we are looking for a sufficient condition which was present in occurrence *. Occurrences 1 and 2 eliminate candidates in exactly the same way as in the inverse method of agreement. In the inverse method of agreement, however, we started with all the possible conditioning properties as candidates, while in the method of difference, we start with the possible conditioning properties that are present in a particular occurrence in which the conditioned property is present. (We shall always call the occurrence that *defines* the candidates "occurrence *" and will number as before the occurrences that *eliminate* some of the candidates.)

If only simple properties are admitted as possible conditioning properties, then occurrence * might only leave one candidate as shown in Example 19. In this example the only possible conditioning property

Example 19

	Possible conditioning properties				Conditioned property
	A	B	C	D	E
Occurrence *:	A	A	A	P	P

present is D. Thus without looking for eliminating occurrences it may be concluded that if one of the possible conditioning properties that is present in occurrence * is a sufficient condition for E, then D is that sufficient condition. In fact, if only simple properties are admitted as possible conditioning properties, then occurrence * might leave no candidates whatsoever.

But there is no reason why negations of the simple properties cannot be admitted as possible conditioning properties, as was done in the treatment of the direct and inverse methods of agreement. If both simple properties and their negations are allowed as possible conditioning properties, then, in an occurrence *, exactly half of the possible conditioning properties will be left as candidates, since exactly half of them must be present in any occurrence. Further occurrences must be sought then in order to eliminate some of these properties, as in the inverse method of agreement.

Let us determine which of the properties present in occurrence * are sufficient conditions for E. In Example 20 D, ∼A, ∼B, and ∼C are the

Example 20

	Possible conditioning properties								Conditioned property
	Simple				Complex				
	A	B	C	D	∼A	∼B	∼C	∼D	E
Occurrence *:	A	A	A	P	P	P	P	A	P
Occurrence 1:	A	P	A	P	A	A	A	A	A
Occurrence 2:	P	P	P	A	P	A	P	P	A

possible conditioning properties present in occurrence * and are the candidates. Occurrences 1 and 2 eliminate D, ∼A, and ∼C. The only one of the candidates which remains is ∼B, leading to the conclusion that if one of the possible conditioning properties that is present in occurrence * is a sufficient condition for E, then ∼B is that sufficient condition.

As has been shown, if simple properties and their negations are allowed as possible conditioning properties, then occurrence * will leave exactly half of the possible conditioning properties as candidates. The least number of additional occurrences needed to eliminate all these candidates but one is one, if that one occurrence is of the right kind, as shown in Example 21. The possible conditioning properties that are present in occurrence * constitute the candidates, and they are B, C, ∼A, and ∼D. Occurrence 1 eliminates B, ∼A, and ∼D since they are absent when E is present. Thus if

Example 21

	Possible conditioning properties								Conditioned property
	Simple				Complex				
	A	B	C	D	∼A	∼B	∼C	∼D	E
Occurrence *:	A	P	P	A	P	A	A	P	P
Occurrence 1:	A	P	A	A	P	A	P	P	A

one of the possible conditioning properties that is present in occurrence °
is a sufficient condition for E, then C is that sufficient condition.

If you look closely at Example 21, you will notice that the reason all
candidates but C were eliminated is that C is the only possible conditioning property that was both present in occurrence ° (where E was present)
and absent in occurrence 1 (where E was absent). All other possible conditioning properties present in occurrence ° were also present in occurrence 1, where E was absent, and thus were eliminated. It follows that
all the possible conditioning properties that were absent in occurrence °
were also absent in occurrence 1 (except for $\sim C$). In other words, there
was only one change in the presence or absence of the possible conditioning properties from occurrence ° to occurrence 1: the change from C
being present and $\sim C$ being absent in occurrence ° to C being absent
and $\sim C$ being present in occurrence 1.[6] When both simple properties and
their negations are allowed to be possible conditioning properties in the
method of difference, this is the only way in which one eliminating occurrence can eliminate all but one of the possible conditioning properties.
This rather special case of the method of difference is what Mill describes
as "the method of difference." However, Mill's view of the method of
difference was too narrow, for, as has been shown, the method has application when several eliminating occurrences, rather than just one, narrow
down the field.

The method of difference may be expanded, in exactly the same way as
in the inverse method of agreement, by allowing conjunctions of simple
properties as possible conditioning properties. Simply remember that we
start with a particular occurrrence, occurrence °, in which E is present.
The candidates will then be all the possible conditioning properties that
are present in occurrence °. We then look for occurrences where E is
absent, so that some of the candidates can be eliminated. A candidate is
eliminated if it is present in an occurrence where E is absent, since a
sufficient condition for E cannot be present when E is absent. If all candidates but one are eliminated, we can conclude that, if one of the possible
conditioning properties present in occurrence ° is a sufficient condition
for E, then the remaining candidate is that sufficient condition. But, as
in the direct and inverse methods of agreement, it is not always possible
to narrow down the field to one candidate. More than one sufficient

---

[6] This one change in the possible conditioning properties corresponds to the
change in the conditioned property: E is present in occurrence ° and absent in
occurrence 1.

condition for *E* may be present in occurrence *. When a man is simultaneously beheaded, shot through the heart, and exposed to a lethal dose of nerve gas, several sufficient conditions for death are present. On the other hand, the eliminating occurrences might eliminate all the candidates. This would show that the list of possible conditioning properties did not include a property that was both present in occurrence * and a sufficient condition for *E*. In such a case other factors that were present in occurrence * must be sought and included in a new, expanded list of possible conditioning properties.

Exercises:

Consider the following example:

Possible conditioning properties								Conditioned property
Simple				Complex				
A	*B*	*C*	*D*	~*A*	~*B*	~*C*	~*D*	*E*
Occurrence*: P	A	A	P	A	P	P	A	P

1. What are the candidates?

2. Describe an eliminating occurrence that would eliminate all the candidates but one.

3. Describe an eliminating occurrence that would eliminate all the candidates.

4. Describe three eliminating occurrences, each of which would eliminate exactly one of the candidates.

5. What would you conclude if you observed the occurrence that you described in Exercise 2?

6. What would you conclude if you observed the occurrence you described in Exercise 3?

7. What would you conclude if you observed the three occurrences you described in Exercise 4?

8. What would you conclude if you observed all the occurrences that you described in Exercises 2 and 4. There are several correct answers to Exercises 2 and 4, and the answer to this question will depend on which ones you chose.

IV.10. THE COMBINED METHODS. Sometimes a property is both a necessary and sufficient condition for another property. It has already been pointed out that in football the complex property "making a touchdown or making a field goal or making a conversion or making a safety" is both a necessary and sufficient condition for scoring. Medical authorities thought until recently that stoppage of the heart for more than a few minutes was both a necessary and sufficient conditon for death. In elementary physics being acted on by a net force is both a necessary and sufficient condition for a change in a body's velocity. Since there is a method for finding necessary conditions—the direct method of agreement—and two methods for finding sufficient conditions—the inverse method of agreement and the method of difference—they may be combined in order to find conditions that are both necessary and sufficient.

In Example 22 the direct and inverse methods of agreement are com-

Example 22

		Possible conditioning properties							Conditioned property
	Simple				Complex				
	A	B	C	D	~A	~B	~C	~D	E
Occurrence 1:	P	A	P	A	A	P	A	P	P
Occurrence 2:	A	P	P	P	P	A	A	A	P
Occurrence 3:	A	P	A	P	P	A	P	A	A
Occurrence 4:	P	A	A	A	A	P	P	P	A

bined into what is called the *double method of agreement*. Occurrence 1 eliminates B, D, $\sim A$, and $\sim C$ and occurrence 2 eliminates A, $\sim B$, $\sim C$, and $\sim D$ as necessary conditions for E in accordance with the *direct* method of agreement, for they are absent when E is present. We can conclude then from occurrences 1 and 2, by the direct method of agreement, that if one of the possible conditioning properties is a necessary condition for E, then C is that necessary condition. In accordance with the *inverse* method of agreement, occurrence 3 eliminates B, D, $\sim A$, and $\sim C$ and occurrence 4 eliminates A, $\sim B$, $\sim C$, and $\sim D$ as sufficient conditions for E, since they are present when E is absent. This again leaves only C. We can conclude from occurrences 3 and 4, by the inverse method of agreement that if one of the possible conditioning properties is a sufficient condition for E, then C is that sufficient condition. Putting these results together leads to the conclusion that if one of the possible conditioning properties is both a necessary and a sufficient condition for E, then C is that property. However, a stronger conclusion may be drawn: If one of the possible conditioning properties is a necessary condition for E, and one of the possible conditioning properties is a sufficient condition for E, then one and the same possible conditioning property is both a necessary and sufficient condition for E, and that property is C.

The *joint method of agreement and difference*, which is illustrated in Example 23, combines the direct method of agreement and the method of difference. The first step is to apply the method of difference to Example 23. Occurrence * sets up as candidates for the sufficient condition for E those properties that are present in occurrence *, namely, A, C, $\sim B$, and $\sim D$. But occurrence 1 shows that neither A nor $\sim B$ nor $\sim D$ can be a sufficient condition for E, since they are all present when E is absent.

Example 23

	Possible conditioning properties							Conditioned property
	Simple				Complex			
	A	B	C	D	$\sim A$	$\sim B$	$\sim C$	$\sim D$	E
Occurrence *:	P	A	P	A	A	P	A	P	P
Occurrence 1:	P	A	A	A	A	P	P	P	A
Occurrence 2:	A	P	P	P	P	A	A	A	P

This leaves only C. Thus we can conclude from occurrence * and occurrence 1 that if one of the possible conditioning properties present in occurrence * is a sufficient condition for E, then C is that sufficient condition.

Now let us apply the direct method of agreement to Example 24. Occurrence * may be used again since, in accordance with the direct method of agreement, it eliminates B, D, $\sim A$, and $\sim C$ as necessary conditions for E. And occurrence 2 further eliminates A, $\sim B$, and $\sim D$ as necessary conditions for E since they also are absent in an occurrence where E is present. This leaves only C. So from occurrence * and occurrence 2, by the direct method of agreement, we can conclude that if one of the possible conditioning properties is a necessary condition for E, then C is that necessary condition. Putting the results of the method of difference and the direct method of agreement together leads to the conclusion that: If one of the possible conditioning properties present in occurrence * is a sufficient condition for E and if one of the possible conditioning properties is a necessary condition for E, then one and the same possible conditioning property that is present in occurrence * is both a necessary and sufficient condition for E, and that property is C.

In comparing the example of the joint method of agreement and difference with the previous example of the double method of agreement, note that occurrences *, 1, and 2 of Example 23 are the same, respectively, as occurrences 1, 4, and 2 of Example 22. Notice also that Example 22, using the double method of agreement, takes four occurrences to narrow down the field to C, while Example 23, using the joint method of agreement and difference, takes only three occurrences. Does this mean that the joint method of agreement and difference is, in some way, a more efficient method than the double method of agreement? Not at all. Less occurrences are needed in Example 23 than in Example 22 because the conclusion drawn from Example 23 is weaker than that drawn from Example 22. From Example 23 we may conclude that if one of the possible conditioning properties *which is present in occurrence* * is a sufficient condition for E and one of the possible conditioning properties is a necessary condition for E, then C is both the necessary and the sufficient condition. If we want to remove the restriction "which is present in occurrence *" then the extra occurrence that appears in Example 22 is needed, and the double method of agreement must be used. Consequently from Example 22 the stronger conclusion may be drawn that if one of the possible conditioning properties is a sufficient condition for E and one of the possible conditioning properties is a necessary condition for E, then C is both the necessary and the sufficient condition.

Whether the joint method of agreement and difference or the double method of agreement is chosen depends on what previous knowledge we have. Suppose we have observed an occurrence and have good reason to believe that one of the possible conditioning properties which is present in that occurrence is a sufficient condition for E. We would then designate that occurrence as occurrence * and proceed with the joint method of agreement and difference. If, however, we had good reason to believe only that one or another of the possible conditioning properties is a sufficient condition for E, we would have to rely on the double method of agreement. The combined methods are equally efficient, but they are appropriate in different circumstances.

The combined methods may be expanded to include other complex properties (disjunctions and conjunctions of simple properties and the negations of simple properties), but a discussion of these more involved forms of Mill's methods belongs in more advanced texts. Remember, however, that everything that has been said about Mill's methods, and everything that can be said about their more involved forms, rests on two simple principles of elimination:

i. A necessary condition for E cannot be absent when E is present.

ii. A sufficient condition for E cannot be present when E is absent.

These two principles are more important to remember than Mill's methods themselves, and they should always be borne in mind when a mass of data is being analyzed.

Exercises:

Suppose you have observed the following occurrences:

		Possible conditioning properties							Conditioned property
		Simple				Complex			
	A	B	C	D	$\sim A$	$\sim B$	$\sim C$	$\sim D$	E
Occurrence 1:	P	P	A	A	A	A	P	P	P
Occurrence 2:	P	A	A	A	A	P	P	P	A
Occurrence 3:	A	P	P	P	P	A	A	A	P

1. Suppose you know that one of the possible conditioning properties is a necessary condition for E. Which one is it? What occurrences did you use and which of Mill's methods did you apply?

2. Suppose you know that one of the possible conditioning properties which is present in occurrence 1 is a sufficient condition for E. Which one is it? What occurrences did you use and which one of Mill's methods did you apply?

3. Suppose you know that one of the possible conditioning properties is a necessary condition for E and that one of the possible conditioning properties which is present in occurrence 1 is a sufficient condition for E. Do you know whether one possible conditioning property is both a necessary and sufficient condition for E? If so, which one is it and which one of Mill's methods did you use?

4. Suppose you know that one of the possible conditioning properties is a necessary condition for E. You also know that one of the possible conditioning properties is a sufficient condition for E, but you do not know whether it is a property that is present in occurrence 1. Furthermore, you have observed an additional occurrence:

	A	B	C	D	$\sim A$	$\sim B$	$\sim C$	$\sim D$	E
Occurrence 4:	A	A	P	P	P	P	A	A	A

Do you know whether one possible conditioning property is both a necessary and a sufficient condition for E? If so, which one is it and which one of Mill's methods did you use?

5. Suppose you had only observed occurrences 1 and 2 but you knew that one of the possible conditioning properties was both a necessary and a sufficient condition for E. Using the two principles of elimination, can you tell which one it is?

IV.11. THE APPLICATION OF MILL'S METHODS. The conclusions we drew from various applications of Mill's methods always began with phrases such as "If one of the possible conditioning properties is a necessary condition for E . . . ," or "If one of the possible conditioning properties which is present in occurrence ° is a sufficient condition for E . . . ," etc. It would seem that our confidence that Mill's methods have found a necessary condition, or a sufficient condition, or a necessary and sufficient condition depends on our confidence that the list of possible conditioning properties contains the requisite kind of condition. But how can we be sure that this list does contain the type of condition being sought?

One suggestion might be to include *all* properties as possible conditioning properties and to rely on some principle of the uniformity of nature to guarantee that each conditioning property has some necessary and some sufficient conditions. There are many things wrong with this suggestion, but the most practical objection is that there are simply too many properties to take into account. Even if we are interested only in the properties that are present in a given occurrence, as in the method of difference, not all properties that are present can be considered. In any occurrence there are countless properties present. When you sneeze, there are hundreds of chemical reactions going on within your body: various electrical currents are circulating in your nerve fibers; you are being bombarded by various types of electromagnetic radiation; diverse happenings, great and small, surround you. It would be an impossible task to measure and catalog all these things and eliminate them, one by one, by Mill's methods in order to find a sufficient condition for sneezing.

For Mill's methods to be of any use, there must be some way of ascertaining what factors are likely to be relevant to the conditioned property in which we are interested; there must be some way of setting up a list of reasonable length of possible conditioning properties which probably contains the necessary or sufficient conditions being sought. The only way to do this is to apply inductive logic to a previously acquired body of evidence. Mill's methods are of no use unless we already have some inductive knowledge to guide us in setting up the list of possible conditioning properties.

Mill's methods are useful in science, but their usefulness depends on inductively based judgments as to what factors are likely to be relevant to a given conditioned property. Of course, inductively based judgments are not infallible. We may be mistaken in believing that the list of possible conditioning properties contains a necessary or a sufficient condition. The occurrences observed may eliminate all of the possible conditioning properties. If this happens, all the evidence at our disposal must be reëxamined, and perhaps new evidence must be sought, in order to find new properties that are probably relevant to the conditioned property under investigation. Once the inductive judgment has been made as to which additional properties must be considered, Mill's methods may then be reapplied. In the search for necessary and sufficient conditions, Mill's methods are part of the picture, but they are not the whole picture. The most basic, and least understood, part of the process is the setting up of lists of possible conditioning properties.

Imagine the following scientific experimental situation in which Mill's methods might be applied. Suppose we have three new drugs that hold promise for the cure of a hitherto incurable disease: drug A, drug B, and drug C. We administer various combinations of these drugs and note whether the patient is cured or not. The results are tabulated in Example 24, where "A" means drug A has been administered, "B" means drug B has been administered, and "C" means drug C has been administered. "E"

Example 24

	Possible conditioning properties			Conditioned property
	A	B	C	E
Occurrence 1:	P	P	A	P
Occurrence 2:	P	A	P	P
Occurrence 3:	A	P	A	A
Occurrence 4:	A	A	P	A
Occurrence 5:	A	A	A	A

means the patient has been cured. Occurrence 5 represents the cases of all the previous patients who had not taken any of these drugs and who had not been cured. The cases of patients to whom various combinations of the new drugs have been administered are tabulated under occurrences 1 through 4. Example 24 constitutes a case of the double method of agreement and it warrants the conclusion that if one of the possible conditioning properties is a necessary condition for E, and one of the possible conditioning properties is a sufficient condition for E, then A is both the necessary and the sufficient condition for E. Thus these results lead to the conclusion that, to the best of our knowledge, the administration of drug A is both a necessary and a sufficient condition for a cure of the disease.

But suppose that someone tries other combinations of the drugs and gets the results shown in Example 25. Occurrence 7 shows that A is not a sufficient condition for E. Therefore if we wished to find a sufficient condition for E, we would have to expand our list of possible conditioning properties. Suppose now that biochemical theory suggests that there may be a

Example 25

| | Possible conditioning properties | | | Conditioned property |
	A	B	C	E
Occurrence 6:	P	A	A	P
Occurrence 7:	P	P	P	A
Occurrence 8:	A	P	P	A

chemical interaction if the three drugs are administered simultaneously, and that such a chemical interaction might cancel out their effectiveness against the disease. The sum of our observations would then suggest that what may be happening in occurrence 7 is that drugs B and C are interacting and preventing drug A from curing the disease. (We could imagine different occurrences that would suggest that two drugs are effective only in combination.) Drug A seems to be effective when taken alone (occurrence 6), or when taken with B but without C (occurrence 1), or when taken with C but without B (occurrence 2). This suggests that the complex property, $A \& \sim(B \& C)$, that is, taking drug A but not in conjunction with both drug B and drug C, is really the sufficient condition for E. And if we were to add this complex property to our list of possible conditioning properties, and use all the eight occurrences, we would find that it is then the only possible conditioning property that is present whenever E is present and absent whenever E is absent. In this way we can reapply the double method of agreement to an enlarged set of possible conditioning properties, in the face of additional occurrences, in order to revise our conclusion and make it more sophisticated.

But we might not be finished even at this point. Suppose that another researcher were to point out that all our tests have been made on patients in whom the disease was at an early stage, and that many diseases are more easily cured in their early stages than in their advanced stages. This would suggest that our complex property only appears to be a sufficient condition for E, because we have not tested our drugs on advanced cases of the disease. What we would now have to do is to take this additional factor into account in our list of possible conditioning properties. We could introduce a new property, D, which is said to be present when the disease is in its advanced stages and absent otherwise. In all the occurrences where drugs have been administered so far, D has been absent. Now we would have to find various occurrences where D was present. That is, we should administer various combinations of drugs to patients in advanced stages of the disease and note the resuts. If the treatment that effected a cure before were to still effect a cure, then we would not have to revise our belief that $A\&{\sim}(B\&C)$ is a sufficient condition for E. But if our treatment failed in advanced cases, then we might have to say that the sufficient condition for being cured is having the disease in an early stage and receiving the correct combination of drugs. That is, we would have to say that $A\&{\sim}(B\&C)$ is not a sufficient condition for E, but that ${\sim}D\&A\&{\sim}(B\&C)$ is a sufficient condition for E.

We could imagine an endless stream of developments which might force us to add more and more complex and simple properties to our list of possible conditioning properties and to continually reëvaluate our results. Someone might develop a new drug that effects a cure in the absence of drug A and thus show that A is not a necessary condition for E. Additional research might suggest other factors that might be relevant and whose relationship to E we might wish to examine. It is by such a process that Mill's methods, in conjunction with a continual search for new occurrences, and new relevant possible conditioning properties, contribute to the growth of scientific knowledge.

Suggested readings

Arthur Pap, *An Introduction to the Philosophy of Science* (Glencoe, Ill.: The Free Press, 1962), pp. 151–55.

Georg Henrik Von Wright, *A Treatise on Induction and Probability* (Patterson, N.J.: Littlefield, Adams & Co., 1960), chap. 4 and chap. 6, pt. 4. (This book is quite difficult and requires a thorough grasp of deductive logic.)

The following books may be consulted for a more historical treatment of Mill's methods:

Irving M. Copi, *Introduction to Logic* (2nd ed.) (New York: The Macmillan Company, 1961).

Morris Cohen and Ernest Nagel, *An Introduction to Logic and Scientific Method* (New York: Harcourt, Brace & World, Inc., 1934).

Nicholas Rescher, *Introduction to Logic* (New York: Saint Martin's, 1964).

IV.12. SUFFICIENT CONDITIONS AND FUNCTIONAL RELATIONSHIPS.

The preceding treatment of Mill's methods in terms of necessary and sufficient conditions proceeded entirely in qualitative terms. One may wonder what relevance, if any, that discussion has for sciences which have moved from qualitative to quantitative language. Here, ascriptions of cause or statements of necessary and sufficient conditions have been replaced by functional relationships expressed by mathematical equations. The basic logic of the situation, however, is not as different as it may seem. An equation expressing a functional relationship between physical quantities is tantamount to not one but an infinite number of statements to the effect that one physical property is a sufficient condition for another.

To understand this, we must look first at the relation between properties and physical quantities. Consider a physical quantity, for example, temperature, as measured on a given scale (e.g., degrees Kelvin). We make a factual claim about a state of a physical system when we say that its temperature (in degrees Kelvin) has a certain value. Temperature (so measured) is thus a *relation* between states of physical systems and (non-negative real) numbers. This is to say no more than:

> For every non-negative real number, x, there is associated a unique *physical property, having the temperature* x *in degrees Kelvin.*

A physical quantity can thus be seen as not one but rather an infinite family of physical properties. The properties in such a family are *mutually exclusive* (a physical system cannot have two different temperatures at the same time) and *jointly exhaustive* (a physical system in a given state must have some temperature or other) over the states of the appropriate type of physical system (the concept of temperature has no meaning when applied, for instance, to the nucleus of an atom). An appropriate set of real numbers serves as a *fruitful filing system* for the physical properties in such a family. We can thus say that:

> A *physical quantity* is a family of physical qualities, mutually exclusive and jointly exhaustive over the states of the intended class of physical systems, *indexed* by some set of real numbers.

We said that the indexing of the physical quantities by the index set of real numbers forms a *fruitful* filing system. It is fruitful just in that it, together with the filing systems of other physical quantities, enables us to formulate physical laws in terms of mathematical equations. To see how this works, let us consider a few simple equations. First the equation $x = 2y$. This equation gives concise expression to an infinite number of statements, of which a few are:

If y is 0, x is 0.
If y is 1, x is 2.
If y is $3\frac{1}{2}$, x is 7.

In general, for each value of y, the equation correlates a unique value of x. We give expression to this fact by saying that here x is a *function* of y. This equation also makes y a function of x, since for every value of x it correlates a unique value for y (i.e., $\frac{1}{2}x$). It does not always follow, however, that if x is a function of y, y is a function of x. Consider the equation $x = y^2$. Here, each value of y determines a unique value of x, but the converse is not true. If x is $+4$, y may be either $+2$ or -2. Thus x is a function of y, but y is not a function of x.

What does this mean in physical terms when the variables of the equation represent physical quantities? If the variables represent physical quantities measured on fixed scales (e.g., temperature Kelvin) then, as we have seen, each numerical value of a variable represents a physical quality (e.g., having a temperature of 10 degrees Kelvin). If a physical quantity, Q_2, is a *function* of another, Q_1, then for every value v_i of Q_1 there is a uniquely determined value v_j of Q_2 such that whenever a physical system has v_i of Q_1 it has v_j of Q_2. That is, having v_i of Q_1 is a *sufficient condition* for having v_j of Q_2. Thus, in terms of our view of physical quantities as families of physical qualities, we may say that:

> If Q_2 is a function of Q_1, then for every member of the family Q_1, there is some member of the family Q_2 *for which it is a sufficient condition.*

This generalizes in a straightforward way to functions of several variables. For example, consider the ideal gas law:

$$V = k\frac{T}{P}$$

where V is volume, T is temperature and P is pressure. k is called a *system-dependent constant* since it varies from system to system (e.g., different balloons filled with gas) but remains constant over different states of the same system (e.g., heating a balloon, or submerging it to 200 fathoms). The equation establishes V as a function of k, T, and P in that each triple of values for k, T, and P uniquely determines a value for V. Thus in conjunction:

$$k = 1 \text{ } and \text{ } T = 100 \text{ } and \text{ } P = 50$$

is a sufficient condition for $V = 2$.

In general, we can say that if a quantity, Q_0, is a function of several others, $Q_1 \ldots Q_n$, then for every conjunctive physical property which contains as conjuncts just one member from each of the families $Q_1 \ldots Q_n$, there is a member of the family Q_0 for which it is a sufficient condition. Mathematical equations establishing functional relations between physical quantities thus allow succinct expression of extremely rich claims about sufficient conditions.

Since we are still, at basis, dealing with sufficient conditions, the fundamental principles that we used to analyze Mill's methods must still apply, although in a slightly more complicated way. Instead of one conditioning property, we have the family of properties comprising a physical quantity (the *dependent* variable). We must find a way for establishing, for each member of this family, a list of possible conditioning properties. This is a two-stage process. The first stage is to construct a list of physical quantities whose values are likely to be relevant in determining the value of the dependent variable. We can call this our list of *independent variables*. The second stage is to construct a list of likely looking *functions* which make the dependent variable a function of our independent variables. For each conditioned property (value of the dependent variable), each of these functions determines one or more complex properties which are possible sufficient conditions for it. For example, consider the two functions:

$$\text{(i) } V = k \, \frac{T}{P} \text{ and (ii) } V = k \, \frac{T^2}{P}$$

Function (i) would make the following, among others, sufficient conditions for $V = 1$:

$$k = 1 \text{ } and \text{ } T = 1 \text{ } and \text{ } P = 1$$
$$k = 1 \text{ } and \text{ } T = 2 \text{ } and \text{ } P = 2$$

Function (ii) also makes

$$k = 1 \text{ } and \text{ } T = 1 \text{ } and \text{ } P = 1$$

a sufficient condition for $V = 1$, but disagrees with function (i) in making

$$k = 1 \text{ and } T = 2 \text{ and } P = 2$$

a sufficient condition for $V = 2$ rather than for $V = 1$. Since $V = 1$ and $V = 2$ are mutually exclusive physical properties, in any occurrence at least one of them must be absent. We have, then, only to look for an occurrence where $k = 1$ and $T = 2$ and $P = 2$ in order to eliminate either the hypothesis that function (i) gives the correct sufficient conditions or the hypothesis that condition (ii) does. The method operative here is thus a straightforward application of the inverse method of agreement. The only new twist is that we have a family of conditioned properties which are mutually exclusive, so that if one is present, the rest must be absent.[7]

Although the mechanism for the elimination of the proposed functions is quite clear here, the process for setting up the list of possible functions is, as before, quite murky. Such is to be expected, since the first process is really deductive whereas the latter is genuinely inductive. Nevertheless, the analysis given so far enables us to shed some light on the process of isolating relevant independent variables.

Remember that if P is a sufficient condition for C, then so is P and Q (and, of course, P and not-Q). There are, then, some very cumbersome sufficient conditions around, but obviously the most knowledge is gained by finding the shortest ones. In terms of functions, this means that if a quantity, Q_0, is a function of another, Q_1, it is also a function of Q_1 and Q_2 for any quantity Q_2. Again, the most interesting functions are stated in terms of the minimum number of variables needed to do the job. Suppose we start with a list of likely conditioning quantities $Q_1, Q_2, \ldots, Q_n$, vary them independently and find that one of them, say Q_1, doesn't make any difference in the conditioned quantity. That is, for different fixed combinations of values for $Q_2 \ldots Q_n$, the value of the conditioned quantity remains the same when the value of Q_1 is varied. Then we have good reason to believe that values of Q_1 would be excess fat in statements of sufficient conditions for the conditioned quantity. In other words, we have good (inductive) reason for believing

---

[7] Note that this means that the complex conditioning properties include conjunctions of simple properties and the negations of simple properties—which is just what we need (see footnote 5, p. 100).

that Q_1 is not a *relevant* variable. This process of reducing our list of conditioning quantities is called *isolating the relevant variables.*

The second stage in setting up the conditioning properties was to select a likely list of functions which make the dependent variable a function of the remaining independent variables. It is difficult to say anything very informative about the selection process. Sometimes we are guided by the sorts of functional relationships which have already been found to hold in similar physical situations, but it is difficult to say what *"similar"* means here. Sometimes we seem to be guided by considerations of *simplicity* of the expressions which designate the function. But, except in certain special cases, simplicity is a highly elusive concept.

To the question, "Why do we have this two-stage method of formulating statements of sufficient conditions?" we have already seen a relatively superficial (though correct) answer. That is, this method allows the succinct formulation of statements of such power and scope that they would otherwise exceed the resources of our language. But there is another, more profound, reason: that *the two stages are not inductively independent.* To see what I mean, consider a new physical quantity, T°, which is just like temperature Kelvin except that when temperature in degrees Kelvin equals 10, $T^{\circ} = 90$ and when temperature in degrees Kelvin equals 90, $T^{\circ} = 10$. T° comprehends exactly the same physical qualities as temperature, and uses the same set of numbers to index them, but the filing system is different. Imagine now, formulating the ideal gas law in terms of T° rather than temperature. Suddenly, the simple becomes more complex[8] (and by the same token, the complex can become more simple). Our basic physical magnitudes come to us, then, not simply as artless vehicles for the expression of factual claims, but rather as bearers of inductive wisdom. It is they, rather than other families of physical qualities, which have found expression in our language precisely because they have been found to enter into simply expressible functional relationships in a wide variety of physical contexts.[9] Language comes to us with inductive commitments—commitments so deeply ingrained that it is easy to overlook them. But, as we learned from Goodman in the

---

[8] The student who knows some advanced logic is invited to consider the proposition that under such a change, the formerly simple may become ineffable.

[9] The most basic of such relationships consist of the correlation of independent methods of measuring a physical quantity.

last chapter, overlooking them leads to an excessively simple-minded view of the nature of the inductive process.

Suggested readings

On physical quantities:

S. S. Stevens, "On the Theory of Scales of Measurement," *Science*, 1946, pp. 677–80.

B. Ellis, *Basic Concepts of Measurement* (London: Cambridge Univ. Press, 1966).

Kranz, Luce, Suppes, and Trevsky, *Foundations of Measurement*, Vol. 1 (New York: Academic Press, 1971), chap. 1.

On simplicity:

W. V. O. Quine, "On Simple Theories of a Complex World," *Synthese* Vol. 15 (1963): 103–6, reprinted in *Probability, Confirmation, and Simplicity*, ed. Foster and Martin (New York: Odyssey Press, 1966).

Nelson Goodman, "Safety, Strength and Simplicity," *Philosophy of Science*, Vol. XXVIII (1961), pp. 150–151.

IV.13. LAWLIKE AND ACCIDENTAL CONDITIONS. In Section IV.5 we defined a sufficient condition as follows:

A property, *F*, is a sufficient condition for a property, *G*, if and only if *whenever F is present, G is present.*

Hence, the following are all legitimate statements of sufficient conditions:

1. *Being a brother* is a sufficient condition for *being male.*

2. *Being over six feet tall* is a sufficient condition for *being over five feet tall.*

3. *Being pure water at a pressure of one atmosphere and a temperature of 100 degrees centigrade* is a sufficient condition for *boiling.*

4. *Having an inertial mass of one kilogram* is a sufficient condition for *having a gravitational mass of one kilogram.*[10]

5. *Eating dinner at the Paris Noodle on January 12, 1972,* is a sufficient condition for *being under six feet tall.*

---

[10] Inertial mass is measured with respect to Newton's second law, gravitational mass with respect to his law of universal gravitation.

6. Nelson Goodman had only dimes, quarters, and half-dollars in his pocket on VE day,[11] so *being a coin in Nelson Goodman's pocket on VE day* is a sufficient condition for *being made of silver.*

It is obvious from these examples that there are strikingly different *grades* of sufficiency. The sufficiency of the condition in Example 1 is due, in a most transparent way, to the meanings of the terms involved. We may call it an *analytic* sufficient condition. Example 2 also depends on the concepts involved, rather than the way we find the world to be, so we shall also call it an analytic sufficient condition. However, Example 2 should remind us that an account of analyticity is not always so easy to give as in the case of Example 1. It is not clear whether Example 3 is analytic or not. Is having a certain boiling point part of what we mean by being pure water? Is the boiling point of pure water involved in the definition of the centigrade scale? If the answer is yes to either of these questions, then we may have an analytic sufficient condition. If we have independent definitions of pure water and temperature centigrade then Example 3 states a sufficient condition which is informative about the way the world operates. Actual practice tends to shift from one set of meanings to another depending on what is most convenient to the occasion. Thus, actual practice does not provide an unambiguous answer as to whether Example 3 is an analytic sufficient condition or not. Such a semantically muddled state of affairs is common in human language, ordinary and scientific, and in such cases an unambiguous answer is only to be had by making a *decision* as to how the words are to be used on a particular occasion. Examples 4, 5, and 6 are all synthetic, but 4 is clearly different in kind from 5 and 6. Example 4 states a condition which is sufficient *by virtue of physical law.* In this respect it resembles Example 3, when Example 3 is interpreted as a synthetic statement. Examples 5 and 6, however, state conditions which are sufficient *simply by happenstance.* It simply *happened* that no one over six feet tall came to the Paris Noodle to eat dinner that day. It just *happened* that Nelson Goodman had no pennies in his pocket on VE day. We say that these truths are *accidental* rather than *lawlike.*

Although each of the distinctions between grades of sufficiency raises important and interesting questions, we shall focus here on the last one: *the distinction between accidental and lawlike sufficient conditions.* This

---

[11] Victory in Europe, World War II.

is an important distinction for inductive logic. The establishment of either sort of sufficient condition may be an inductive affair, but the roles they play are so different that one would suspect that inductive logic should treat them differently. It is lawlike sufficient conditions which make up the body of science. Statements of accidental sufficient conditions like 5 and 6 may, like any other factual statement, set up the application of a scientific theory, but they never form part of such a theory itself. The examples that we used to illustrate Mill's methods were, accordingly, all examples of lawlike sufficient conditions (or necessary conditions—all the distinctions being made here obviously apply to necessary conditions also).

Now, does this imperil our analysis of Mill's methods? Not at all. Our analysis depended only on the principle that a *sufficient condition cannot be present when the conditioned property is absent*. This principle of elimination follows from the definition of *sufficient condition* and thus holds for *all* sufficient conditions; accidental, lawlike, or analytic (likewise for necessary conditions). The story that we have told about Mill's methods is nothing but the truth. It is, however, far from the whole truth.

Mill's methods apply to analytic sufficient conditions, but eliminating other conditioning properties is surely not the most efficient way to arrive at *being a brother* as a sufficient condition for *being male*. It would be a hopelessly incompetent mathematician or logician who relied on the experimental method for his theorems. A scientist, on the other hand, would not even want an analytic sufficient condition in his list of conditioning properties, for knowing an analytic sufficient condition gives us no information about the way the world behaves. Neither would a scientist want a property like *being a coin in Nelson Goodman's pocket on VE day* on his list of possible sufficient conditions for *being composed of silver*. He knows that the overwhelming likelihood is that if this turns out to be a sufficient condition, it will turn out to be an accidental sufficient condition.[12]

This raises two questions:

(A) How do we distinguish lawlike from accidental sufficient conditions?

(B) Why is it that lawlike conditions find a place in the body of science whereas accidental ones do not?

_____

[12] One can imagine bizarre circumstances in which it might be a lawlike sufficient condition, so the property is not *fated* to be, at best, an accidental sufficient condition.

The answer to the second question, if it is to have any philosophical importance, must flow from considerations of the function of scientific law. And anything better than an *ad hoc* answer to the first question must flow from a satisfactory answer to the second.

Looking at Examples 1 through 6 it is easy to conjecture that the difference between accident and law is the difference between part and whole; that laws are truths about the whole universe, throughout space and time, whereas truths are restricted parts of it (e.g., the Paris Noodle and Nelson Goodman's pocket for the specified periods of time) may be accidental.[13]

Such a view has its attractions. Surely the most striking examples of accidental conditions stem from generalizations of spatio-temporally limited scope. And the preoccupation of science with *lawlike* sufficient conditions is neatly explained by the *universality* of science. Science is concerned with patterns which recur throughout the universe, rather than with gossip about a particular spatio-temporal region. This concern flows from the essential pursuits of science: *explanation and prediction.* Science always explains an event by showing it, in some way,[14] to be an instance of a general pattern, rather than just a freak occurrence. As for prediction, our generalizations about the Paris Noodle and Nelson Goodman's pocket are obviously not very powerful predictive instruments, because they don't cover much territory and typically *we don't know about the sufficient conditions until we have already covered the territory!* Both the contents of Goodman's pocket and the clientele of the Paris Noodle at the times in question had to be completely surveyed before confidence could be placed in our statements of sufficient conditions. And given such a complete survey, there is nothing left for them to predict. Since no complete survey of the universe is possible, generalizations about it must be known, if at all, while there is still predictive life left in them.

Suppose we accordingly try to define a law as a true generalization which does not name specific times, places, or individuals. Isn't it possible that even the general descriptive machinery we have left may pick out

---

[13] Truths about restricted parts of the universe *that are logical consequences of laws,* e.g., the statement that every object in Nelson Goodman's pocket on VE day obeys the law of gravitation, would of course be lawlike rather than accidental.

[14] In *what way* the particular event must be related to the general pattern is a matter of extensive debate.

a small finite class of objects? For instance, isn't it possible that a description of Nelson Goodman's pocket on VE day down to the finest detail, down to the trajectories of subatomic particles, could be so specific without containing names for times, places, or individuals, that the only thing in the whole universe which would answer to it would be Nelson Goodman's pocket on VE day. Then, according to our definition, *being a coin enclosed in such a structure* would have to be a lawlike sufficient condition for *being composed of silver*. But it is clearly accidental. In fact, it is *doubly* accidental, for it would be something of an accident that Goodman's pocket would be the *only* structure in the universe answering the description in question.

What has gone wrong? One natural line of thought is to conjecture that the trouble lies in defining spatio-temporal limitation of scope *via* the terms in which the generalization is couched, rather than by the objects to which it refers. Why not say that a law is a true generalization which does not refer to any spatio-temporally limited (or alternatively, to any finite) class of objects? Then

All coins enclosed in a structure of type I are composed of silver.

would fail to be a law, even if true, if Nelson Goodman's pocket on VE day constituted the only structure of type I.

But wait! Why do we assume that this generalization is *only about* coins enclosed in structures of type I? To be sure, if we know that a certain object is such a coin, we know that it is *crucial* to the generalization. It is crucial in that, if it turns out not to be silver, it falsifies the generalization. But if we know of another object that it is *not silver*, then similarly we know it to be crucial to the generalization. It is crucial in that if it turns out to be a coin enclosed in a structure of type I, it will falsify the generalization. In all fairness, then, we ought to allow that our generalization is *also about* objects not composed of silver. Another way to put the same point is to note that *being a coin enclosed in a structure of type I* is a sufficient condition for *being composed of silver* just in case *not being composed of silver* is a sufficient condition for *not being a coin enclosed in a structure of type I*. Thus our generalization refers both to coins enclosed in a structure of type I and to objects not made of silver. A little further discussion might convince us that it refers to everything else as well.[15] But we have already gone far enough

---

[15] Saying of each thing that it is either not a coin enclosed in a structure of type I or it is silver (or both).

to see that we are on the wrong track. The class of objects referred to by our generalization is no longer spatio-temporally limited or finite.

The attempt to locate the dividing line between accidental and lawlike sufficient conditions in considerations of spatio-temporal limitation of scope seems to have come to a dead end. And if the problems so far raised for this approach are not enough, consider the following example (due to Professor Carl Hempel):

> 7. It seems likely that there is no body of pure gold in the universe whose mass equals or exceeds 100,000 kilograms. If so, *being a body composed of pure gold* is a sufficient condition for *having a mass of less an 100,000 kilos.*

Note that our belief in the foregoing is quite compatible with the belief in an infinite universe strewn with an infinite number of bodies composed of pure gold *and* an infinite number of bodies having a mass of more than 100,000 kg.

Yet, for all that, we would consider such a sufficient condition not a matter of law but rather an accident—a "global accident," if you please. A world might obey the same physical laws as ours, and yet contain huge masses of gold just as a world with the same laws might have particles moving with different velocities. What then is the difference between such global accidents and true laws?[16]

A major difference seems to be that laws are crucial to the structure of our whole view of the world in a way that accidental generalizations are not. If astronomers announced the discovery of a large interstellar body of pure gold, we would find it surprising, but not disturbing. It would arouse our curiosity and our desire for an explanation. The falsification of a physical law, on the other hand, would call for revision throughout a whole system of beliefs and would destroy a whole tissue of explanations. Tranquillity is restored only when a new law reorders the chaos.

One way of viewing this difference is to regard laws not merely as beliefs about the world but, in addition, as contingent rules for changing our beliefs under the pressure of new evidence. I now believe my harpsichord to be safely at rest in Goleta, California. If I would learn that a huge net force were being applied to it, say by a hurricane, I would revise that belief in accordance with the laws of physics and fear for its

---

16 The distinction is not merely a philosophical nicety, but is important for the analysis of scientific theories; for instance, in the foundations of thermodynamics.

safety. It is not surprising that our system of beliefs should suffer a greater disturbance when rules normally used for changing beliefs must themselves be revised in comparison to situations in which they remain intact.

It is of course true that an accidental generalization, or indeed any statement we believe to be true, plays a role in determining how we change our beliefs under the pressure of new evidence. But the role appears to be different from that played by laws. Let us compare. If I am told on good authority that a new heavenly body of mass greater than 100,000 kg. has been discovered, I will assume that this is not a mass of pure gold. But if later investigations convince me that it is, in fact, pure gold I will not (as in the case of the harpsichord) revise my previous belief and conclude that it must really weigh less than 100,000 kilos. Rather, I will give up my belief that all bodies composed of pure gold have a mass of less than 100,000 kilos.

But consider the coins in Goodman's pocket on VE day. You may have extremely strong grounds for believing that all these coins are silver; say you were present at the time, observed Goodman turning his pockets inside out yielding just three coins, that you tested them chemically and found them to be silver, etc. Now if someone convinces you that he has one of the coins in Goodman's pocket on VE day you will assume that it is silver. And if he then fishes out a copper cent, exclaiming "This is it!" you will revise your opinions both as to the origin of the coin and the veracity of its´possessor. Thus, the fact that a belief is held with extreme tenacity does not guarantee that it is functioning as a law, even though laws are typically more stable and central pieces of our intellectual equipment than mere factual judgments.

Perhaps the matter can be clarified if we consider the farfetched sort of circumstances under which *being a coin in Goodman's pocket on VE day* would be considered a lawlike sufficient condition for *being made of silver*. Suppose that our grounds for believing that all these coins are silver is that we know Goodman's pockets had a certain physical structure; that this structure sets up a force field which allows only silver articles to enter (or, more fancifully, one which transmutes all other elements to silver). If the suggestion that laws have a special place as rules for changing beliefs has any currency then we should be able to find differences between such application of this sufficient condition in the lawlike and accidental cases.

Human observation is fallible, and there is some likelihood, however small, that we missed a coin when examining Goodman's pockets. (Perhaps it stuck in that little corner of the pocket that doesn't turn inside out; perhaps this pair of pants had *two* watch pockets; etc.) Suppose that there is such a coin. If we are suddenly informed of its existence, what are we to think of its composition? *In the accidental case* we have no clue what to think and if it turns out to be copper we will not find this disturbing over and above our initial disturbance at having missed it. *In the lawlike case,* the inference rule still applies and we will be quite confident that it is silver. If it turns out to be copper, we will hasten to reexamine the structure of Goodman's pocket and if we find no fault in our previous beliefs about it, we will be forced to seek for some revised physical theory to account for these facts.

Laws then, *do* seem to have a special status as rules for revising our beliefs. This special status is perhaps most easily seen in our reasoning about *what might have been.* We will say, of a glass of pure, cold water (at a pressure of one atmosphere):

(A) If this water *had been* heated to 100 degrees centigrade it *would have* boiled.

because we believe that:

(B) All pure water at a pressure of one atmosphere and a temperature of 100 degrees centigrade boils.

is a *law.* (A) is said to be a *counterfactual* conditional since, as the water has *not* been heated, its if-clause is contrary to fact. The law (B) is said to *support* the counterfactual condition (A). If we review our examples, we will find that laws support counterfactuals in a way that accidental generalizations do not. Suppose I have a box with an inertial mass of 3/5 of a kilogram. I say without trepidation that if this box *had* had an inertial mass of 1 kg., it *would have* had a gravitational mass of 1 kg. But if a certain man is $6\frac{1}{2}$ feet tall I will certainly *not* say that if he had eaten dinner in the Paris Noodle on January 12, 1972, he would have been under 6 feet tall. I will say that if a net force had been applied to my harpsichord, it would have moved. But I will not say that if this penny had been in Goodman's pocket on VE day it would have been silver nor will I say that if Jupiter were made of pure gold it would have a mass of 100,000 kilograms.

Romantic metaphysicians have held that statements of what might have been are objective statements about parallel worlds or branches of time. More cautious and critical thinkers hold that correct counterfactuals are fables constructed according to our contingent rules for changing beliefs.

Reasoning about what might have been has value only as practice for reasoning about what might be.

It should be now clear that lawlike and accidental conditions *are* different, and you have some general indication of how they are different, but the specification of differences has not been precise. How exactly do laws function as contingent rules of inference? What are the rules for changing our beliefs about laws? Just what is needed for a law to support a given counterfactual? Despite an enormous amount of work there is, as yet, no generally satisfactory solution to these and related problems. They remain a major area of concern for the philosophy of science.

Suggested readings

Roderick Chisholm, "The Contrary-to-Fact Conditional," in *Readings in Philosophical Analysis*, ed. Feigl & Sellars (New York: Appleton-Century-Crofts, Inc., 1949), pp. 482–97.

Nelson Goodman, *Fact, Fiction and Forecast* (Cambridge, Mass.: Harvard University Press, 1955).

Ernest Nagel, *The Structure of Science* (New York: Harcourt, Brace & World, 1961), chap. 4, "The Logical Character of Scientific Laws."

V

THE PROBABILITY CALCULUS

V.1. INTRODUCTION. The theory of probability resulted from the cooperation of two eminent seventeenth-century mathematicians and a gambler. The gambler, Chevalier de Mere, had some theoretical problems with practical consequences at the dice tables. He took his problems to Blaise Pascal who in turn entered into correspondence with Pierre de Fermat, in order to discuss them. The mathematical theory of probability was born in the Pascal-Fermat correspondence.

We have used the word "probability" rather freely in the discussion so far, with only a rough, intuitive grasp of its meaning. In this chapter we will learn the mathematical rules that a quantity must satisfy in order to qualify as a probability. With that knowledge in hand, we will proceed in Chapter VI to examine the reasons for believing that epistemic and inductive probabilities should be probabilities in the mathematical sense.

V.2. PROBABILITY, ARGUMENTS, STATEMENTS, AND PROPERTIES. The word "probability" is used for a number of distinct concepts. Earlier I pointed out the difference between inductive probability, which applies to arguments, and epistemic probability, which applies to statements. There is yet another type of probability, which applies to properties. When we speak of the probability *of* throwing a "natural" in dice, or the probability *of* living to age 65, we are ascribing probabilities to properties. When we speak of the probability *that* John Q. Jones will live to age 65, or the probability *that* the next throw of the dice will come up a natural, we are ascribing probabilities to statements. Thus there are at least three different types of probability which apply to three different types of things: arguments, statements, and properties.

Luckily, there is a common core to these various concepts of probability: Each of these various types of probability obeys the rules of the mathematical theory of probability. Futhermore, the different types of probability are interrelated in other ways, some of which were brought out in the discussion of inductive and epistemic probability. In Chapter V it will be shown how these different concepts of probability put flesh on the skeleton of the mathematical theory of probability. Here, however, we shall restrict ourselves to developing the mathematical theory. The mathematical theory is often called the *probability calculus*. In order to facilitate the framing of examples we shall develop the probability calculus as it applies to *statements*. But we shall see later how it can also accommodate arguments and properties.

Remember that the truth tables for "∼," "&," and "v" enable us to find out whether a complex statement is true or false if we know whether its simple constituent statements are true or false. However, truth tables tell us nothing about the truth or falsity of the simple constituent statements. In a similar manner, the rules of the probability calculus tell us how the probability of a complex statement is related to the probability of its simple constituent statements, but they do not tell us how to determine the probabilities of simple statements. The problem of determining the probability of simple statements (or properties or arguments) is a problem of inductive logic, but it is a problem that is not solved by the probability calculus.

Probability values assigned to complex statements range from 0 to 1. Although the probability calculus does not tell us how to determine the probabilities of simple statements, does not assign the extreme values of 0 and 1 to special kinds of complex statements. In Section IV.3 we discussed complex statements that are *true* no matter what the facts are. These statements were called tautologies. Since a tautology is guaranteed to be true, no matter what the facts are, it is assigned the highest possible probability value.

>   **Rule 1:** If a statement is a tautology, then its probability is equal to 1.

Thus just as the complex statement $sv{\sim}s$ is true no matter whether its simple constituent statement, s, is true or false, so its probability is 1 regardless of the probability of the simple constituent statement.

We also discussed another type of statement that is *false* no matter what the facts are. This type of statement, called the self-contradiction, is assigned the lowest possible probability value.

>   **Rule 2:** If a statement is a self-contradiction, then its probability is equal to 0.

Thus just as the complex statement $s\&{\sim}s$ is false no matter whether its simple constituent statement, s, is true or false, so its probability is 0 regardless of the simple constituent statement.

When two statements make the same factual claim, that is, when they are true in exactly the same circumstances, they are logically equivalent. Now if a statement that makes a factual claim has a certain probability, another statement that makes exactly the same claim in different words should be equally probable. The statement "My next throw of the dice will come up a natural" should have the same probability as "It is *not* the case that my next throw of the dice will *not* come up a natural." This fact is reflected in the following rule:

> **Rule 3:** If two statements are logically equivalent, then they have the same probability.

By the truth table method it is easy to show that the simple statement p is logically equivalent to the complex statement that is its double negation, $\sim\sim p$, since they are true in exactly the same cases.

	p	$\sim p$	$\sim\sim p$
Case 1:	T	F	T
Case 2:	F	T	F

Thus the simple statement "My next throw of the dice will come up a natural" has, according to Rule 3, the same probability as its double negation, "It is *not* the case that my next throw of the dice will *not* come up a natural."

The first two rules cover certain special cases. They tell us the probability of a complex statement if it is either a tautology or a contradiction. The third rule tells us how to find the probability of a complex contingent statement from its simple constituent statements, if that complex statement is logically equivalent to one of its simple constituent statements. But there are many complex contingent statements that are not logically equivalent to any of their simple constituent statements, and more rules shall be introduced to cover them. The next two sections present rules for each of the logical connectives.

Exercises:

Instead of writing "The probability of p is $\frac{1}{2}$," we shall write, for short "$\mathrm{Pr}(p) = \frac{1}{2}$." Now suppose that $\mathrm{Pr}(p) = \frac{1}{2}$ and $\mathrm{Pr}(q) = \frac{1}{4}$. Find the probabilities of the following complex statements, using Rules 1 through 3 and the method of truth tables:

1. pvp.   5. $\sim(pv\sim p)$.
2. $q\&q$.   6. $\sim\sim(pv\sim p)$.
3. $q\&\sim q$.   7. $pv(q\&\sim q)$.
4. $\sim(q\&\sim q)$.   8. $q\&(pv\sim p)$.

V.3. DISJUNCTION AND NEGATION RULES. The probability of a disjunction pvq is most easily calculated when its disjuncts, p and q, are *mutually exclusive* or inconsistent with each other. In such a case the probability of the disjunction can be calculated from the probabilities of the disjuncts by means of the *special disjunction rule*. We shall use the notation introduced in the exercises on p. 132, writing "The probability of p is x" as: "$\text{Pr}(p) = x$."

Rule 4: If p and q are mutually exclusive, then $\text{Pr}(pvq) = \text{Pr}(p) + \text{Pr}(q)$.

For example, the statements "Socrates is both bald and wise" and "Socrates is neither bald nor wise" are mutually exclusive. Thus if the probability that Socrates is both bald and wise is $\frac{1}{2}$ and the probability that Socrates is neither bald nor wise is $\frac{1}{4}$, then the probability that Socrates is either both bald and wise *or* neither bald nor wise is $\frac{1}{2} + \frac{1}{4}$, or $\frac{3}{4}$.

We can do a little more with the special alternation rule in the following case: Suppose you are about to throw a single six-sided die and that each of the six outcomes is equally probable; that is:

$\text{Pr}(\text{the die will come up a } 1) = \frac{1}{6}$
$\text{Pr}(\text{the die will come up a } 2) = \frac{1}{6}$
$\text{Pr}(\text{the die will come up a } 3) = \frac{1}{6}$
$\text{Pr}(\text{the die will come up a } 4) = \frac{1}{6}$
$\text{Pr}(\text{the die will come up a } 5) = \frac{1}{6}$
$\text{Pr}(\text{the die will come up a } 6) = \frac{1}{6}$

Since the die can show only one face at a time, these six statements may be treated as being mutually exclusive.[1] Thus the probability of getting

---

[1] Actually the statements are not mutually exclusive in the logical sense. We cannot show that they are inconsistent with each other by the method of truth tables, and it is logically possible that the die might change shape upon being thrown so as to display two faces simultaneously. To treat this case rigorously, we would have to use the general disjunction rule, along with a battery of assumptions: $\text{Pr}(1\&2) = 0$, $\text{Pr}(2\&3) = 0$, $\text{Pr}(1\&3) = 0$, etc. However, we shall see that the result is the same as when we use the special disjunction rule, and treat these statements as if they were mutually exclusive.

a 1 or a 6 may be calculated by the special disjunction rule as follows:

$$\Pr(1v6) = \Pr(1) + \Pr(6) = \tfrac{1}{6} + \tfrac{1}{6} = \tfrac{1}{3}$$

The probability of getting an even number may be calculated as

$$\Pr(\text{even}) = \Pr(2v4v6) = \Pr(2) + \Pr(4) + \Pr(6)$$
$$= \tfrac{1}{6} + \tfrac{1}{6} + \tfrac{1}{6} = \tfrac{1}{2}$$

The probability of getting an even number that is greater than 3 may be calculated as

$$\Pr(\text{even greater than 3}) = \Pr(4v6) = \Pr(4) + \Pr(6) = \tfrac{1}{6} + \tfrac{1}{6} = \tfrac{1}{3}$$

The probability of getting an even number or a 3 may be calculated as

$$\Pr(\text{even or 3}) = \Pr(2v4v6v3) = \tfrac{4}{6} = \tfrac{2}{3}$$

Finally, calculating the probability of getting either a 1, 2, 3, 4, 5, or 6 (that is, the probability that the die will show one face or another) gives $\tfrac{6}{6}$, or 1.

We will now apply the special disjunction rule to a case of more general interest. It can be shown, by the method of truth tables, that any statement p is inconsistent with its negation, $\sim p$. Since p and $\sim p$ are therefore mutually exclusive, the special disjunction rule permits the conclusion that

$$\Pr(pv\sim p) = \Pr(p) + \Pr(\sim p)$$

But the statement $pv\sim p$ is a tautology, so by Rule 1,

$$\Pr(pv\sim p) = 1$$

Putting these two conclusions together gives

$$\Pr(p) + \Pr(\sim p) = 1$$

If the quantity $\Pr(p)$ is subtracted from both sides of the equation, the sides will remain equal, so we may conclude that

$$\Pr(\sim p) = 1 - \Pr(p)$$

This conclusion holds good for any statement, since any statement is inconsistent with its negation, and for any statement p its disjunction with its negation, $pv\sim p$, is a tautology. This therefore establishes a general negation rule, which allows us to calculate the probability of a negation from the probability of its constituent statement:

Rule 5: $\Pr(\sim p) = 1 - \Pr(p)$.

Suppose in the example using the die we wanted to know the probability of not getting a 3:

$$\Pr(\sim 3) = 1 - \Pr(3) = 1 - \tfrac{1}{6} = \tfrac{5}{6}$$

Note that we get the same answer as we would if we took the long road to solving the problem and confined ourselves to using the special disjunction rule:

$$\begin{aligned}
\Pr(\sim 3) &= \Pr(1v2v4v5v6) \\
&= \Pr(1) + \Pr(2) + \Pr(4) + \Pr(5) + \Pr(6) \\
&= \tfrac{1}{6} + \tfrac{1}{6} + \tfrac{1}{6} + \tfrac{1}{6} + \tfrac{1}{6} = \tfrac{5}{6}
\end{aligned}$$

We shall apply the special disjunction rule one more time in order to establish another generally useful rule. For any two statements, p, q, we can show by the truth table method that the complex statements $p\&q$, $p\&\sim q$, and $\sim p\&q$ are inconsistent with each other. As shown below, there is no case in which two of them are true:

	p	q	$\sim p$	$\sim q$	$p\&q$	$p\&\sim q$	$\sim p\&q$
Case 1:	T	T	F	F	T	F	F
Case 2:	T	F	F	T	F	T	F
Case 3:	F	T	T	F	F	F	T
Case 4:	F	F	T	T	F	F	F

Since they are mutually exclusive, we can apply the special disjunction rule and conclude:

    a. $\Pr[(p\&q)v(p\&\sim q)] = \Pr(p\&q) + \Pr(p\&\sim q)$
    b. $\Pr[(p\&q)v(\sim p\&q)] = \Pr(p\&q) + \Pr(\sim p\&q)$
    c. $\Pr[(p\&q)v(p\&\sim q)v(\sim p\&q)] = \Pr(p\&q) + \Pr(p\&\sim q)$

But the complex statement $(p\&q)v(p\&\sim q)$ is logically equivalent to the simple statement p, as is shown by the following truth table:

	p	q	$\sim q$	$p\&q$	$p\&\sim q$	$(p\&q)v(p\&\sim q)$
Case 1:	T	T	F	T	F	T
Case 2:	T	F	T	F	T	T
Case 3:	F	T	F	F	F	F
Case 4:	F	F	T	F	F	F

Since according to Rule 3 logically equivalent statements have the same probability, equation (a) may be rewritten as

a′. $\Pr(p) = \Pr(p\&q) + \Pr(p\&{\sim}q)$

A similar truth table will show that the complex statement $(p\&q)v({\sim}p\&q)$ is logically equivalent to the simple statement q. Therefore equation (b) may be rewritten as

b′. $\Pr(q) = \Pr(p\&q) + \Pr({\sim}p\&q)$

Finally, a truth table will show that the complex statement $(p\&q)v(p\&{\sim}q)$ $v({\sim}p\&q)$ is logically equivalent to the complex statement pvq, which enables us to rewrite equation (c) as

c′. $\Pr(pvq) = \Pr(p\&q) + \Pr(p\&{\sim}q) + Pr({\sim}p\&q)$

Now let us add equations (a′) and (b′) together to get

d. $\Pr(p) + \Pr(q) = 2\,\Pr(p\&q) + \Pr(p\&{\sim}q) + \Pr({\sim}p\&q)$

If we subtract the quantity $\Pr(p\&q)$ from both sides of the preceding equation, we get

d′. $\Pr(p) + \Pr(q) - \Pr(p\&q) = \Pr(p\&q) + \Pr(p\&{\sim}q) + \Pr({\sim}p\&q)$

If equation (d′) is compared with equation (c′) we see that $\Pr(pvq)$ is equal to the same thing as $\Pr(p) + \Pr(q) - \Pr(p\&q)$. This establishes a general disjunction rule that is good for all disjunctions, whether the disjuncts are mutually exclusive or not:

Rule 6: $\Pr(pvq) = \Pr(p) + \Pr(q) - \Pr(p\&q)$.

If some of the algebra used to establish the general disjunction rule has left you behind, the following diagram may help to make the reasoning clear:

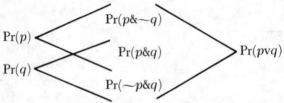

When $\Pr(p)$ is added to $\Pr(q)$, then $\Pr(p\&q)$ is counted twice. But to get $\Pr(pvq)$, it should be counted only once. Thus to get $\Pr(pvq)$, we add

$\Pr(p)$ and $\Pr(q)$ and then subtract $\Pr(p\&q)$ to make up for having counted it twice. In the case in which p and q are mutually exclusive, this makes no difference, because when p and q are mutually exclusive, $\Pr(p\&q) = 0$. No matter how many times 0 is counted, we will always get the same result. For example, by the general disjunction rule, $\Pr(pv{\sim}p) = \Pr(p) + \Pr({\sim}p) - \Pr(p\&{\sim}p)$. But the statement $p\&{\sim}p$ is a self-contradiction, so its probability is zero. Thus we get the same result as if we had used the special disjunction rule. Counting $\Pr(p\&q)$ twice *does* make a difference when p and q are *not* mutually exclusive. Suppose we use the general disjunction rule to calculate the probability of the complex statement pvp:

$$\Pr(pvp) = \Pr(p) + \Pr(p) - \Pr(p\&p)$$

But since the complex statement $p\&p$ is logically equivalent to the simple statement p, $\Pr(p\&p) = \Pr(p)$. So we get

$$\Pr(pvp) = \Pr(p) + \Pr(p) - \Pr(p) = \Pr(p)$$

We know this is the correct answer, because the complex statement pvp is also logically equivalent to the simple statement p.

The example with the die shall be used to give one more illustration of the use of the general disjunction rule. Suppose that we want to know the probability that the die will come up an even number or a number less than 3. There is a way to calculate this probability using only the special disjunction rule:

$$\Pr(\text{even v less than 3}) = \Pr(1v2v4v6)$$
$$= \Pr(1) + \Pr(2) + \Pr(4) + \Pr(6) = \tfrac{4}{6} = \tfrac{2}{3}$$

We may use the special disjunction rule because the outcomes 1, 2, 4, and 6 are mutually exclusive. However, the outcomes "even" and "less than 3" are not mutually exclusive, since the die might come up 2. Thus we may apply the general disjunction rule as follows:

$$\Pr(\text{even v less than 3})$$
$$= \Pr(\text{even}) + \Pr(\text{less than 3}) - \Pr(\text{even\&less than 3})$$

Now we may calculate $\Pr(\text{even})$ as $\Pr(2v4v6)$ by the special disjunction rule; it is equal to $\tfrac{1}{2}$. We may calculate $\Pr(\text{less than 3})$ as $\Pr(1v2)$ by the special disjunction rule; it is equal to $\tfrac{1}{3}$. And we may calculate $\Pr(\text{even\&} \text{less than 3})$ as $\Pr(2)$, which is equal to $\tfrac{1}{6}$. So, by this method,

$$\Pr(\text{even v less than 3}) = \tfrac{1}{2} + \tfrac{1}{3} - \tfrac{1}{9} = \tfrac{2}{3}$$

The role of the subtraction term can be seen clearly in this example. What we have done is to calculate Pr(even v less than 3) as

$$Pr(2v4v6) + Pr(1v2) - Pr(2)$$

so the subtraction term compensates for adding in Pr(2) twice when we add Pr(even) and Pr(less than 3). In this example use of the general disjunction rule was the long way of solving the problem. But in some cases it is necessary to use the general disjunction rule. Suppose you are told that

$$Pr(p) + \tfrac{1}{2}$$
$$Pr(q) = \tfrac{1}{3}$$
$$Pr(p\&q) = \tfrac{1}{4}$$

You are asked to calculate Pr(pvq). Now you cannot use the special disjunction rule since you know that p and q are not mutually exclusive. If they were, Pr(p&q) would be 0, and you are told that it is $\tfrac{1}{4}$. Therefore you must use the general disjunction rule in the following way:

$$Pr(pvq) = Pr(p) + Pr(q) - Pr(p\&q)$$

$$= \tfrac{1}{2} + \tfrac{1}{3} - \tfrac{1}{4} = \tfrac{7}{12}$$

In Section IV.12, we compared the rules of the probability calculus to the way in which the truth tables for the logical connectives relate the truth or falsity of a complex statement to the truth or falsity of its simple constituent statements. We are now at the point where we must qualify this comparison. We can always determine the truth or falsity of a complex statement if we know whether its simple constituent statements are true or false. But we cannot always calculate the probability of a complex statement from the probabilities of its simple constituent statements. Sometimes, as in the example above, in order to calculate the probability of the complex statement pvq, we need not only know the probabilities of its simple constituent statements, p and q, we also need to know the probability of another complex statement, $p\&q$. We shall discuss the rules that govern the probabilities of such conjunctions in the next section. However, we shall find that it is not always possible to calculate the probability of a conjunction simply from the probabilities of its constituent statements.

Exercises:

1. Suppose you have an ordinary deck of 52 playing cards. You are to draw one card. Assume that each card has a probability of $\frac{1}{52}$ of being drawn. What is the probability that you will draw:

    a. The ace of spades?

    b. The queen of hearts?

    c. The ace of spades or the queen of hearts?

    d. An ace?

    e. A heart?

    f. A face card (king, queen, or jack)?

    g. A card that is not a face card?

    h. An ace or a spade?

    i. A queen or a heart?

    j. A queen or a non-spade?

2. $\Pr(p) = \frac{1}{2}$, $\Pr(q) = \frac{1}{2}$, $\Pr(p\&q) = \frac{1}{8}$. What is $\Pr(pvq)$?

3. $\Pr(r) = \frac{1}{2}$, $\Pr(s) = \frac{1}{4}$, $\Pr(rvs) = \frac{3}{4}$. What is $\Pr(r\&s)$?

4. $\Pr(u) = \frac{1}{2}$, $\Pr(t) = \frac{3}{4}$, $\Pr(u\&\sim t) = \frac{1}{8}$. What is $\Pr(uv\sim t)$?

V.4. CONJUNCTION RULES AND CONDITIONAL PROBABILITY.

Before the rules that govern the probability of conjunctions are discussed, it is necessary to introduce the notion of *conditional probability*. We may write $\Pr(q$ given $p)$ as the probability of *q on the condition that p*. This probability may or may not be different from $\Pr(q)$. We shall deal with the concept of conditional probability on the intuitive level before a precise definition for it is introduced.

In the example with the die, we found that the probability of throwing an even number was $\frac{1}{2}$. However, the probability of getting an even number *given that* a 2 or a 4 is thrown is not $\frac{1}{2}$ but 1. And the probability of casting an even number *given* that a 1 or a 3 is thrown is 0. To take a little more complicated example, suppose that the die remains unchanged and you are to bet on whether it will come up even, with a special agreement that if it comes up 5 all bets will be off and it will be thrown again. In such a situation you would be interested in the probability that it will come up even *given that* it will be either a 1, 2, 3, 4, or 6. This probability should be greater than $\frac{1}{2}$ since the condition excludes one of the ways in which the die could come up odd. It is–in fact, $\frac{3}{5}$. Thus the probabilities of "even," given three different conditions, are each different from the probability of "even" by itself:

    a. $\Pr(\text{even}) = \frac{1}{2}$

    b. Pr(even *given* 2v4) = 1
    c. Pr(even *given* 1v3) = 0
    d. Pr(even *given* 1v2v3v4v6) = $\frac{3}{5}$

Conditional probabilities allow for the fact that if a certain statement, p, is known to be true, this may affect the probability to be assigned to another statement, q. The most striking cases occur when there is a deductively valid argument from p to q:

    p = The next throw of the die will come up 2
        v
        the next throw of the die will come up 4.
    _____
    q = The next throw of the die will come up even.

In this case, Pr(q *given* p) = 1:[2]

    Pr(even *given* 2v4) = 1

Suppose there is a deductively valid argument from p to $\sim q$:

    p = The next throw of the die will come up 1
        v
        the next throw of the die will come up 3.
    _____
    $\sim q$ = The next throw of the die will *not* come up even.

In this case, Pr(q *given* p) = 0:

    Pr(even *given* 1v3) = 0.[3]

There are, however, important cases where neither the argument from p to q nor the argument from p to $\sim q$ is deductively valid and yet Pr(q *given* p) differs from Pr(q), as in the previous example with the die:

    Pr(even *given* 1v2v3v4v6) = $\frac{3}{5}$
    Pr(even) = $\frac{1}{2}$

---

[2] We must make one qualification to this statement. When p is a self-contradiction, then for any statement q there is a deductively valid argument from p to q *and* a deductively valid argument from p to $\sim q$. In such a case, Pr(q *given* p) has no value.

[3] We must make one qualification to this statement. When p is a self-contradiction, then for any statement q there is a deductively valid argument from p to q *and* a deductively valid argument from p to $\sim q$. In such a case, Pr(q *given* p) has no value.

There are other cases where the knowledge that p is true may be completely irrelevant to the probability to be assigned to q. For example, it was said that the probability that the next throw of the die will come up even is $\frac{1}{2}$. We could say that the probability that the next throw of the die will come up even, given that the President of the United States sneezes simultaneously with our throw, is still $\frac{1}{2}$. The President's sneeze is irrelevant to the probability assigned to "even." Thus the two statements "The next throw of the die will come up even" and "The President of the United States will sneeze simultaneously with the next throw of the die" are *independent*.[4]

We can now give substance to the intuitive notions of conditional probability and independence by defining them in terms of pure statement probabilities. First we will define conditional probability:

Definition 12: *Conditional probability:*[5]

$$Pf(q \text{ given } p) = \frac{\Pr(p\&q)}{\Pr(p)}$$

Let us see how this definition works out in the example of the die:

b. $\Pr(\text{even given } 2v4) = \dfrac{\Pr[\text{even}\&(2v4)]}{\Pr(2v4)} = \dfrac{\Pr(2v4)}{\Pr(2v4)} = .1$

c. $\Pr(\text{even given } 1v3) = \dfrac{\Pr[\text{even}\&(1v3]}{\Pr(1v3)} = \dfrac{0}{\frac{1}{3}} = 0$

d. $\Pr(\text{even given } 1v2v3v4v6) = \dfrac{\Pr[\text{even}\&(1v2v3v4v6)]}{\Pr(1v2v3v4v6)}$

$$= \frac{\Pr(2v4v6)}{\Pr(1v2v3v4v6)} = \frac{\frac{3}{6}}{\frac{5}{6}} = \frac{3}{5}$$

Notice that the conditional probabilities computed by using the definition accord with the intuitive judgments as to conditional probabilities in the die example. We may test the definition in another way. Consider the special case of $\Pr(q \text{ given } p)$, where p is a tautology and q is a contingent statement. Since a tautology makes no factual claim, we would not expect

---

[4] This type of independence is called probabilistic or stochastic independence. It should not be confused with the mutual logical independence discussed in deductive logic. Stochastic independence of two statements is neither a necessary nor a sufficient condition for their mutual logical independence.

[5] When $\Pr(p) = 0$ the quotient is not defined. In this case there is no $\Pr(q \text{ given } p)$.

knowledge of its truth to influence the probability that we would assign to the contingent statement, q. The probability that the die will come up even given that it will come up either even or odd should be simply the probability that it will come up even. In general, if we let T stand for an arbitrary tautology, we should expect $\Pr(q$ given $T)$ to be equal to $\Pr(q)$. Let us work out $\Pr(q$ given $T)$, using the definition of conditional probability:

$$\Pr(q \text{ given } T) = \frac{\Pr(T\&q)}{\Pr(T)}$$

But the probability of a tautology is always equal to 1. This gives

$$\Pr(q \text{ given } T) = \Pr(T\&q)$$

When T is a tautology and q is any statement whatsoever, the complex statement $T\&q$ is logically equivalent to the simple statement q. This can always be shown by truth tables. Since logically equivalent statements have the same probability, $\Pr(q$ given $T) = \Pr(q)$.[6] Again the definition of conditional probability gives the expected result.

Now that conditional probability has been defined, that concept can be used to define independence:

> **Definition 13:** *Independence:* Two statements p and q are independent if and only if $\Pr(q$ given $p) = \Pr(q)$.

We talk of two statements p and q being independent, rather than p being independent of q and q being independent of p. We can do this because we can prove that $\Pr(q$ given $p) = \Pr(q)$ if and only if $\Pr(p$ given $q) = \Pr(p)$. If $\Pr(q$ given $p) = \Pr(q)$, then, by the definition of conditional probability,

$$\frac{\Pr(p\&q)}{\Pr(p)} = \Pr(q)$$

Multiplying both sides of the equation by $\Pr(p)$ and dividing both sides by $\Pr(q)$, we have

---

[6] We could have constructed the probability calculus by taking conditional probabilities as basic, and then defining pure statement probabilities as follows: The probability of a statement is defined as its probability *given* a tautology. Instead we have taken statement probabilities as basic, and defined conditional probabilities. The choice of starting point makes no difference to the system as a whole. The systems are equivalent.

$$\frac{\Pr(p\&q)}{\Pr(q)} = \Pr(p)$$

But by the definition of conditional probability, this means $\Pr(p$ given $q)$ = $\Pr(p)$.

This proof only works if neither of the two statements has 0 probability. Otherwise one of the relevant quotients would not be defined. To take care of this eventuality, we may add an additional clause to the definition and say that two statements are also independent if at least one of them has probability 0. It is important to realize the difference between independence and mutual exclusiveness. The statement about the outcome of the throw of the die and the statement about the President's sneeze are independent, but they are not mutually exclusive. They can very well be true together. On the other hand, the statements "The next throw of the die will come up an even number" and "The next throw of the die will come up a 5" are mutually exclusive, but they are not independent. $\Pr(\text{even}) = \frac{1}{2}$, but $\Pr(\text{even given } 5) = 0$. $\Pr(5) = \frac{1}{6}$, but $\Pr(5 \text{ given even})$ = 0. In general, if p and q are mutually exclusive they are not independent, and if they are independent they are not mutually exclusive.[7]

Having specified the definitions of conditional probability and independence, the rules for conjunctions can now be introduced. The *general conjunction rule* follows directly from the definition of conditional probability:

Rule 7: $\Pr(p\&q) = \Pr(p) \times \Pr(q$ given $p)$.

The proof is simple. Take the definition of conditional probability:

$$\Pr(q \text{ given } p) = \frac{\Pr(p\&q)}{\Pr(p)}$$

Multiply both sides of the equation by $\Pr(p)$ to get

$$\Pr(p) \times \Pr(q \text{ given } p) = \Pr(p\&q)$$

which is the general conjunction rule. Since, when p and q are independent, $\Pr(q$ given $p) = \Pr(q)$, we may substitute $\Pr(q)$ for $\Pr(q$ given $p)$ in the general conjunction rule, thus obtaining

$$\Pr(p) \times \Pr(q) = \Pr(p\&q)$$

---

[7] The exception is when at least one of the statements is self-contradiction and thus has probability 0.

Of course, the substitution may only be made in the special case when p and q are independent. This result constitutes the *special conjunction rule:*

> **Rule 8:** If p and q are independent, then $\Pr(p \& q) = \Pr(p) \times \Pr(q)$.

The general conjunction rule is more basic than the special conjunction rule. But since the special conjunction rule is simpler, its application will be illustrated first. Suppose that two dice are thrown simultaneously. The basic probabilities are as follows:

Die A	Die B
$\Pr(1) = \frac{1}{6}$	$\Pr(1) = \frac{1}{6}$
$\Pr(2) = \frac{1}{6}$	$\Pr(2) = \frac{1}{6}$
$\Pr(3) = \frac{1}{6}$	$\Pr(3) = \frac{1}{6}$
$\Pr(4) = \frac{1}{6}$	$\Pr(4) = \frac{1}{6}$
$\Pr(5) = \frac{1}{6}$	$\Pr(5) = \frac{1}{6}$
$\Pr(6) = \frac{1}{6}$	$\Pr(6) = \frac{1}{6}$

Since the face shown by die A presumably does not influence the face shown by die B, or vice versa, it shall be assumed that all statements claiming various outcomes for die A are independent of all the statements claiming various outcomes for die B. That is, the statements "Die A will come up a 3" and "Die B will come up a 5" are independent, as are the statements "Die A will come up a 6" and "Die B will come up a 6." The statements "Die A will come up a 5" and "Die A will come up a 3" are not independent; they are mutually exclusive (when made in regard to the same throw).

Now suppose we wish to calculate the probability of throwing a 1 on die A and a 6 on die B. The special conjunction rule can now be used:

$$\Pr(1 \text{ on } A \& 6 \text{ on } B) = \Pr(1 \text{ on } A) \times \Pr(6 \text{ on } B)$$
$$= \frac{1}{6} \times \frac{1}{6} = \frac{1}{36}$$

In the same way, the probability of each of the 36 possible combinations of results of die A and die B may be calculated as $\frac{1}{36}$, as shown in Table 1. Note that each of the cases in the table is mutually exclusive of each other case. Thus by the special alternation rule, the probability of case 1 v case 3 is equal to the probability of case 1 plus the probability of case 3.

Table 1

		Possible results when throwing two dice			
Case	Die A	Die B	Case	Die A	Die B
1	1	1	19	4	1
2	1	2	20	4	2
3	1	3	21	4	3
4	1	4	22	4	4
5	1	5	23	4	5
6	1	6	24	4	6
7	2	1	25	5	1
8	2	2	26	5	2
9	2	3	27	5	3
10	2	4	28	5	4
11	2	5	29	5	5
12	2	6	30	5	6
13	3	1	31	6	1
14	3	2	32	6	2
15	3	3	33	6	3
16	3	4	34	6	4
17	3	5	35	6	5
18	3	6	36	6	6

Suppose now that we wish to calculate the probability that the dice will come up showing a 1 or a 6. There are two ways this can happen: a 1 on die A and a 6 on die B (case 6), or a 6 on die A and a 1 on die B (case 31). The probability of this combination appearing may be calculated as follows:

$$\Pr(1 \text{ and } 6) = \Pr[(1 \text{ on } A \,\&\, 6 \text{ on } B) \text{ v } (1 \text{ on } B \,\&\, 6 \text{ on } A)]$$

Since the cases are mutually exclusive, the special disjunction rule may be used to get

$$\Pr[(1 \text{ on } A \,\&\, 6 \text{ on } B) \text{ v } (1 \text{ on } B \,\&\, 6 \text{ on } A)]$$
$$= \Pr(1 \text{ on } A \,\&\, 6 \text{ on } B) + \Pr(1 \text{ on } B \,\&\, 6 \text{ on } A)$$

But it has already been shown, by the special conjunction rule, that

$$\Pr(1 \text{ on } A \,\&\, 6 \text{ on } B) = \tfrac{1}{36}$$
$$\Pr(1 \text{ on } B \,\&\, 6 \text{ on } A) = \tfrac{1}{36}$$

so the answer is $\tfrac{1}{36} + \tfrac{1}{36}$, or $\tfrac{1}{18}$.

The same sort of reasoning can be used to solve more complicated problems. Suppose we want to know the probability that the sum of spots showing on both dice will equal 7. This happens only in cases 6, 11, 16, 21, 26, and 31. Therefore

$$
\begin{aligned}
\Pr(\text{total of } 7) = \Pr[\,&(1 \text{ on } A \,\&\, 6 \text{ on } B) \\
\text{v }&(2 \text{ on } A \,\&\, 5 \text{ on } B) \\
\text{v }&(3 \text{ on } A \,\&\, 4 \text{ on } B) \\
\text{v }&(4 \text{ on } A \,\&\, 3 \text{ on } B) \\
\text{v }&(5 \text{ on } A \,\&\, 2 \text{ on } B) \\
\text{v }&(6 \text{ on } A \,\&\, 1 \text{ on } B)]
\end{aligned}
$$

Using the special disjunction rule and the special conjunction rule $\Pr(\text{total of } 7) = \frac{6}{36}$, or $\frac{1}{6}$.

In solving a particular problem, there are often several ways to apply the rules. Suppose we wanted to calculate the probability that both dice will come up even. We could determine in which cases both dice are showing even numbers, and proceed as before, but this is the long way to solve the problem. Instead we can calculate the probability of getting an even number on die A as $\frac{1}{2}$ by the special disjunction rule:

$$
\begin{aligned}
\Pr(\text{even on } A) &= \Pr(2 \text{ on } A \text{ v } 4 \text{ on } A \text{ v } 6 \text{ on } A) \\
&= \Pr(2 \text{ on } A) + \Pr(4 \text{ on } A) + \Pr(6 \text{ on } A) \\
&= \tfrac{3}{6} = \tfrac{1}{2}
\end{aligned}
$$

and calculate the probability of getting an even number on die B as $\frac{1}{2}$ by the same method. Then, by the special conjunction rule,[8]

$$
\begin{aligned}
\Pr(\text{even on } A \,\&\, \text{even on } B) &= \Pr(\text{even on } A) \times \Pr(\text{even on } B) \\
&= \tfrac{1}{2} \times \tfrac{1}{2} = \tfrac{1}{4}
\end{aligned}
$$

We apply the *general conjunction rule* when two statements are not independent. Such is the case in the following example. Suppose you are presented with a bag containing 10 gumdrops, 5 red and 5 black. You are to shake the bag, close your eyes and draw out a gumdrop, look at it, eat it, and then repeat the process once more. We shall assume that, at the time of each draw, each gumdrop in the bag has an equal probability of being drawn. The problem is to find the probability of drawing two red gumdrops.

---

[8] It can be shown that the statements "Die A will come up even" and "Die B will come up even" are independent, on the basis of the independence assumptions made in setting up this example.

To solve this problem we must find the probability of the conjunction Pr(red on 1 & red on 2). We will first find Pr(red on 1). We will designate each of the gumdrops by a letter: $A, B, C, D, E, F, G, H, I, J$. We know that we will draw one of these on the first draw, so

$$\text{Pr}(A \text{ on } 1 \text{ v } B \text{ on } 1 \text{ v } C \text{ on } 1 \text{ v} \ldots \text{v } J \text{ on } 1) = 1$$

Now, by the special disjunction rule,

$$\text{Pr}(A \text{ on } 1) + \text{Pr}(B \text{ on } 1) + \text{Pr}(C \text{ on } 1) + \ldots + (\text{Pr}(J \text{ on } 1) = 1$$

Since each of the gumdrops has an equal chance of being drawn, and there are 10 gumdrops, therefore

$$\text{Pr}(A \text{ on } 1) - \tfrac{1}{10}$$
$$\text{Pr}(B \text{ on } 1) = \tfrac{1}{10}$$
$$\vdots$$
$$\text{Pr}(J \text{ on } 1) = \tfrac{1}{10}$$

We said that there were five red ones. We will use the letters $A, B, C, D,$ and E to designate the red gumdrops and the remaining letters to designate the black ones. By the special disjunction rule, the probability of getting a red gumdrop on draw 1 is

$$\text{Pr}(A \text{ on } 1 \text{ v } B \text{ on } 1 \text{ v } C \text{ on } 1 \text{ v } D \text{ on } 1 \text{ v } E \text{ on } 1)$$
$$= \text{Pr}(A \text{ on } 1) + \text{Pr}(B \text{ on } 1) + \text{Pr}(C \text{ on } 1) + \text{Pr}(D \text{ on } 1) + \text{Pr}(E \text{ on } 1)$$
$$= \tfrac{5}{10} = \tfrac{1}{2}$$

We shall have to use the general conjunction rule to find Pr(red on 1 & red on 2), since the statements "A red gumdrop will be drawn the first time" and "A red gumdrop will be drawn the second time" are not independent. If a red gumdrop is drawn the first time, this will leave four red and five black gumdrops in the bag with equal chances of being drawn on the second draw. But if a black gumdrop is drawn the first time, this will leave five red and four black gumdrops awaiting the second draw. Thus the knowledge that a red one is drawn the first time will influence the probability we assign to a red one being drawn the second time, and the two statements are not independent. Applying the general conjunction rule, we get

$$\text{Pr}(\text{red on } 1 \,\&\, \text{red on } 2) = \text{Pr}(\text{red on } 1) \times \text{Pr}(\text{red on } 2 \text{ given red on } 1)$$

We have already found Pr(red on 1). Now we must calculate Pr(red on 2 given red on 1). Given that we draw a red gumdrop on the first draw, there will be nine gumdrops remaining: four red and five black. We must draw one of them, and they each have an equal chance of being drawn. By reasoning similar to that used above, each has a probability of $\frac{1}{9}$ of being drawn, and the probability of drawing a red one is $\frac{4}{9}$. Therefore

Pr(red on 2 given red on 1) $= \frac{4}{9}$

We can now complete our calculations:

Pr(red on 1 & red on 2) $= \frac{1}{2} \times \frac{4}{9} = \frac{1}{9}$

We can calculate Pr(black on 1 & red on 2) in the same way:

Pr(black on 1) $= \frac{1}{2}$
Pr(red on 2 given black on 1) $= \frac{5}{9}$

Therefore by the general conjunction rule,

Pr(black on 1 & red on 2) $= \frac{1}{2} \times \frac{5}{9} = \frac{5}{18}$

At this point the question arises as to what the Pr(red on 2) is. We know Pr(red on 2 given red on 1) $= \frac{4}{6}$. We know Pr (red on 2 given black on 1) $= \frac{5}{9}$. But what we want to know now is the probability of getting a red gumdrop on the second draw before we have made the first draw. We can get the answer if we realize that *red on 2* is logically equivalent to

(red on 1 & red on 2) v (not-red on 1 & red on 2)

Remember that the simple statement q is logically equivalent to the complex statement $(p\&q)v(\sim p\&q)$. Therefore

Pr(red on 2) $=$ Pr[(red on 1 & red on 2) v (not-red on 1 & red on 2)]

By the special disjunction rule,

Pr(red on 2) $=$ Pr(red on 1 & red on 2) $+$
Pr(red on 1 & red on 2)

We have caculated Pr(red on 1 & red on 2 as $\frac{2}{9}$. We have also calculated

Pr (not-red on 1 & red on 2) $=$ Pr(black on 1 & red on 2) $= \frac{5}{18}$

Therefore

Pr(red on 2) $= \frac{2}{9} + \frac{5}{18} = \frac{4}{18} + \frac{5}{18} = \frac{9}{18} = \frac{1}{2}$

The same sort of applications of conditional probability and the general conjunction rule would apply to card games where the cards that have been played are placed in a discard pile rather than being returned to the deck. Such considerations are treated very carefully in manuals on poker and blackjack. In fact, some gambling houses have resorted to using a new deck for each hand of blackjack in order to keep astute students of probability from gaining an advantage over the house.

Exercises:

1. $Pr(p) = \frac{1}{2}$, $Pr(q) = \frac{1}{2}$, p and q are independent.
   a. What is $Pr(p\&q)$?
   b. Are p and q mutually exclusive?
   c. What is $Pr(pvq)$?

2. Suppose two dice are rolled, as in the example above.
   a. What is the probability of both dice showing a 1 ("snake-eyes")?
   b. What is the probability of both dice showing a 6 ("boxcars")?
   c. What is the probability that the total number of spots showing on both dice will be either 7 or 11 ("a natural")?

3. A coin is flipped three times. Assume that on each toss $Pr(\text{heads} = \frac{1}{2}$ and $Pr(\text{tails}) = \frac{1}{2}$. Assume that the tosses are independent.
   a. What is $Pr(3 \text{ heads})$?
   b. What is $Pr(2 \text{ heads and } 1 \text{ tail})$?
   c. What is $Pr(1 \text{ head and } 2 \text{ tails})$?
   d. What is $Pr(\text{head on toss } 1 \text{ \& tail on toss } 2 \text{ \& head on toss } 3)$?
   e. What is $Pr(\text{at least } 1 \text{ tail})$?
   f. What is $Pr(\text{no heads})$?
   g. What is $Pr(\text{either } 3 \text{ heads or } 3 \text{ tails})$?

4. Suppose you have an ordinary deck of 52 cards. A card is drawn and is not replaced, then another card is drawn. Assume that on each draw each of the cards then in the deck has an equal chance of being drawn.
   a. What is $Pr(\text{ace on draw } 1)$?
   b. What is $Pr(10 \text{ on draw } 2 \text{ given ace on draw } 1)$?
   c. What is $Pr(\text{ace on draw } 1 \text{ \& } 10 \text{ on draw } 2)$?
   d. What is $Pr(10 \text{ on draw } 1 \text{ \& ace on draw } 2)$?
   e. What is $Pr(\text{an ace and a } 10)$?
   f. What is $Pr(2 \text{ aces})$?

5. The probability that George will study for the test is $\frac{4}{5}$. The probability that he will pass the test given that he studies is $\frac{3}{5}$. The probability that he will pass the test given that he does not study is $\frac{1}{10}$. What is the probability that George will pass the test? Hint: The simple statement "George will pass the test" is logically equivalent to the complex statement "Either George will study and pass the test or George will not study and pass the test."

V.5. EXPECTED VALUE OF A GAMBLE. The attractiveness of a wager depends not only on the probabilities involved, but also on the odds given. The probability of getting a head and a tail on two independ-

ent tosses of a fair coin is $\frac{1}{2}$, while the probability of getting two heads is only $\frac{1}{4}$. But if someone were to offer either to bet me even money that I will not get a head and a tail or give 100 to 1 odds against my getting two heads, I would be well advised to take the second wager. The probability that I will win the second wager is less, but this is more than compensated for by the fact that if I win, I will win a great deal, and if I lose, I will lose much less. The attractiveness of a wager can be measured by calculating its *expected value*. To calculate the expected value of a gamble, first list all the possible outcomes, along with their probabilities and the amount won in each case. A loss is listed as a negative amount. Then for each outcome multiply the probability by the amount won or lost. Finally, add these products to obtain the expected value. To illustrate, suppose someone bets me 10 dollars that I will not get a head and a tail on two tosses of a fair coin. The expected value of this wager for me can be calculated as follows:

Possible outcomes		Probability	Gain	Probability × Gain
Toss 1	Toss 2			
H	H	$\frac{1}{4}$	−$10	−$2.50
H	T	$\frac{1}{4}$	10	2.50
T	H	$\frac{1}{4}$	10	2.50
T	T	$\frac{1}{4}$	− 10	− 2.50
			Expected value:	$0.00

Thus the expected value of the wager for me is $0, and since my opponent wins what I lose and loses what I win, the expected value for him is also $0. Such a wager is called a *fair bet*. Now let us calculate the expected value for me of a wager where my opponent will give me 100 dollars if I get two heads, and I will give him one dollar if I do not.

Possible outcomes		Probability	Gain	Probability × Gain
Toss 1	Toss 2			
H	H	$\frac{1}{4}$	$100	$25.00
H	T	$\frac{1}{4}$	−1	−0.25
T	H	$\frac{1}{4}$	−1	−0.25
T	T	$\frac{1}{4}$	−1	−0.25
			Expected value:	$24.25

The expected value of this wager for me is $24.25. Since my opponent loses what I win, the expected value for him is −$24.25. This is not a fair bet, since it is favorable to me and unfavorable to him.

The procedure for calculating expected value and the rationale behind it are clear, but let us try to attach some meaning to the numerical answer. This can be done in the following way. Suppose that I make the foregoing wager many times. And suppose that over these many times the distribution of results corresponds to the probabilities; that is, I get two heads one-fourth of the time; a head and then a tail one-fourth of the time; a tail and then a head one-fourth of the time; and two tails one-fourth of the time. Then the expected value will be equal to my average winnings on a wager (that is, my total winnings divided by the number of wagers I have made).

I said that expected value was a measure of the attractiveness of a wager. Generally, it seems reasonable to accept a wager with a positive expected gain and reject a wager with a negative expected gain. Furthermore, if you are offered a choice of wagers, it seems reasonable to choose the wager with the highest expected value. These conclusions, however, are oversimplifications. They assume that there is no positive or negative valued associated with risk itself, and that gains or losses of equal amounts of money represent gains or losses of equal amount of value to the individual involved. Let us examine the first assumption.

Suppose that you are compelled to choose an even-money wager either for 1 dollar or for 100 dollars. The expected value of both wagers is 0. But if you wish to avoid risks as much as possible, you would choose the smaller wager. You would, then, assign a negative value to risk itself. However, if you enjoy taking larger risks for their own sake, you would choose the larger wager. Thus although expected value is a major factor in determining the attractiveness of wagers, it is not the only factor. The positive or negative values assigned to the magnitude of the risk itself must also be taken into account.

We make a second assumption when we calculate expected value in terms of money. We assume that gains or losses of equal amounts of money represent gains or losses of equal amounts of value to the individual involved. In the language of the economist this is said to be the assumption that money has a constant marginal utility. This assumption is quite often false. For a poor man, the loss of 1000 dollars might mean he would starve, while the gain of 1000 dollars might mean he would merely live somewhat more comfortably. In this situation, the real loss accompanying a monetary loss of 1000 dollars is much greater than the real gain accompanying a monetary gain of 1000 dollars. A man in these circumstances would be foolish to accept an even money bet of 1000 dollars on the flip of a coin. In terms of money, the wager has an expected value of 0. But in terms of real value, the wager has a negative expected value.

Suppose you are in a part of the city far from home. You have lost your wallet and only have a quarter in change. Since the bus fare home is 35 cents, it looks as though you will have to walk. Now someone offers to flip you for a dime. If you win, you can ride home. If you lose, you are hardly any worse off than before. Thus although the expected value of the wager in monetary terms is 0, in terms of real value, the wager has a positive expected value. In assessing the attractiveness of wagers by calculating their expected value, we must always be careful to see whether the monetary gains and losses accurately mirror the real gains and losses to the individual involved.

Exercises:

1. What is the expected value of the following gamble? You are to roll a pair of dice. If the dice come up a natural, you win 10 dollars. If the dice come up snake-eyes or boxcars, you lose 20 dollars. Otherwise the bet is off.

2. What is the expected value of the following gamble? You are to flip a fair coin. If it comes up heads you win one dollar, and the wager is over. If it comes up tails you lose one dollar, but you flip again for two dollars. If the coin comes up heads this time you win two dollars. If it comes up tails you lose two dollars, but flip again for four dollars. If it comes up heads you win four dollars. If it comes up tails you lose four dollars. But in either case the wager is over.

Hint: The possible outcomes are:

Toss 1	Toss 2	Toss 3
H	None	None
T	H	None
T	T	H
T	T	T

3. Suppose you extended the doubling strategy of Exercise 2 to four tosses. Would this change the expected value?

4. Suppose that you tripled your stakes instead of doubling them. Would this change the expected value?

5. Suppose that you have just enough money to buy needed medicine for yourself or your family. Someone offers to bet you on the flip of a fair coin. If it

comes up heads, he will give you 10 dollars. If it comes up tails, you will give him five dollars. In these circumstances it would be unreasonable for you to accept this normally attractive wager. Why?

V.6. RATIONAL DECISION MAKING AND PROBABILITY AS A GUIDE TO LIFE. We have said that rational human decisions are based on probabilities, and that each decision is in effect a wager with nature. Of course, this is a metaphor rather than a literal statement. We do not bet with nature in the ordinary sense of gambling. Nature is not an opponent, pitted against us, who stands to gain what we lose. And what we risk on our decisions is often less tangible and easily measured than money. But the fact remains that in our decisions we do risk things of value to us and that the rationality of the course of action decided upon depends on the probability that it will accomplish our aims. In line with these observations, we can construct an ideal model of rational decision making which uses the notion of expected value.

Let us suppose that in an ideal choice situation you are confronted with several mutually exclusive courses of action. You must decide which one of these alternative courses of action to follow. Your choice of a course of action may *influence* what will happen to you without *determining* what will happen to you. Generally, there are other factors at work besides your choice of a course of action. For instance, choosing to study for the test may not guarantee that you will pass it, but the probability that you will pass it given that you study may be greater than the probability that you will pass given that you do not study. Associated with each course of action is a range of possible consequences, whose probability is influenced by the choice of that course of action. The situation is summarized in Table 2. The expected value of each course of action in the table can be found by multiplying each of the probabilities of the consequences given the choice of that course of action by the value of that consequence, and then taking the sum of these products. In the absence of any liking or distaste for risk itself, the reasonable thing to do is to choose the course of action that has the highest expected value. Let us see how this rule for rational decision making works in a simple example.

Suppose you are to guess whether the queen is over 40 or not. If you guess correctly, you will be given 1000 dollars. If you guess that the queen is either 40 or younger, and she is in fact over 40, you will win nothing and lose nothing. If you guess that the queen is over 40, and she is in

Table 2

Alternative courses of action	Possible consequences	Probability of the consequence given the choice	Value of the consequence
Course 1:	A	Pr(A given 1)	Val (A)
	B	Pr(B given 1)	Val (B)
	C	Pr(C given 1)	Val (C)
Course 2:	A	Pr(A given 2)	Val (A)
	B	Pr(B given 2)	Val (B)
	C	Pr(C given 2)	Val (C)
Course 3:	A	Pr(A given 3)	Val (A)
	B	Pr(B given 3)	Val (B)
	C	Pr(C given 3)	Val (C)

fact 40 or younger, she will have your tongue cut out. You value your tongue highly, say at one million dollars. The epistemic probability that the queen is over 40, on the basis of all the evidence available to you, is $\frac{9}{10}$. The expected values of the courses of action open to you may be calculated as shown in Table 3. Needless to say, the rational choice is to guess that the queen is 40 or under, even though you would be more likely to be correct if you guessed that she was over 40. By guessing that the queen is 40 or under, you have a smaller chance of winning money, but you eliminate the possibility of losing your tongue.

We said that the model of rational decision making, whose use has just been illustrated, is an ideal model. The ideal may be distant from reality in various ways: (1) The relevant values cannot always be put into monetary terms. Even in the example, it was artificial to assign a monetary value to your tongue. If value cannot be measured in terms of money, how can it be measured? To use units of utility is simply to give the problem another name, for how is utility to be measured? (2) the requisite probabilities are to be gotten from our stock of knowledge, via the rules of inductive logic. But precise and adequate rules of inductive logic have not yet been formulated. The value of the epistemic probability that the queen was over 40 had to be based on intuition and educated guesswork, rather than on precise calculations. (3) In some situations there may be so many courses of action open that to attempt to evaluate them all would mean spending all the time in planning and none in acting.

Table 3

Alternative courses of action	Possible consequences	Probability of the consequence given the choice	Value of the consequence	Pr × Value
Guess over 40	Guess correctly	$\frac{9}{10}$	$ 1,000	$ 900
	Guess too high	$\frac{1}{10}$	−1,000,000	−100,000
	Guess too low	0	0	0
			Expected value:	−$ 99,100
Guess 40 or under	Guess correctly	$\frac{1}{10}$	1,000	100
	Guess too high	0	−1,000,000	0
	Guess too low	$\frac{9}{10}$	0	0
			Expected value:	$ 100

If too much time is spent estimating probabilities and calculating expected gains down to the last decimal point, we will miss opportunities that we might otherwise have seized. To be *too* rational is the ultimate irrationality.

Suggested readings

Irwin D. Bross, *Design for Decision* (New York: The Macmillan Company, 1953).

J. D. Williams, *The Compleat Strategyst* (New York: McGraw-Hill Book Company, Inc., 1954).

The following are recommended for the advanced student:

Rudolf Carnap, *Logical Foundations of Probability* (2nd ed.) (Chicago: University of Chicago Press, 1962), pp. 252–70.

Herbert Simon, "A Behavioral Model of Rational Choice," in *Models of Man* (New York: John Wiley & Sons, Inc., 1957).

V.7. BAYES' THEOREM. You may wonder what the relation is between a conditional probability Pr(q given p) and its converse Pr(p given q). They need not be equal. The probability that Ezekial is an ape, given that he is a gorilla, is 1. But the probability that Ezekial is a gorilla, given that he is an ape, is less than 1. The value of a conditional probability is not determined by the value of its converse alone. But the value of a conditional probability can be calculated from the value of its converse, together with certain other probability values. The basis of this calculation is set forth in *Bayes' theorem*. A simplified version of a proof of Bayes' theorem is presented in Table 4. Step 4 of this table states the simplified version of Bayes' theorem.[9] Note that it allows us to compute conditional probabilities going in one direction—that is, Pr(q given p)—from conditional probabilities going in the opposite direction—that

Table 4

Step	Justification
1. $\Pr(q \text{ given } p) = \dfrac{\Pr(p\&q)}{\Pr(p)}$	Definition of conditional probability
2. $\Pr(q \text{ given } p) = \dfrac{\Pr(p\&q)}{\Pr[(p\&q)\text{v}(p\&{\sim}q)]}$	p is logically equivalent to $(p\&q)\text{v}(p\&{\sim}q)$
3. $\Pr(q \text{ given } p) = \dfrac{\Pr(p\&q)}{\Pr(p\&q) + \Pr(p\&{\sim}q)}$	Special disjunction rule
4. $\Pr(q \text{ given } p) =$	General conjunction rule

$$\frac{\Pr(q) \times \Pr(p \text{ given } q)}{[\Pr(q) \times \Pr(p \text{ given } q)] + [\Pr({\sim}q) \times \Pr(p \text{ given } {\sim}q)]}$$

---

[9] The general form of Bayes' theorem arises as follows: Suppose that instead of simply the two statements q and ${\sim}q$ we consider a set of n mutually exclusive statements, $q_1, q_2, \ldots q_n$, which is *exhaustive*. That is, the complex statement, $q_1\text{v}q_2\text{v} \ldots \text{v}q_n$, is a tautology. Then it can be proven that the simple statement p is logically equivalent to the complex statement $(p\&q_1)\text{v}(p\&q_2)\text{v} \ldots \text{v}(p\&q_n)$. This substitution is made in step 2, and the rest of the proof follows the model of the proof given. The result is

$$\Pr(q_1 \text{ given } p)$$
$$= \frac{\Pr(q_1) \times \Pr(p \text{ given } q_1)}{[(\Pr(q_1) \times \Pr(p \text{ given } q_1)] + [\Pr(q_2) \times \Pr(p \text{ given } q_2)] + \ldots + [\Pr(q_n) \times \Pr(p \text{ given } q_n)]}$$

is, Pr(p given q) and Pr(p given $\sim q$)—together with certain statement probabilities—that is, Pr(q) and Pr($\sim q$). Let us see how this theorem is applied in a concrete example.

Suppose we have two urns. Urn 1 contains eight red balls and two black balls. Urn 2 contains two red balls and eight black balls. Someone has selected an urn by flipping a fair coin. He then has drawn a ball from the urn he selected. Assume that each ball in the urn he selected had an equal chance of being drawn. What is the probability that he selected urn 1, given that he drew a red ball? Bayes' theorem tells us the Pr(urn 1 given red) is equal to

$$\frac{\text{Pr(urn 1)} \times \text{Pr(red given urn 1)}}{[\text{Pr(urn 1)} \times \text{Pr(red given urn 1)}] + [\text{Pr(}\sim\text{urn 1)} \times \text{Pr(red given }\sim\text{urn 1)}]}$$

The probabilities needed may be calculated from the information given in the problem:

$$\text{Pr(urn 1)} = \tfrac{1}{2}$$
$$\text{Pr(}\sim\text{urn 1)} = \text{Pr(urn 2)} = \tfrac{1}{2}$$
$$\text{Pr(red given urn 1)} = \tfrac{8}{10}$$
$$\text{Pr(red given }\sim\text{urn 1)} = \text{Pr(red given urn 2)} = \tfrac{2}{10}$$

If these values are substituted into the formula, they give

$$\text{Pr(urn 1 given red)} = \frac{\tfrac{1}{2} \times \tfrac{8}{10}}{\left(\tfrac{1}{2} \times \tfrac{8}{10}\right) + \left(\tfrac{1}{2} \times \tfrac{2}{10}\right)} = \frac{\tfrac{4}{10}}{\tfrac{4}{10} + \tfrac{1}{10}} = \tfrac{4}{5}$$

A similar calculation will show that Pr(urn 2 given red) $= \tfrac{1}{5}$. Thus the application of Bayes' theorem confirms our intuition that a red ball is more likely to have come from urn 1 than urn 2, and it tells us how much more likely.

It is important to emphasize the importance of the pure statement probabilities Pr(q) and Pr($\sim q$) in Bayes' theorem. If we had not known that the urn to be drawn from had been selected by flipping a fair coin, if we had just been told that it was selected some way or other, we could not have computed Pr(urn 1 given red). Indeed if Pr(urn 1) and Pr($\sim$urn 1) had been different, then our answer would have been different. Suppose that the urn had been selected by throwing a pair of dice. If the dice came up "snake-eyes" (a 1 on each die), urn 1 would be selected; otherwise urn 2 would be selected. If this were the case, then

Pr(urn 1) = $\frac{1}{36}$ and Pr($\sim$urn 1) = Pr(urn 2) = $\frac{35}{36}$. Keeping the rest of the example the same, Bayes' theorem gives

Pr(urn 1 given red)

$$= \frac{\frac{1}{36} \times \frac{8}{10}}{\left(\frac{1}{36} \times \frac{8}{10}\right) + \left(\frac{35}{36} \times \frac{2}{10}\right)} = \frac{\frac{8}{360}}{\frac{8}{360} + \frac{70}{360}} = \frac{8}{78} = \frac{4}{39}$$

This is quite a different answer from the one we got when urns 1 and 2 had an equal chance of being selected. In each case Pr(urn 1 given red) is higher than Pr (urn 1). This can be interpreted as saying that in both cases the additional information that a red ball was drawn would raise confidence that urn 1 was selected. But the initial level of confidence that urn 1 was selected is different in the two cases, and consequently the final level is also.

Exercises:

1. The probability that George will study for the test is $\frac{4}{10}$. The probability that he will pass, given that he studies, is $\frac{9}{10}$. The probability that he passes, given that he does not study, is $\frac{3}{10}$. What is the probability that he has studied, given that he passes?

2. Suppose there are three urns. Urn 1 contains six red balls and four black balls. Urn two contains nine red balls and one black ball. Urn 3 contains five red balls and five black balls. A ball is drawn at random from urn 1. If it is black a second ball is drawn at random from urn 2, but if it is red the second ball is drawn at random from urn 3.

   a. What is the probability of the second ball being drawn from urn 2?

   b. What is the probability of the second ball being drawn from urn 3?

   c. What is the probability that the second ball drawn is black, given that it is drawn from urn 2?

   d. What is the probability that the second ball drawn is black, given that it is drawn from urn 3?

   e. What is the probability that the second ball is black?

   f. What is the probability that the second ball was drawn from urn 2, given that it is black?

   g. What is the probability that the second ball was drawn from urn 3, given that it is black?

   h. What is the probability that the second ball drawn was drawn from urn 2, given that it is red?

   i. What is the probability that the second ball drawn was drawn from urn 3, given that it is red?

    j. What is the probability that the first ball drawn was red, given that the second ball drawn is black?

    k. What is the probability that the first ball is black, given that the second ball is black?

    l. What is the probability that both balls drawn are black?

  3. A fair coin is flipped twice. The two tosses are independent. What is the probability of a heads on the first toss given a heads on the second toss?

Suggested readings

The following may be consulted for further study of the probability calculus:

Richard T. Cox, *The Algebra of Probable Inference* (Baltimore, 1961).

William Feller, *An Introduction to Probability Theory and Its Applications* (2nd ed.) (New York: John Wiley & Sons, Inc., 1957).

The following is recommended for the advanced student:

Rudolf Carnap, *Logical Foundations of Probability* (2nd ed.) (Chicago: University of Chicago Press, 1962), chap. V.

APPENDIX TO CHAPTER V:
SAMPLING AND STATISTICS

A.1. INTRODUCTION. The word "sampling" most readily brings to mind public opinion polls, quality control procedures in industry, and ratings of television programs. But the use of sampling is far more universal than is suggested by these immediate associations. When you take a sip of wine to ascertain the quality of the contents of the bottle, you are sampling. The same is true when you judge the general reliability of a make of automobile on the basis of the experiences of several people who have owned one, or when you decide how honest a man is on the basis of limited observation of his behavior. Whenever you attempt to gain information about a group of things (persons, events, physical objects, actions, etc.) by examining a portion of that group, you are sampling.

The group that is the object of the investigation is called the *population* and the portion that is examined is called the *sample*. When we draw a conclusion as to the composition of the population on the basis of information on the composition of the sample, we shall say that we are making a *statistical inference.*

No very interesting statistical inference is deductively valid. A deductively valid argument whose premises simply describe the sample and say that it is included in the population can only conclude what is true of the population by virtue of the sample being a part of it; for example:

I have examined 10 lions and half of them have had tooth decay. The 10 lions in my sample were all from American zoos.

The population of lions in American zoos at the time of my investigation included at least five with tooth decay.

The evaluation of less trivial types of statistical inference is the business of inductive logic, for if the arguments involved are to have any merit they must be inductively strong. Such inferences are studied in a branch of statistics known as *projective statistics.* Projective statistics is based on the theory of probability and on another branch of statistics: *descriptive statistics.* Descriptive statistics analyzes the various ways in which the composition of a group of things (sample or population) may be succinctly characterized.

A.2. DESCRIPTIVE STATISTICS. Suppose we wish to characterize the composition of a group of people in terms of the scores that its members have made on a standard intelligence test. The most complete characterization of the composition of the group would consist of a tabulation of the number of people who received each score. Such a tabulation is known as a *frequency distribution*. But just because the frequency distribution is so complete a characterization, it runs the risk of overwhelming us with detail. General tendencies and patterns may be difficult to distinguish in a forest of figures. For this reason, descriptive statistics has developed various ways of characterizing the composition of a group which are less complete but more succinct.

Probably the most familiar concepts of descriptive statistics are those associated with the word "average." There are many different types of average, the most common being the mean, median, and mode.

Suppose we have a group of 10 gumdrops and wish to characterize the composition of the group with respect to color. If we characterize the composition of a group simply in terms of *qualitative* categories (such as color) the only type of average that can be applied is the mode. Suppose that the frequency distribution of colors within the group of gumdrops is as follows:

Category	Frequency
Red	5
Green	3
Lavender	1
Black	1

The modal color for this group is red. The *mode* is simply that category which has more members of the group in it than any other.

If, however, our categories are not merely qualitative, but fall in some natural order, we can apply not only the mode but also the median. Suppose we wish to categorize nine cups of coffee with regard to crude temperature categories, as shown in the following frequency distribution:

Category	Frequency
Boiling hot	2
Comfortably hot	2
Tepid	1
Cold	4

The median temperature in this group is tepid. The *median* category is the one in the middle, that is, the one such that there as many things in higher categories as in lower categories. It did not make sense to talk about a median in the gumdrop example because it does not make sense to talk about higher and lower colors, although it does make sense to talk about higher and lower temperatures. We can, however, talk about the mode as well as the median in the example of the cups of coffee. Note that while the "average" cup of coffee, in the sense of median, is tepid, the "average" cup of coffee, in the sense of mode, is cold.

The third kind of average, the mean, is applicable only when the categories are quantitative. Suppose we wish to characterize a group of 100 students in terms of their scores on a 10-point quiz. The frequency distribution of their scores is as follows:

Category (score)	Frequency (number of students)
10	5
9	9
8	26
7	20
6	27
5	8
4	3
3	1
2	0
1	1

We may calculate the mean score by adding up all the individual scores (5 tens, 9 nines, 26 eights, etc.) and dividing the total by the number of individuals (100). The mean score for this group is 6.79. The *mean* quantity for a group is the sum of the quantities for each member of the group divided by the number of members. It did not make sense to talk about the mean in either the gumdrop or the coffee example because the categories were not quantities and could not be added or divided. But it does make sense to talk about both the median and mode, as well as the mean, when the categories are quantitative. A check of the frequency distribution of test scores shows that the median score is 7 and the modal score is 6.

We have surveyed only a small number of the concepts of descriptive statistics. A more thorough treatment may be found in some of the suggested readings listed at the end of this section. However, one point that we have made in connection with various types of average holds in general for descriptive statistics: The types of descriptive statistics which are applicable depend on the types of categories used to characterize the members of the group.

Exercises:

1. Suppose you have a bag containing 100 mineral specimens. You ascertain how many of them fall into each of the following categories: hard enough to scratch glass; hard enough to scratch talc but not hard enough to scratch glass; not hard enough to scratch talc. Given only this information, which type or types of average would be applicable? Why?

2. Nine students take a 100-point quiz. The sores are as follows: 79, 78, 77, 75, 71, and 70, and three zeros. Calculate the mean, median, and modal scores.

Suggested readings

Darrell Huff, *How to Lie With Statistics* (New York: W. W. Norton and Company, Inc., 1954).

For a discussion of the relationship between the types of categories used to characterize the members of a group and the types of descriptive statistics which are applicable, the advanced student should see the following:

S. S. Stevens, "On the Theory of Scales of Measurement," in *Philosophy of Science*, Arthur Danto and Sidney Morgenbesser, eds. (New York: Meridian Books, Inc., 1960), pp. 141–49.

A.3. SAMPLING AND PROJECTIVE STATISTICS. When we know that a certain descriptive statistic correctly characterizes a sample (for example, that the mean weight of a sample of 100 "one-pound" boxes of Sticky Cookies is 14 ounces) and we wish to conclude something about the descriptive statistics which correctly characterizes the population (for example, that the mean weight of all "one-pound" boxes of Sticky Cookies is below one pound) then we are involved in problems of statistical inference. The great majority of the descriptive statistics with which we are presented are arrived at in this way, rather than by an examination of the entire population. The Sunday supplements regularly print statements as to the average (mean) weight of American women between 30 and 40, the average (mean) number of hairs on an adult male Caucasian's head, and the proportion of Americans who are suffering from undiagnosed mental illness. It should be rather obvious that none of these figures were obtained from a complete survey of the population, but rather by inference from samples.

In general, the inference from sample statistics to population statistics is, at best, inductively strong. Common sense tells us that some types of samples provide a firmer basis for such inferences than others. Someone who claims that the mean weight of Japanese men is over 200 pounds on the basis of a sample composed solely of Sumo wrestlers would not convince many people. Such a sample is said to be *biased* by virtue of the fact that one must be quite heavy to be a Sumo wrestler. Although the Sumo wrestler sample is so blatantly biased that it would mislead no one, samples can be biased in more subtle ways. Consider, for example, a poll taken on a New York streetcorner in which every tenth person who passes the streetcorner is interviewed. This may appear to be a way of obtaining an unbiased sample of the opinions of New Yorkers. But suppose that the poll deals with attitudes toward the welfare state and that it is taken on streetcorners in the heart of the financial district during lunch hour on weekdays. We would certainly not expect such a sample to be representative of the entire population of New York. It is clear then that for the inference from the sample to the population to be inductively strong, the sample must be unbiased.

But even an unbiased sample may not be much good if the sample is too small. An unbiased sample of one New Yorker would not be of much help in telling us the percentage of New Yorkers who are female. A new drug would hardly be judged medically safe if it had been tried on a sample of only 10 people. For the inference from the sample to the population to be inductively strong, the sample must be sufficiently large, and the larger the better.

Common sense has given us some rules of thumb for evaluating statistical inferences. If we are to go farther we must venture into the domain of projective statistics. Projective statistics brings the theory of probability to bear on the problem of statistical inference by requiring that a sample be *random*. Saying that a sample is random does not refer to any characteristics of the sample itself, but rather to the selection process used to pick the sample out from the population. A random-selection process has two main virtues. The first is that it eliminates bias from sampling. The second is that if we know that a sample had been picked by a random-selection process and if we know a few things about the population from which it was selected, we can sometimes calculate the probability that the sample will resemble the population.

There are various types of random-selection processes. We shall examine four of them. Let us suppose that we have a herd of 10 elephants as
our population, and wish to find out something about the average weight
of the elephants, but that because of the difficulties involved we can afford
to weigh only 4 of them. One way to eliminate bias would be to select
our sample by the following process: We number the elephants 1 through
10. We then roll a 10-sided, well-balanced die and weigh the elephant
whose number comes up. We roll the die three more times and weigh
the indicated elephants in order to come up with a list of four weights.
A sample selected in this way is called a *simple random sample with
replacement*. The phrase "with replacement" alludes to the fact that if
the sample is taken in this manner, the same elephant may be included
more than once in the sample, since his number may come up on more
than one throw of the die. We might say that after the first elephant is
selected to be a member of the sample, it is *replaced* in the population
and is thus eligible to be selected again. A selection procedure gives us
a simple random sample with replacement if:

> 1. Each member of the population has an equal probability of
> being selected as the first member of the sample.
> 2. Each member of the population, including those selected as
> previous members of the sample, has an equal chance of being
> selected as the nth member of the sample.

A simple random sample with replacement, although unbiased, is typically an inefficient way of gaining information about a population. It
would be silly to weigh the same elephant four times. The natural thing
to do would be to require that the sample be composed of four different
elephants. We could use the same sampling procedure except that if on
the second, third, or fourth throw of the die the number of an elephant
already selected came up, we would roll again until we got a different
number. A sample obtained by such a procedure is called a simple random sample without replacement. A selection procedure gives us a simple
random sample without replacement if:

> 1. Each member of the population has an equal probability of
> being selected as the first member of the sample.
> 2. Each member of the population, excluding those selected as
> previous members of the sample, has an equal chance of being
> selected as the nth member of the sample.

In other words, in a simple random sample without replacement of size n, each group of n distinct members of the population has an equal chance of constituting the sample. Thus this type of sample is just as unbiased as a simple random sample with replacement, but it avoids the risk of loss of information through duplication in the sample. If the only information that we have about the population is a list of its members, then a simple random sample without replacement is the best bet, and the larger the sample the better.

However, if we have some additional information about the population, we may be in a position to make good use of a different type of random sample. Suppose we know that the herd of elephants is composed of five adult elephants and five baby elephants. Using either of the types of simple random sampling we run the risk of getting a sample composed of all babies or all adults. In either case, the average weight of the sample would surely not be representative of the average weight of the herd. In order to exclude such a possibility, we may select our sample of four elephants by taking a simple random sample of two from the adults and a simple random sample of two from the babies. Such a sampling procedure is called *stratified random sampling*. The adults and the babies constitute the two *strata*. We have stratified random sampling with replacement or without replacement depending on whether the constituent simple random samples are taken with or without replacement. Notice that the feature of this example that made stratified random sampling desirable was our knowledge that baby elephants tend to have a much lower weight than adult elephants. A stratified random sample is preferable to a simple random sample if and only if we can divide the population into strata such that members of one stratum are relatively alike, and members of different strata are relatively different, with respect to the property in which we are interested.

The concepts introduced here form only a small part of the topics dealt with in projective statistics. A more detailed discussion is beyond the scope of this book.

Exercises:

1. From an ordinary deck of playing cards, a sample of four cards is selected by simple random sampling with replacement. What is the probability that all four selections will be aces?

2. From an ordinary deck of playing cards, a sample of four cards is selected by simple random sampling without replacement. What is the probability that all four selections will be aces?

3. Pollsters trying to predict the outcomes of national elections always use stratified random samples. Why do you suppose that they do so? If you were conducting such a poll, how would you choose your strata?

Suggested readings

Morris J. Slonim, *Sampling in a Nutshell* (New York: Simon and Schuster, 1960), pp. 1–53.

The following is recommended for the advanced student:

Herman Chernoff and Lincoln E. Moses, *Elementary Decision Theory* (New York: John Wiley & Sons, Inc., 1959).

VI

WHY EPISTEMIC AND INDUCTIVE PROBABILITIES *ARE* PROBABILITIES

VI.1. INTRODUCTION. The concepts of epistemic and inductive probability were introduced in Chapter I as numerical measures grading degree of rational belief in a statement and degree of support which the premises of an argument give its conclusion. In Chapter V we encountered a mathematical characterization of probabilities and conditional probabilities. Here, we inquire why epistemic and inductive probabilities obey the mathematical rules laid down for probabilities and conditional probabilities.

VI.2. THE PROBABILITY CALCULUS IN A NUTSHELL. In discussing these questions it will be useful to have as concise a characterization of the mathematical conception of a probability as is possible. Here is the classic one, due to Kolmogarov:

> **Definition 1:** A probability (on statements) is a rule assigning each statement, S, a unique probability, $Pr(S)$, such that:
> a. No probability is less than zero.
> b. If T is a tautology, $Pr(T) = 1$
> c. If P; Q are mutually exclusive, then $Pr(PvQ) = Pr(P) + Pr(Q)$.

Let us see how this brief characterization yields the longer one of Chapter V. Rules 1 and 4 of Chapter V are explicitly contained in Definition 1 as 1b and 1c. We saw in Chapter V that these two rules yield the negation rule. Since $Pv{\sim}P$ is a tautology and $P;{\sim}P$ are mutually exclusive,

$$Pr(P) + Pr({\sim}P) = 1$$

Rule 5: $Pr({\sim}P) = 1 - Pr(P)$

Since the denial of a contradiction is a tautology, 1b and Rule 5 show that if C is a contradiction:

$$1 = Pr(C) - 1$$

Rule 2: $\Pr(C) = 0$

It is not so obvious that Rule 3 ("if two statements are logically equivalent, they have the same probability") is a consequence of Definition 1, but it is. Suppose P is logically equivalent to Q. Then P; $\sim Q$ are mutually exclusive for $\sim Q$ is true when P is false and false when P is true. (If the foregoing statement is not obvious, review what logical equivalence means and prove it.) By the same token, $Pv\sim Q$ is a tautology. So by 1b and 1c: $\Pr(P) + \Pr(-Q) = 1$. Using the negation rule:

$$\Pr(P) + 1 - \Pr(Q) = 1$$
$$\Pr(P) = \Pr(Q)$$

We have now only to show that Definition 1 restricts the possible probability values to the range from 0 to 1, for everything else in Chapter V was shown to follow from what we have here developed. We will demonstrate this by showing something much more general and interesting. First, a few preliminaries.

Definition 2: Q is a logical consequence of P just if Q is true in every case in which P is true.

So, for example, R is a logical consequence of R & S, as is S; and RvS is a logical consequence of R and of S.

	R	S	R & S	$R \vee S$
Case 1:	T	T	T	T
Case 2:	T	F	F	T
Case 3:	F	T	F	T
Case 4:	F	F	F	F

Notice that a tautology is a logical consequence of everything, since a tautology is true in all cases. And everything is a logical consequence of a contradiction, since a contradiction is never true. We will now show the *Logical Consequence Principle*:

If Q is a logical consequence of P, then $\Pr(Q)$ must be at least as great as $\Pr(P)$.

Then, of course, every probability must fall in the interval from 0 to 1. If Q is a logical consequence of P then either P and Q are true in exactly the same cases or Q is true in the cases where P is, plus some extra cases. In the former instance P and Q are logically equivalent and thus have the same probability. Let us, then, look at the latter. For example:

	P	Q	$(Q \& - P)$
Case 1:	T	T	F
Case 2:	F	F	F
Case 3:	T	T	F
Case 4:	T	T	F
Case 5:	F	T	T
Case 6:	F	F	F
Case 7:	T	T	F
Case 8:	F	T	T

Here Q is a logical consequence of P. It is true in the cases where P is [1, 3, 4, 7] plus some extra ones [5, 8]. At the right is the statement, $Q\&\sim P$, which is true in *just these extra cases* and false otherwise. Notice that $(Q\&\sim P)$ *and* P *are mutually exclusive.* Next notice that $Pv(Q\&\sim P)$ *is logically equivalent to* Q since $(Q\&\sim P)$ adds just the required extra cases to P. Then:

$$\Pr(Q) = \Pr[Pv(Q\&\sim P)] = \Pr(P) + \Pr(Q \& \sim P)$$

Since $\Pr(Q\&\sim P)$ is at worst zero, $\Pr(Q)$ must be at least as great as $\Pr(P)$.

This result completes the argument that Definition 1 captures the probability calculus as developed in Chapter V. It is, however, of more than incidental importance. It assures the *probabilistic validity of deductive argument.* If

$$P_1$$
$$P_2$$
$$.$$
$$.$$
$$.$$
$$\underline{P_n}$$
$$C$$

is a (truth-functionally) deductively valid argument, then the conclusion, C, is a logical consequence of the conjunction of the premises $P_1 \& P_2 \ldots \& P_n$. Our result shows that our conclusion *must be at least as probable as the conjunction of the premises.*

Think of the disastrous consequences if this were *not* true! We could have good reason for believing that all the premises of an argument are true, deduce the conclusion from them, and *not* have equally good reason for thereby believing the conclusion. Under such circumstances it would be hard to imagine a rationale for applying deductive logic.

The probabilistic validity of deductive argument provides a justification for applying deductive logic to situations where we are entitled to assign high probability to the conjunction of the premises but are not entitled to be certain of their truth. There are strong arguments to the effect that this covers almost all applications of deductive logic to empirical knowledge.

Exercises:

1. Show:
   a. If *P* is a logical consequence of *Q* and *Q* is a logical consequence of *P*, then *P* is logically equivalent to *Q*.
   b. If *P* is a logical consequence of *Q* and *Q* is a logical consequence of *R*, then *P* is a logical consequence of *R*.
   c. If *P* is logically equivalent to *Q*, then *P* and *Q* are logical consequences of the same statements and have as logical consequences the same statements.

2. Show that if *R* is a logical consequence of *P* and of *Q* and *R* has as a logical consequence *PvQ*, then *R* is logically equivalent to either *P* or to *Q* or to *PvQ*.

3. Study the following truth table:

	P	Q	R	~P&Q&R	P&Q&~R	(~P&Q&R)v(P&Q&~R)
Case 1:	T	T	T	F	F	F
Case 2:	T	T	F	F	T	T
Case 3:	T	F	T	F	F	F
Case 4:	T	F	F	F	F	F
Case 5:	F	T	T	T	F	T
Case 6:	F	T	F	F	F	F
Case 7:	F	F	T	F	F	F
Case 8:	F	F	F	F	F	F

Then:
   a. Show that for *any* case in *any* truth table you can construct a sentence which is true in that case and false in all other cases.

b. Show that for any *set* of cases in *any* truth table you can construct a sentence true in those cases and false in all other cases.

VI. 3. THE LOGICAL CONSEQUENCE PRINCIPLE ALONE IS NOT ENOUGH.

The Logical Consequence Principle is both plausible and powerful. It is hardly open to dispute that if Q is true in every case in which P is, Q must have at least as good a chance of being true as P. We should be pleased that Definition 1 of the previous section leads to this result; we should have been dismayed if it had not.

It is interesting to ask here how far the Logical Consequence Principle will take us toward mathematical probability as characterized by Definition 1. It leads immediately to the principle that logically equivalent statements have the same probability since P and Q are logically equivalent just in case each is a logical consequence of the other. It leads to the fact that there must be a maximum probability value, shared by all tautologies, and a minimum probability value, shared by all contradictions. But even if we arbitrarily choose 1 as the maximum and 0 as the minimum probability, the logical consequence principle does not thereby lead to the additivity of probabilities of mutually exclusive sentences, that is:

1 c. If P; Q are mutually exclusive then $\Pr(PvQ) = \Pr(P) + \Pr(Q)$

This can be most easily seen by considering a new quantity, *plausibility*, which is defined in terms of probability as on the graph in Figure 1. (To find a statement's plausibility from its probability, first find its probability on the horizontal axis, go straight up to the curve and straight over to its plausibility on the vertical scale.) Notice that the curve defining plausibility is so drawn that greater probabilities lead to greater plausibilities and greater plausibilities arise only from greater probabilities. That is:

Probability $(A) >$ Probability (B)
    if and only if
Plausibility of $(A) >$ Plausibility (B)

The upshot of this is that if we were to arrange some statements in order of increasing plausibility, we would place them *in the same order* as we would if we were arranging them in order of increasing probability. A short way of saying this is to say that probability and plausibility are *ordinally similar*.

It is now easy to see that plausibility must satisfy the Logical Consequence Principle. If Q is a logical consequence of P then the probability of Q must be at least as great as the probability of P (since we showed, in the last section, that probability satisfies the logical consequence principle). Since plausibility is ordinally similar to probability, plausibility of Q must be at least as great as plausibility of P.

However, plausibility need not add for mutually exclusive statements. Assume that some statement, P, is as likely as not; so:

$$Pr(P) = Pr(\sim P) = \tfrac{1}{2}$$

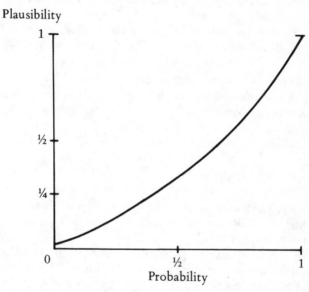

Figure 4

Referring to Figure 4, we see that the *plausibility* values of P and of $\sim P$ are $\tfrac{1}{4}$. We also see that since $Pr(Pv\sim P) = 1$, the plausibility of $(Pv\sim P) = 1$. So plausibility of $(Pv\sim P)$ is definitely *not* equal to plausibility of (P) plus plausibility of $(\sim P)$.

Although plausibility satisfies the logical consequence principle, and has a maximum of 1 and a minimum of zero, it is not a probability.

To understand the need for the extra property of additivity which distinguishes a probability we must look to quantitative applications of probability. In the next few sections, we shall consider the oldest and most general quantitative application of probabilities—that of a guide for the intelligent gambler.

Exercises for the advanced student:

1. The following principle has been proposed for any grading of rational degree of belief.

I. For any statements, R, S, T, if R and T are mutually exclusive and S and T are mutually exclusive, then the degree of belief in R is greater than the degree of belief in S, if and only if *the* degree of belief in RvT should be greater than the degree of belief in SvT.

  a. Show that probability satisfies principle I and that any quantity ordinally similar to probability does also.

  b. Show that any quantity representing degree of belief which:

   i. Satisfies principle I,

   ii. Gives logically equivalent sentences the same probability, and

   iii. Requires that tautologies have the maximum probability and contradictions the minmum

  must satisfy the logical consequence principle.

2. Consider a language containing only two simple statements, P, Q, together with every complex statement which can be built out of them using &, v, $\sim$.

  a. Show that every statement in the language is logically equivalent to one of the following sixteen statements:

   $P\&\sim P$; $-P\&-Q$; $-P\&Q$; $-P$; $P\&-Q$; $-Q$; $(P\&-Q)v(-P\&Q)$; $-Pv$ $-Q$; $P\&Q$; $(P\&Q)v(-P\&-Q)$; Q; $-PvQ$; P; $Pv-Q$; PvQ; $Pv\sim P$.
   (Hint: Look at the truth table for all these statements.)

  b. Assuming $\Pr(P\&Q) = .41$; $\Pr(P\&\sim Q) = .29$; $\Pr(-P\&Q) = .2$; $\Pr(-P\&$ $-\&Q) = .1$; calculate the probability values for each of the foregoing statements.

  c. Consider the quantity representing a degree of belief which takes as values just the foregoing probabilities except that $(-Pv-Q)$ and $(-PvQ)$ switch values. That is, for any statement R, $D(R) = \Pr(R)$ except that $D(-Pv-Q) = .71$ and $D(-PvQ) = .69$

   i. Show that D satisfies the Logical Consequence Principle.
   (Hint: to verify that the Logical Consequence Principle is not violated you need only verify that no sentence of which $-PvQ$ is a consequence has a probability greater than .69 and no statement which is a consequence of $-P\&-Q$ has a probability less than .71.)

   ii. Show that D *violates* principle 1.
   (Hint: $-PvQ$ is logically equivalent to $(P\&Q)v\sim P$ and $-Pv-Q$ is logically equivalent to $(P\&\sim Q)v\sim P$.)

3. Exercises 1 and 2 show that satisfying the Logical Consequence Principle is not a sufficient condition for being ordinally similar to probability. Show that satisfying principle I also fails to be sufficient for ordinal similarity to probability. (This is a *difficult* problem. The required proof can be found in the first of the

suggested readings. Conditions which are sufficient to guarantee ordinal similarity to probability may be found in both of the suggested readings.)

Suggested readings

Kronz, Luce, Suppes, and Trevsky, *Foundations of Measurement* (New York: Academic Press, 1971).

Richard Cox, *The Algebra of Probable Inference* (Baltimore, Md.: The Johns Hopkins Press, 1961).

VI.4. BETS. A bet on a statement, P, is an arrangement by which the bettor collects a certain sum, a, if P is true and forfeits a certain sum, b, if P is false. The situation can be characterized in a payoff table:

P	Net Gain
T	$+a$
F	$-b$

The total amount involved, $a + b$, is the *stake* and the ratio $\dfrac{b}{a}$ is the *odds*. For instance, if I agree to pay you \$2 if the Senators win and you to pay me \$1 if they lose, the stake is \$3 and I am giving you 2 to 1 odds that they win.

A bet on one statement may also constitute a bet on another statement. In the most trivial case, if two statements are logically equivalent then a bet on one is equally a bet on the other. In the next most trivial case a negative bet on $\sim P$ is identical to a positive bet on P.

$\sim P$	Net Gain	P
T	$-b$	F
F	$+a$	T

If B_1 and B_2 are betting arrangements, their *sum* is an arrangement by which the bettor fulfills his obligations under both B_1 and B_2. For example:

	B_1			B_2	
P	Net Gain		Q	Net Gain	
T	a		T	c	
F	$-b$		F	$-d$	

Sum of B_1 and B_2

P	Q	Net Gain
T	T	$a + c$
T	F	$a - d$
F	T	$c - b$
F	F	$-(b + d)$

It should be clear that the sum of two bets *need not* be a bet on any given statement. A bet on a statement, S, pays a certain value if S is true and costs a certain value if S is false. There is no differentiation about *ways* that S can be true or *ways* that S can be false. So if in the payoff table for the sum bet, there are at least three different figures under net gain, the sum bet cannot be interpreted as a bet on any statement.

But otherwise, a sum bet may be a bet on some one statement. For instance, suppose that I bet $100 at 2 to 1 odds that the Plumbers will win. Later, getting nervous at the amount of money I have risked, I hedge with a side bet against the Plumbers at the same odds. The sum of these two bets is a bet on the proposition that the Plumbers will win, at the original odds but at half the original stakes. Suppose I now become convinced that the Plumbers are in deep trouble and hedge by betting against them again, though by this time the best odds I can get are even money. The sum of this third bet with the preceding is again a bet on the same statement.

Plumbers Win	Bet 1	Bet 2	Sum of 1 and 2	Bet 3	Sum of 3 with 1 and 2
T	+$100	−$ 50	+$ 50	−$40	+$10
F	−$200	+$100	−$100	+$40	−$60

I have succeeded in reducing the stakes still further, but only at the cost of giving six to one odds.

Let us move to a more interesting case of a sum bet being a bet on a statement. Suppose that P and Q are mutually exclusive, that B_1 is a bet on P for stakes $(a + b)$ at odds $\frac{b}{a}$ and B_2 is a bet on Q_n:

P	Q	B_1	B_2	Sum of B_1 and B_2
T	F	a	$-d$	$a - d$
F	T	$-b$	c	$c - b$
F	F	$-b$	$-d$	$-(b + d)$

Since P and Q are mutually exclusive, there are only three possible combinations of truth values. If the sum bet has a different payoff value in each of the three cases, we know that it is not a bet on any statement. But what if the payoff values in the first two cases are the same (that is $a - d = c - b$)? Then the bettor wins this value in either of these cases, *that is whenever PvQ is true* and loses $b + d$ in the third case, *that is when PvQ is false.* So if $a - d = c - b$, the sum bet is a bet on PvQ with stakes $(a - d) + (b + d) = (a + b)$ and odds $\dfrac{b + d}{a - d}$. Under what conditions does this interesting phenomenon occur? It doesn't take much algebra to show that $a - d = c - b$ just in case $a + b = c + d$, that is just in case the stakes of our bets on P and Q are equal. In summary,

> *If P and Q are mutually exclusive, the sum of bets on P and on Q at equal stakes is a bet on PvQ at the same stakes.*

There is another kind of betting arrangement which is of general interest and which is not a bet on any statement. This is the sort of bet that is called off if certain conditions are not met; call it a *conditional bet.* If the bet is on Q and the conditions to be met are specified by P, then it is called, not surprisingly, a bet on Q conditional on P and gives rise to the following sort of payoff table:

P	Q	Payoff
T	T	a
T	F	$-b$
F	T	0
F	F	0

A little reflection should convince you that many of the betting situations that we get ourselves into are conditional bets. Sometimes we may wish that even more of them were. If so, it should come as good news that we can always construct a betting arrangement conditional on P by a simple hedging strategy.

Consider the sum of two bets, the first being a bet on $P \& Q$ and the second being a bet on $\sim P$.

P	Q	$P\&Q$	Bet 1	$\sim P$	Bet 2	Sum of Bets 1 and 2
T	T	T	c	F	$-f$	$c - f$
T	F	F	$-d$	F	$-f$	$-(d + f)$
F	T	F	$-d$	T	e	$e - d$
F	F	F	$-d$	T	e	$e - d$

If we arrange Bet 2 so that our winnings on $\sim P$, e, equal our losses from bet 1, d, the sum of bets 1 and 2 will be a bet on Q conditional on P, as follows:

P	Q	Sum of Bets 1 and 2
T	T	$c - f$
T	F	$-(d + f)$
F	T	0
F	F	0

In summary: The sum of two bets, the first on $P \& Q$ and the second on $\sim P$ with the winnings on the second being equal to the losses on the first, is a bet on Q conditional on P.

Exercise:

    If you bet someone a dollar at 2 to 1 odds that P:
        a. What is *your* payoff table for P?
        b. What is *your* payoff table for $\sim P$?
        c. What is *his* payoff table for P?
        d. What is *his* payoff table for $\sim P$?

VI.5. FAIR BETS. Remember from Chapter V that the *expected value* of a betting arrangement is the sum of the quantities obtained by multiplying the payoff in a given case by the probability of that case. For example, the bet:

Bet 1

P	Payoff
T	a
F	$-b$

has an expected value of $a\Pr(P) - b\mathrm{Pv}(-P)$ and the betting arrangement:

Bet 2

P	Q	Payoff
T	T	a
T	F	b
F	T	c
F	F	$-d$

has an expected value of $a\Pr(P\&Q) + b\Pr(P\&-Q) + c\Pr(-P\&Q) - d\Pr(-P\&-Q)$.

If the expected value of a bet is positive, it is called a *favorable* bet; if negative, it is an *unfavorable* bet; if zero, it is a *fair* bet. Whether a bet is fair, favorable, or unfavorable depends on how the probabilities balance out the odds. Consider Bet 1 on P. It is fair just in case:

$$a\Pr(P) - b\Pr(-P) = 0$$
$$a\Pr(P) - b[1 - \Pr(P)] = 0$$
$$a\Pr(P) - b + b\Pr(P) = 0$$
$$a\Pr(P) + b\Pr(P) = b$$
$$\Pr(P)[a + b] = b$$
$$\Pr(P) = \left(\frac{b}{a + b}\right)$$

The quantity $\dfrac{b}{a + b}$ is called the *betting quotient* for P. So we can say that a bet on P is fair just in case the probability of P equals the betting quotient for P.

Suppose we have fair bets on P and Q:

P	Payoff
T	a
F	$-b$

Q	Payoff
T	c
F	$-d$

Must the sum of these two bets be fair? The sum bet:

P	Q	Payoff
T	T	$a + c$
T	F	$a - d$
F	T	$c - b$
F	F	$-b - d$

is fair if and only if:

$$\Pr(P\&Q)(a + c) + \Pr(P\&-Q)(a - d) + \Pr(-P\&Q)(c - b)$$
$$+ \Pr(-P\&-Q)(-b - d) = 0$$

or:

$$a\Pr(P\&Q) + c\Pr(P\&Q) + a\Pr(P\&-Q) - d\Pr(P\&-Q) + c\Pr(-P\&Q)$$
$$- b\Pr(-P\&Q) - b\Pr(-P\&-Q) - d\Pr(-P\&-Q) = 0$$

or:

$$a[\Pr(P\&Q) + \Pr(P\&-Q)] - b[\Pr(-P\&Q) + \Pr(-P\&-Q)]$$
$$+ c[\Pr(-P\&Q) + \Pr(P\&Q)] - d[\Pr(P\&-Q) + \Pr(-P\&-Q)] = 0$$

or:

$$a\Pr(P) - b\Pr(-P) + c\Pr(Q) - d\Pr(-Q) = 0$$

But since our bet on P is fair, $a\Pr(P) - b\Pr(-P) = 0$; and since our bet on Q is fair, $c\Pr(Q) - d\Pr(-Q) = 0$. So if bets on two statements are fair their sum is fair.[1]

The argument is summarized in Figure 5. Each square contains the payoff for one case of the sum bet multiplied by the probability of that case (e.g., in the upper left-hand square $\Pr(P\&Q)(a + c) = a\Pr(P\&Q) + c\Pr(P\&Q)$. Thus, the expected value of the sum bet is just the sum of everything in all the squares. The squares are divided into triangles to suggest a way of adding. The quantities in the lower left triangles are added downward and summed at the bottom of the columns. The quantities in the upper right triangles are added to the right. The sum of the quantities at the bottom of the columns is the expected value of the

---

[1]Note that this is not the only way that the sum bet can be fair. If the expected value of one bet is $+e$ and that of the other is $-e$, then the sum bet will be fair.

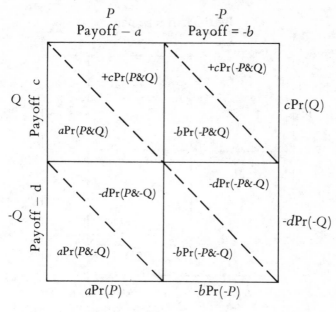

Figure 5

bet on P; the sum of the quantities a the right of the rows is the expected value of the bet on Q. *So we have shown that the expected value of the sum of bets on* P *and on* Q *is the sum of the expected values of those bets.* Of course, then, if two bets are fair, their sum bet is fair.

So far, we have only talked about the sum of two fair *bets*, rather than two fair *betting arrangements*. Remember, a bet on a statement, P, admits of only two possibilities—P is true or P is false—and specifies a unique payoff in each case. As we saw in the last section, the sum of the two bets (on statements) is a betting arrangement, which typically is not a bet on any statement. Thus, we have still to ask whether the sum of any two fair *betting arrangements* is a fair betting arrangement. The answer, happily, is yes—by the same sort of argument we used in the simpler case. The argument is indicated in Figure 6. Again the lower left triangles are summed downwards and when they are added at the bottom we find that their sum equals the expected value of betting arrangement 1. Likewise the sum of all the contents of all the upper right triangles equals the expected value of betting arrangement 2. But the sum of all the triangles is just the expected value of the sum betting arrangement.

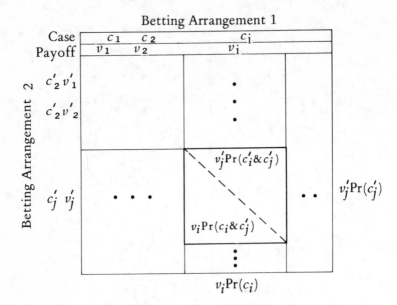

Figure 6

So we know in general that:

> The expected value of a sum of betting arrangements is the sum of the expected values of the individual betting arrangements.

and in particular that:

> A sum of fair betting arrangements is fair.

Perhaps you may think that this is not very surprising and that we have been, perhaps, belaboring the obvious. Well and good! Think then how surprising it would be if this were not true—in fact how *disastrous* it would be for making decisions under uncertainty. We could undertake a series of fair risks and yet have no assurance that the total arrangement was not unfair.

What is surprising is not that probabilities, as measures of belief, lead to such well believed concepts of expected value and fair bets but that probabilities are the *only* kinds of measures of belief which will do so.

Imagine us using some new measure of belief, call it plausibility (Pl), to take the place of probability. Again, we will call a bet on a statement S

S	Payoff
T	a
F	$-b$

fair just in case the betting quotient for S, $\dfrac{b}{a+b}$, equals the plausibility of S.

Now remember that the foregoing bet of S *is* also a bet on $\sim$S with negative payoff $(-b)$ if $\sim$S is true and a negative loss $(-a)$ if $\sim$S is false.[2]

$\sim$S	Payoff
T	$-b$
F	$-(-a)$

The betting quotient for $\sim$S is

$$\frac{-a}{(-a)+(-b)} = \frac{a}{a+b}$$

Now suppose S has a certain plausibility, Pl(S). If a bet on S is fair, the betting quotient for S must equal that plausibility:

$$\text{Pl}(S) = \frac{b}{a+b}$$

Since this bet is also a bet on $\sim$S and since it is fair, the betting quotient for $\sim$S must equal its plausibility.

$$\text{Pl}(\sim S) = \frac{a}{a+b}$$

Notice that plausibility is beginning to resemble probability since:

$$\text{Pl}(\sim S) = 1 - \text{Pl}(S)$$

Now let's look at the case where we have two mutually exclusive statements, P; Q. Suppose we find the proper betting quotients $\dfrac{b}{a+b}$

---

[2] Remember that "a bet on a statement, P, is an arrangement by which the bettor collects a certain sum, a, if P is true and forfeits a certain sum, b, if P is false. These quantities may be negative. Thus a bet of P is literally also a bet on $\sim P$. This argument thus depends on *fairness* being a property of the arrangement rather than on the way it is described (as bet on P or bet on $\sim P$, etc.).

and $\dfrac{d}{c + d}$ to assure fair bets. Keeping to these quotients, we can choose the stakes so that they are equal on the bets ($a + b = c + d$). In section VI.4 we saw that under such circumstances the sum of these bets is a bet on PvQ with betting quotient $\dfrac{b + d}{(a - d) + (b + d)}$. (If you don't understand where this came from, go back to section VI.4 and work it out.) This is just $\dfrac{b + d}{a + b} = \dfrac{b}{a + b} + \dfrac{d}{a + b}$. Since we assumed the stakes were equal, $a + b = c + d$. So the betting quotient for PvQ is equal to $\dfrac{b}{a + b} + \dfrac{d}{c + d}$; that is, to the sum of the betting quotients for P and for Q.

At this point we need to add one modest assumption about fairness to make any headway:

> *If a bet is a sum of fair bets it is fair.*

Given this assumption it follows that:

> *If P and Q are mutually exclusive then $Pl(PvQ) = Pl(P) + Pl(Q)$.*

Taken together with the foregoing fact about negation [i.e., that $Pl(\sim S) = 1 - Pl(S)$] this shows us the $Pl(Pv\sim P) = 1$ and $Pl(P\&\sim P) = 0$. Remember now from IV.4 that if two statements are logically equivalent, a bet on one is equally a bet on the other. Thus every tautology must have plausibility 1 and every contradiction plausibility 0. It would be hard to imagine anything less worthy of belief than $P\&\sim P$ or more worthy than $Pv\sim P$. If we make this final assumption,

> *A tautology has the maximum plausibility and a contradiction the minimum*

we have insured that all the clauses of Definition 1, section VI.2, have been met and thus that plausibility must, in fact, be probability.

> To sum up: *If plausibility meets the following conditions, it is probability:*
>
> (i)   A bet on a statement, S, is fair if and only if the betting quotient for S equals the plausibility of S.
>
> (ii)   If two bets are fair, their sum bet is fair.
>
> (iii)   A tautology has the maximum plausibility value and a contradiction the minimum.

Exercises:

1. I bet on P with you, with the betting quotient for P being $\dfrac{a}{a+b}$ and the stakes being $a + b$ with a and b both positive quantities. Describe your bet on $-P$ with me.

2. More precisely, when we bet *with* someone he enters into an arrangement where our winnings are his losses, and *vice versa*. That is, the entries on his payoff table are the negative of the corresponding payoffs in our table. Call his bet the *complement* of our bet.

Consider the principle that *a bet is fair if and only if its complement is fair*. Using the results of Exercise 1, show that this principle can replace the use of negative winnings and losses in the argument for:

$$Pl(S) + Pl(\sim S) = 1$$

3. What kind of bets give rise to betting quotients greater than 1 or less than 0? (Hint: if a and b are both positive, $\dfrac{a}{a+b}$ must be between 0 and 1. If a is positive and b is zero, $\dfrac{a}{a+b} = 1$. If b is positive and a is zero, $\dfrac{a}{a+b} = 0$. What if a and b are both negative?)

4. Give an intuitive argument as to why the kinds of bets that give rise to betting quotients less than 0 or greater than 1 could not reasonably be described as fair no matter how plausible or implausible the statement in question. Remember that a bet that is favorable or unfavorable is not fair.

5. Suppose we allowed some statements to have greater plausibility than a tautology, and some less than a contradiction, but kept to the other restrictions. So, for example: $Pr(P) = 2$ and $Pr(\sim P) = 1 - Pr(P) = -1$. Suppose also that we calculate the expected value of a bet on P in the normal way as $a\,Pr(P) - b\,Pr(-P)$.

    a. Show that these plausibility values would give an expected value of 0 to some of the types of bets discussed in Exercises 3 and 4.

    b. Show that these plausibility values would violate the following principle:

        If Bet 1 and Bet 2 differ only in that Bet 2 has a greater payoff in one case than Bet 1, then Bet 2 has at least as great an expected value as Bet 1.

6. When we showed that if fair bets and expected values are to work reasonably, plausibility must be probability, our demonstration was based on minimal assumptions about fair bets. If we assume more about fair bets, the argument becomes very short. Assume that the expected value of *betting arrangement* is the sum of the products of the plausibility of a case and the payoff in that case. We will consider only unfair bets.

a. Consider:

Bet 1		Bet 2	
P	Payoff	$P v \sim P$	Payoff
T	a	T	a
F	a	F	$-b$

Show that they are the same bet.

b. Assume the following *sure-thing* principle: *If a bet pays off a fixed amount,* a, *in every possible case, then the expected value of that bet must be* a. Under this assumption, show that the plausibility of tautology must be 1 and the plausibility of $\sim S$ must be $1 - \mathrm{Pl}(S)$.

c. Suppose that P and Q are mutually exclusive. Consider the betting arrangement:

P	Q	Payoff
T	F	a
F	T	a
F	F	a

Using the rule for calculating expected value and the sure-thing principle, relate $\mathrm{Pl}(P\&\neg Q)$; $\mathrm{Pl}(\neg P\&Q)$; $\mathrm{Pl}(\neg P\&\neg Q)$. Assuming that logically equivalent statements have the same plausibility, show that $\mathrm{Pl}(P) + \mathrm{Pl}(Q) = \mathrm{Pl}(P v Q)$

d. Show that logically equivalent statements must have the same plausibility.

VI.6. THE DUTCH BOOK. If you are so foolish and your bookie is so clever that you conclude a series of bets with him such that he wins the sum bet *no matter what happens* he is said to have made a *Dutch Book* against you.

The following striking fact is often cited as a justification for the assumption that epistemic probabilities should obey the rules of the probability calculus:

If you count as fair any bet on S if the betting quotient for S equals the plausibility of S, and if you are willing to make any series of bets each of which you regard as fair, then *if your plausibility values do not obey the rules of the probability calculus a Dutch Book can be made against you.*

Against the background of the previous two sections, the reasons for this theorem should be fairly transparent. Let us take the conditions for being a probability in order.

1a: No probability is less than zero.

If you have done the exercises you have already discovered the unpleasant results of taking plausibilities less than 0. Such plausibilities would lead me to regard a bet on P as fair, which would result in a loss whether P is true or false. For example, a plausibility of $-.10$ would lead me to regard the following bet as fair

P	Payoff
T	-110
F	-10

since the betting quotient is $\dfrac{b}{a + b} = \dfrac{10}{(-110) + 10} = -.10$. In general, any plausibility value, ϵ, for S will justify as fair a bet on S with winnings a if S is true and losses b if S is false just in case $\dfrac{a}{b} = \dfrac{1 - \epsilon}{\epsilon}$. (Exercise: Show that this is true.) Thus, if ϵ is negative, it will justify a bet with negative winnings (a) and positive losses (b).

1b. If T is a tautology, $\Pr(T) = 1$.

Any plausibility greater than 1 will get us into what we just discussed because if ϵ is greater than 1, $\dfrac{1 - \epsilon}{\epsilon}$ is negative. Suppose, on the other hand, we underestimate a tautology and give it plausibility less than 1. Then there will be some odds at which we consider it fair to bet against T (i.e., bet on T with negative winnings and negative losses). This is a bet we are sure to regret. For example, suppose we assign a plausibility of .75 to a tautology. This justifies a bet where $a = \$-25$ and $b = \$-75$. My bookie need only do a truth table to collect my \$25.

1c: If P; Q are mutually exclusive, then $\Pr(PvQ) = \Pr(P) + \Pr(Q)$.

We have already learned that if P and Q are mutually exclusive, the sum of bets on P and on Q of equal stakes is a bet on PvQ such that the betting quotient on PvQ is the betting quotient on P plus the betting quotient on Q. Since I am committed to accepting any series of bets, each member of which I consider as fair, my bookie can always compel me to act *as if*

$Pl(PvQ) = Pl(P) + Pl(Q)$ by placing separate bets at equal stakes on P and Q. He makes a bet on P which I consider fair. This means that the betting quotient for P equals what I take to be $Pl(P)$. Likewise with Q at equal stakes. The sum of these bets is a bet on (PvQ) which I would consider fair if and only if I took $Pl(PvQ)$ to equal $Pl(P) + Pl(Q)$. But we are assuming that I take $Pl(PvQ)$ to have *another* value which establishes a different betting quotient for what I take to be a fair bet. I am offering my bookie two separate sets of odds on PvQ! Obviously, the thing for him to do is bet on PvQ at one set of odds and against PvQ at the other, choosing the most lucrative odds and catching me in the middle. For example, suppose the effective fair betting ratio on PvQ resulting from separate bets on P and Q is .6 while the betting ratio I judge directly to be fair is .5. Then I will judge to be fair separate bets on P and Q whose sum will pay me \$4 if PvQ is true and cost me \$6 if PvQ is false. I will also judge a bet to be fair which costs me \$5 if PvQ is true and pays me \$5 if PvQ is false. If my bookie makes all these bets he will win \$1 from me no matter what happens. The whole story is in the following table:

P	Q	Bet on P	Bet on Q	Sum of P; Q	Bet on PvQ	Sum of Bets on P; Q; PvQ
T	F	7	-3	4	-5	-1
F	T	-3	7	4	-5	-1
F	F	-3	-3	-6	$+5$	-1

If you understand the principles at work, you should be able to now show for yourself how this can be done in general.

The moral of the story is important. The Dutch Book being made against me results from my having two different effective betting quotients for PvQ. If we regard the odds that a person is willing to give on P a measure of his degree of belief on P, my problems stem from my having two incompatible degrees of belief. The most extreme case of this disease would occur if I gave a proposition degrees of belief 0 and 1, thus in effect believing with certainty both P and $\sim P$. Thus, if degrees of belief are held to be tied to betting quotients and betting behavior[3] in the manner indicated, the additivity requirement for probability is a kind of *consistency requirement* for degrees of belief. The fact that we

---

[3] That a series of bets may be made if the bets individually are fair.

do use our epistemic probabilities as weights for determining what risks to take in uncertain situations makes this the strongest argument to the effect that epistemic probabilities *are* probabilities.

The argument lacks one step of being complete. We have shown that if you violate the rules of the probability calculus you lay yourself open to a Dutch Book. But we have not shown that compliance with those rules protects you against a Dutch Book. Does it? Stop now, if you do not know, and think about the answer.

The answer is, of course, implicit in section VI.5. When someone makes a Dutch Book against you he entices you into a sum bet such that it is a sum of individual bets which you consider to be fair, but which itself guarantees you a loss in every case. Now if you are dealing in genuine probabilities (rather than some wacky plausibilities with values less than 0 or greater than 1) you will consider the sum bet to be unfair. The expected value of the sum bet is the sum of the products of the payoffs and the corresponding probabilities. Some of the probabilities will be positive; none will be negative. All the payoffs will be negative; so will the expected value.

Now we proved in section VI.5 that if we are using genuine probabilities to define fairness, *if two bets are fair, their sum bet is fair, and if two betting arrangements are fair their sum is fair.* It follows that if you are using genuine probabilities, no sequence of bets you consider fair can constitute a Dutch Book against you.

Exercises:

1. Suppose someone assigns a plausibility to $P \vee Q$ different from the sum of the plausibilities he assigns to P and to Q. Give explicit instructions for making a Dutch Book against him.

2. Show that if you are using genuine probabilities, no sequence of bets you consider fair or favorable can constitute a Dutch Book against you.

3. If you conclude a series of bets such that there is no possible circumstance under which you can win on the sum bet and there is some possible circumstance under which you can lose on the sum bet, we will say that you are the victim of a semi-Dutch Book. (This concept is due to Shimony, as are the following theorems.)

    a. Prove that if you assign probability 1 to any statement other than a tautology, you lay yourself open to a semi-Dutch Book.

    b. Show that if you adhere to the rules of the probability calculus and assign probability 1 only to tautologies, you are not open to a semi–Dutch Book.

Suggested readings

Abner Shimony, "Scientific Inference," in *The Nature and Function of Scientific Theories*, ed. Robert Colodny (Pittsburgh: University of Pittsburgh Press, 1970), pp. 79–172.

Richard Jeffrey, *The Logic of Decision* (New York: McGraw-Hill Book Company, 1965).

VI.7. CONDITIONALIZATION. In the preceding sections we have discussed why *epistemic* probabilities should, in fact, be probabilities. The question of *inductive* probabilities has been left open. In this section, let us approach the question of inductive probabilities from rather a different angle than that of Chapter 1; that is, via the rule of conditionalization.

Let us assume, for the moment, that we are operating within a certainty model. We get to know more and more things with certainty and these items pile up, so to speak, in an ever-growing stock of knowledge. Suppose we have a certain "initial" set of epistemic probabilities; Pr_i; and our senses toss a new item of knowledge, P, into our stock of knowledge. How are we to move to a "final" set of epistemic probabilities, Pr_f, which accommodate our new item of knowledge in a rational fashion? The rule of conditionalization gives this answer:

> **Rule C:** For any statement Q, take its new probability to be its old probability conditional on the new item of knowledge, i.e., $Pr_f(Q) = Pr_i(Q$ given $P)$.

Note that Rule C gives P the new value of 1, a status commensurate with its new-found certainty. Rule C, however, can also effect a change in the epistemic probability of nearly every other statement. What justification is there for making these changes according to this rule? For the answer we must go back to bets once more.

Remember that the sum of bets on $P\&Q$ and on $\sim P$ is, if the stakes are right, a bet on Q conditional on P with a payoff table as represented below:

P	Q	Payoff
T	T	a
T	F	$-b$
F	T	0
F	F	0

This betting arrangement is fair just in case its expected value is zero, that is:

$$a\Pr(P\&Q) - b\Pr(P\&-Q) = 0$$

or:

$$\frac{\Pr(P\&Q)}{\Pr(P\&-Q)} = \frac{b}{a}$$

Note that several sets of probability values will render such a bet fair. For example, if $a = \$1$ and $b = \$2$, then $\Pr(P\&Q) = \frac{2}{3}$ and $\Pr(P\&{\sim}Q) = \frac{1}{3}$ renders the bet fair, as does $\Pr(P\&Q) = \frac{2}{6}$ and $\Pr(P\&{\sim}Q) = \frac{1}{6}$. The first set of values makes $\Pr(P) = 1$ and the second set makes $\Pr(P) = \frac{1}{2}$. In fact, *any* value of P is compatible with our conditional bet so long as it is[4] divided up into $\Pr(P\&Q)$ and $\Pr(P\&-G)$ in the same ratio as b to a.

In other words, the bet is fair just in case:[5]

$$\Pr(P\&Q) = \frac{b}{a+b} \Pr(P)$$

$$\Pr(P\&{\sim}Q) = \frac{a}{a+b} \Pr(P)$$

or

$$\frac{\Pr(P\&Q)}{\Pr(P)} = \Pr(Q \text{ given } P) = \frac{a}{a+b}$$

$$\frac{\Pr(P\&{\sim}Q)}{\Pr(P)} = \Pr({\sim}Q \text{ given } P) = \frac{a}{a+b}$$

If we call $\dfrac{b}{a+b}$ the *betting quotient on Q conditional on* P, which seems reasonable, we can now say that a conditional bet is fair when the conditional betting quotients equal the corresponding conditional probabilities.

Now the interesting thing to notice about all this is the connection between a conditional bet's *remaining* fair under a belief change and that change taking place by conditionalization. Suppose a bet of Q conditional on P with conditional betting quotient $\dfrac{b}{a+b}$ is fair on a

---

[4] If not zero.

[5] Or $\Pr(P) = 0$ or $a = b = 0$.

set of initial probabilities Pr_i. Then $\dfrac{Pr_i(P\&Q)}{Pr_i(P)} = Pr_i(Q$ given $P) =$ $\dfrac{b}{a+b}$. Suppose now that a change to a new set of probabilities is made by conditionalizing on P. Then $Pr_f(P\&Q) = Pr_i(P\&Q$ given $P) =$ $Pr_i(Q$ given $P)$ and $Pr_f(P) = Pr_i(P$ given $P) = 1$. Thus, $\dfrac{Pr_f(P\&Q)}{Pr_f(P)} =$

$\dfrac{Pr_i(Q \text{ given } P)}{1} = \dfrac{b}{a+b}$. So, *if beliefs are changed by conditionaliza-tion on* P, *fair bets conditional on* P *remain fair.*

Very nice. But what's nicer is that conditionization is the *only* method for changing beliefs under these circumstances[6] which has this property. Suppose a bet on Q conditional on P is fair before and after a belief change from Pr_i to Pr_f. Then $\dfrac{Pr_i(P\&Q)}{Pr_i(P)} = \dfrac{b}{a+b} =$

$\dfrac{Pr_f(P\&Q)}{Pr_f(P)}$. If this belief is a result of P becoming *certain*, then $Pr(P) = 1$. Furthermore, $Pr_f(P\&Q)$ must equal $Pr_f(Q)$ for $Pr_f(Q) = Pr_f(P\&Q) =$ $Pr_f(-P\&Q)$ and $Pr_f(\sim P\&Q)$ must be 0, since $Pr_f(P) = 1$. So $Pr_f(Q) =$ $\dfrac{Pr_i(P\&Q)}{Pr_i(P)}$ and the change has taken place by conditionalization. *The only method of changing beliefs such that* P *becomes certain and bets conditional on* P *which are fair remain fair is conditionalization on* P[7]. If this is true, a Dutch Book argument cannot be far away. We have shown that if someone does *not* change his beliefs according to Rule C, the conditional betting quotient which he regards as assuring a fair bet on Q conditional on P will *change* upon the acquisition of P as an item of knowledge. If the bookie knows *how* the bettor will change his betting quotients he is clearly in a position to guarantee a profit if P occurs. By making conditional bets before and after that occurrence, he is essentially betting on Q at two different sets of odds. We have already seen how a bookie can assure himself a profit in such a situation. If $Pr_i(Q$ given $P)$ is less than $Pr_f(Q$ given $P)$, he will bet initially *on* Q conditional on P and finally *against* Q conditional on P. If $Pr_i(Q$ given $P)$ is greater than $Pr_f(Q$ given $P)$, he will bet initially *against* Q conditional on P and finally *on* Q conditional on P. Choosing the stakes correctly, he guarantees himself a profit if P occurs. Furthermore, he breaks even

---

[6] Certainty model.

[7] Excepting cases where $Pr(P) = 0$ or $a = b = 0$.

if P does not occur, since all bets are conditional on P. Only one more small step is required to achieve a proper Dutch Book. The bookie considers the amount, a, that he has guaranteed he will win if P occurs, and makes a side bet of $\frac{1}{2}a$ on $\sim P$, guaranteeing himself net winnings of $\frac{1}{2}a$, come what may.

The virtues of conditionalization having been firmly established, now let us look a little more closely at the workings of the certainty model with the rule of conditionalization. As we travel through life, with our eyes open, we come to know more and more things. This growth of knowledge is represented by the adding of statements $(O_1, O_2, \ldots O_n)$ to our stock of knowledge. Upon the addition of a new item of knowledge, O_n, to our stock of knowledge, we revise our belief structure by passing from old epistemic probabilities, Pr_n to new epistemic probabilities $Pr_{(n+1)}$ by conditionalization on O_n.[8] So for any statement Q, $Pr_{(n+1)}(Q) = Pr_n(Q \text{ given } O_n)$, and

$$Pr_{(n+2)}(Q) = Pr_{n=1}(Q \text{ given } Q_{n+1})$$

but

$$Pr_{n+1}(Q \text{ given } O_{n+1}) =$$

$$\frac{Pr_{n+1}(Q \& O_{n+1})}{Pr_{n+1}(O_{n+1})} =$$

$$\frac{Pr_n(Q \& O_{n+1} \text{ given } O_n)}{Pr_n(O_{n+1} \text{ given } O_n)} =$$

$$\frac{Pr_n(Q \& O_{n+1} \& O_n)/Pr_n(O_n)}{Pr_n(O_{n+1} \& O_n)/Pr_n(O_n)} =$$

$$\frac{Pr_n(Q \& O_{n+1} \& O_n)}{Pr_n(O_{n+1} \& O_n)} =$$

$$Pr_n(Q \text{ given } O_n \& O_{n+1}).$$

So two steps can be compressed into one. First conditionalizing on O_n and moving from the resulting distribution by conditionalizing on O_{n+1} is equivalent to moving from the original distribution by conditionalizing on the conjunction $O_n \& O_{n+1}$. It follows that we can compress any finite number of steps into one.

The set of epistemic probabilities, $Pr_{(n+1)}(Q)$ arrived at by successive conditionalizations on items in a stock of knowledge $(O_1, O_2 \ldots O_n)$

---

[8] We are assuming that $Pr_n(O_n) > 0$, so that the conditional probabilities are well defined.

is identical to the set of probabilities which would be arrived at by conditionalization on the conjunction of all those items of knowledge, $Pr_1(Q$ *given* $O_1 \& O_2 \& \ldots \& O_n)$.

$Pr_1(Q$ given $O_1 \& O_2 \& \ldots \& O_n)$ is a measure of the firmness with which $O_1 \& O_2 \& \ldots \& O_n$ supports Q. Since Pr_1 is not the result of a conditionalization, it does not depend upon the contents of our stock of knowledge. This suggests that we might identify it as the *inductive* probability of the argument:

$$O_1$$
$$O_2$$
$$\cdot$$
$$\cdot$$
$$\cdot$$
$$\frac{O_n}{Q}$$

This identification is vouchsafed by Definition 5 of Chapter I:

> In the certainty model the epistemic probability of a statement is the inductive probability of that argument which has that statement as its conclusion and whose premises consist of all the observation reports which comprise our stock of knowledge.

and it answers the question with which we began this section. *"Inductive probabilities" must, in fact, be conditional probabilities.*

In Chapter I, we started with inductive probabilities and, in the certainty model, defined epistemic probabilities in terms of them. In this section we started with epistemic probabilities and, within the assumptions of the certainty model, recovered inductive probabilities. The approach of Chapter I is that of Carnap; that of this section is associated with the Bayesian school. That they coincide to such an extent is a pleasant and informative fact.

Exercise:

Show that if I move from an initial set of probabilities, first by conditionalizing on P, then on Q, then on R, to a final set of probabilities, then for any statements S and T:

$$\frac{Pr_f(P \& Q \& R \& S)}{Pr_f(P \& Q \& R \& T)} = \frac{Pr_i(P \& Q \& R \& S)}{Pr_i(R \& Q \& R \& T)}$$

(provided the initial probabilities are positive).

VI.8. FALLIBILITY. A man would be rash indeed if his acts of observation all resulted in *certainty* in an associated observation statement. In fact, there are reasons to believe that it is never rational to be certain (in the sense of assigning epistemic probability of 1) of any observational statement. The first reason is Shimony's argument that assigning probability 1 or 0 to any statement not a logical truth or a contradiction respectively lays us open to a quasi–Dutch Book. The other reasons have emerged from much threshing about by epistemologists in this century. The threshing is perhaps not yet over, and no brief summary of its results is likely to be regarded as fair by all sides. Nevertheless, what I take to be the heart of the matter is this: no matter what language we use to describe our observations, the act of observation and the act of believing a sentence attributing a certain character to that observation are distinct.[9] Doing one does not entail doing the other. The link between them is causal, not logical. If I am of sound mind and body, adopt a modest observation language, and am proficient in its use, this causal process may be highly reliable as a means for generating true beliefs. But there is no reason whatsoever to believe that it is infallible.

In such circumstances it is hard to see how it would be reasonable to be certain. Remember that certainty for us means an epistemic probability equal to 1. And if $\Pr(P) = 1$, the bet

P	Payoff
T	0
F	$-b$

is fair no matter how great b is. It is common folk knowledge that someone who says he is certain and who even *feels* certain, may shrink from putting his money where his mouth is. Certainty of the sort in which we are interested involves the willingness to risk *everything* if you are wrong over against no gain if you are right.

If all this has not convinced you that certainty is never warranted for contingent statements, I hope it has at least convinced you that there are *some* times when we wish to change our beliefs under the pressure of new evidence where the certainty model is inappropriate. We need, then, a way of changing our epistemic probabilities when an

---

[9] N.B. "Distinct" means "not identical." It does not mean "disjoint"; it does not mean "unrelated."

observation raises our degree of belief in a statement, without raising it all the way to 1.

Suppose that an observation causes us to change our degree of belief in P from $\text{Pr}_i(P)$ to $\text{Pr}_f(P)$. We might hope that our rule for changing beliefs in such a situation would be such that bets conditional on P and bets conditional on $\sim P$ which are fair before the change remain fair. We saw in section VI.7 that bets conditional on P remain fair just in case the ratio of $\text{Pr}(P\&Q)$ to $\text{Pr}(P\&\sim Q)$ remains constant. And this ratio remains constant just in case the conditional probabilities $\text{Pr}(Q$ given $P)$ and $\text{Pr}(\sim Q$ given $P)$ remain constant. By the same token, fair bets conditional on $\sim P$ remain fair just in case the conditional probabilities $\text{Pr}(Q$ given $\sim P)$ and $\text{Pr}(\sim Q$ given $\sim P)$ remain constant. Thus if fair bets conditional on P and on $\sim P$ are to remain fair:

$$\text{Pr}_f(P\&Q) = \text{Pr}_f(P)\text{Pr}_i(Q \text{ given } P)$$

$$\text{Pr}_f(P\&\sim Q) = \text{Pr}_f(P)\text{Pr}_i(\sim Q \text{ given } P)$$

$$\text{Pr}_f(\sim P\&Q) = \text{Pr}_f(\sim P)\text{Pr}_i(Q \text{ given } \sim P)$$

$$\text{Pr}_f(\sim P\&\sim Q) = \text{Pr}_f(\sim P)\text{Pr}_i(\sim Q \text{ given } \sim P)$$

and

$$\text{Pr}_f(Q) = \text{Pr}_f(P\&Q) + \text{Pr}_f(\sim P\&Q)$$

Putting these together we have:

Jeffrey's Rule: If our new information is represented as a change in degree of belief in P from $\text{Pr}_i(P)$ to $\text{Pr}_f(P)$, then for any statement Q, take:

$$\text{Pr}_f(Q) = \text{Pr}_f(P)\text{Pr}_i(Q \text{ given } P) + \text{Pr}_f(\sim P)\text{Pr}_i(Q \text{ given } \sim P)$$

Notice that Jeffrey's rule is a generalization of Rule C. In the special case where $\text{Pr}_f(P) = 1$, Jeffrey's rule reduces to Rule C. Notice also that Jeffrey's rule can be viewed as a weighted average of Rule C to both P and to $\sim P$. Conditionalizing on P, $\text{Pr}_f(Q)$ would be $\text{Pr}_i(Q$ given $P)$. Conditionalizing on $\sim P$, $\text{Pr}_f(Q)$ would be $\text{Pr}_i(Q$ given $\sim P)$. Averaging these results, weighting the average by $\text{Pr}_f(P)$ and $\text{Pr}_f(\sim P)$, gives us Jeffrey's rule.

We have, then, a viable fallibility model for changing from one set of epistemic probabilities to another. But now it is not so easy as it was in the certainty model to represent an epistemic probability as the result of an inductive probability operating on a stock of knowledge. What observation gives us now is not a set of certain sentences

$0_1, 0_2, \ldots$, but rather a set of observational probabilities, $Pr_0(0)_1$); $Pr_0(0_2)$; .... The observational probabilities are to be the outcome solely of the observation, not of inductive reasoning, for the point is to separate out the factors of observation and induction.

In the certainty model we showed that conditionalizing first on 0_1, then on 0_2, etc., gave the same result as conditionalizing on their conjunction 0_1 & 0_2. Hence the possibility of "factoring" our epistemic probability into a stock of knowledge and a set of inductive probabilities. In general there is no long conjunction and associated probability to which we can apply Jeffrey's rule and get the same set of epistemic probabilities as we would have gotten from successive applications of that rule.

Suppose we attempt to define our epistemic probability as the result of applying Jeffrey's rule successively to each item in our stock of knowledge, taking inductive probabilities as the conditional probabilities in the first step, the resulting epistemic conditional probabilities as conditional probabilities for the next step, and so on. This will not do, for several reasons. The first is that the final result differs depending on the *order* in which the items in our stock of knowledge are taken in this process. This will not work, since the *same data* coupled with the same inductive probabilities should generate the same epistemic probability. The second reason is that at each stage in this process the observational probability is taken as the final probability. In the certainty model if P is observed, it becomes certain. Well and good. Its final probability becomes 1. But if we are sophisticated enough to realize that observations may fall short of certainty, we should be sophisticated enough to realize that observational probability need not be the only factor influencing final probability. Final probability is rather the result of the interaction of observational probability with theories which we may hold on the basis of previous observations.

Let me illustrate. Suppose I see a bird at twilight which I clearly identify as a raven. Because the light is not so good, the probability I can assign to him being black on the basis of that observation is only .8. Suppose further that I hold the theory that all ravens are black and that this theory is buttressed by massive numbers of previous observations. In such a situation the final probability I assign to the statement that the raven is black will be higher than the observational probability, and quite properly so. Otherwise I could disconfirm lots of theories just by running around at night.

All right, my *theory* (which is really the conduit of the force of previous observations) *pulls up* the observational probability in this case.

It is just as easy to think of cases where *it pulls it down*, say where I think I see a water buffalo on the San Bernardino Freeway at 3 A.M.

This interaction between theory and observation, which determines the final probabilities which go into Jeffrey's rule, is a process for which we have no nice analysis. But just such an analysis is needed if we are to explain epistemic probabilities in the fallibility model as the product of a stock of observational knowledge and a set of inductive probabilities.

Exercises:

1. Start with initial probabilities $\Pr(P\&Q) = 1/3$; $\Pr(P\&\sim Q) = .001$; $\Pr(\sim P\&Q) = 1/3$; $\Pr(\sim P\&\sim Q) = 1/3$. Apply Jeffrey's rule taking $\Pr_f(P) = .99$. Calculate $\Pr_f(P\&Q)$; $\Pr_f(P\&+Q)$; $\Pr_f(\sim P\&Q)$; $\Pr_f(\sim P\&Q)$. Now taking this set of probabilities as initial probabilities, apply Jeffrey's rule taking $\Pr_f(Q) = .99$. Calculate the final probabilities of all the same statements.

Now repeat the process in opposite order; that is, first apply Jeffrey's rule on Q at $\Pr_f(Q) = .99$, then on P at $\Pr(P) = .99$. Compare this set of final probabilities with the previous one.

2. Suppose we move from $\Pr_i$ to $\Pr_f$ by applying Jeffrey's rule to P, taking $\Pr_f(P)$ to have some value between 0 and 1. Suppose also that $\Pr_i(S) = 1$ only if S is a tautology and $\Pr_f(S) = 0$ only if S is a contradiction.

   a. Show that $\Pr_f(S) = 1$ if S is a tautology and $\Pr_f(S) = 0$ only if S is a contradiction.

   b. Show that for any contingent statements S and T,

   $$\frac{\Pr_i(P\&S)}{\Pr_i(P\&T)} = \frac{\Pr_f(P\&S)}{\Pr_f(P\&T)}$$

   and

   $$\frac{\Pr_i(\sim P\&S)}{\Pr_i(\sim P\&T)} = \frac{\Pr_f(\sim P\&S)}{\Pr_f(\sim P\&T)}$$

   c. If $\Pr_i(P) = a$ and $\Pr_f(P) = b$, show that first applying Jeffrey's rule to $\Pr_i$ with $\Pr_f(P) = b$ and then applying it to that set of probabilities with $\Pr_f(P) = a$ gets you back to the initial set of probabilities.

Suggested readings

Rudolf Carnap, "Inductive Logic and Rational Decisions," in *Studies in Inductive Logic and Probability*, ed. Carnap and Jeffrey (Los Angeles: University of California Press, 1971) pp. 5–31.

Richard Jeffrey, *The Logic of Decision* (New York: McGraw Hill Book Company, 1965).

Paul Teller, "Conditionalization, Observation and Change of Preference," forthcoming in *Synthese*.

VII

INTERPRETATIONS OF THE PROBABILITY CALCULUS

VII.1. INTRODUCTION. Chapter V showed how the probability calculus is developed in terms of statement probabilities and how conditional probabilities can be interpreted as argument probabilities. Since the logical connectives can be used to construct complex properties out of simple ones just as they are used to construct complex statements out of simple ones, the probability calculus could just as well have been developed in terms of property probabilities.

If we take the presentation of the probability calculus given in Chapter V, interpret p, q, etc., as properties, substitute "universal property" for "tautology" and "null property" for contradiction, we have the probability calculus in terms of properties. Corresponding to each property there is a group or *set* of individuals which possesses that property. For instance, a certain set of physical objects corresponds to the property "weighs over 600 pounds." The set that corresponds to the complex property $-A$ is called the *complement* of the set that corresponds to A. The set that corresponds to the complex property AvB is called the *union* of the set that corresponds to A and the set that corresponds to B. The set that corresponds to the complex property $A\&B$ is called the *intersection* of the set that corresponds to A with the set that corresponds to B. The set that corresponds to a universal property is called the *universal set*, and the set that corresponds to a null property is called the *null set*, or empty set (since no individuals possess a null property).

In mathematical texts the probability calculus is often developed in terms of sets and their complements, unions, and intersections. As far as we are concerned, there is no essential formal difference between this approach and the approach that develops the probability calculus in terms of the properties to which the sets correspond. But no matter how the probability calculus is developed, the calculus itself does not tell us what "probability" means. And until we know what "probabilty" means we shall not know how to determine the basic probabilities.

To give a precise definition of "probability" is to give an *interpretation* of the probability calculus. The definition must of course be such that probabilities obey the rules of the probability calculus. Otherwise it would not be a definition of "probability" but a definition of something else. In other words, the rules of the probability calculus *partially* specify the meaning of the word "probability," and an interpretation of the probability calculus must *completely* specify that meaning, without coming into conflict with the partial specification implicit in the rules of the calculus.

It would be a mistake, however, to assume that there can be only one legitimate interpretation of the probability calculus. The word "probability" is ambiguous; it has more than one meaning. Consequently there is more than one legitimate interpretation of the probability calculus. (Just how many distinct meanings are associated with the word probability is still a matter of debate: in fact, there are a few philosophers who would disagree with my statement that the word "probability" is ambiguous.) In this chapter we will discuss interpretations of the probability calculus and their importance for inductive logic.

VII.2 DESCRIPTIVE AND INDUCTIVE PROBABILITY. The word "probability" has at least two distinct functions in our language. We have concentrated on inductive probability, whose function is to grade the strength of inductive arguments, to evaluate the amount of support that the factual information contained in the premises gives to the factual claim made by the conclusion.

But sometimes the word "probability" is used not to evaluate the support for a given factual claim, but to make a factual claim. If you were to say that the probability of a man born in the twentieth century living to age 60 is $\frac{5}{10}$, you might mean simply that 50 per cent of the men born in the twentieth century will live to age 60. If this is what you meant, then you would be making a definite factual claim. You would be using the word "probability" *descriptively*. Of course, inductive and epistemic probability will come into the picture when we try to *evaluate* this factual claim. For instance, the epistemic probability of the statement "The probability of a man born in the twentieth century living to age 60 is $\frac{5}{10}$" might be quite low on the basis of knowledge of present birth rates, lack of economic progress by underdeveloped nations, and the predilection of the great powers for playing nuclear roulette.

It is generally agreed that the descriptive use of "probability" can be accounted for by the *frequency interpretation* of the probability calculus.[1] The frequency interpretation is an interpretation of the probability calculus as formulated in terms of properties, with conditional probabilities as basic. In Pr(A given B), the property B is called the *reference property*, and the set of all individuals that have that property is called the *reference class*. For example, in Pr(living to age 60 given being a man born in the twentieth century), the reference property is "(being a man born in the twentieth century)," and the reference class is the set of all men born in the twentieth century. The frequency interpretation identifies Pr(A given B) with the *relative frequency* of the property A within the reference class. That is:

$$\text{Pr}(A \text{ given } B) = \frac{\text{The number of individuals having } A\&B}{\text{The number of individuals having } B}$$

(Note that Pr(A given B) has no value when B is null since then the denominator of the fraction is 0.) For example, the probability of a man born in the twentieth century living to age 60 would be equal to the number of men born in the twentieth century who live to the age of 60 divided by the number of men born in the twentieth century.

This definition provides a straightforward interpretation of the probability calculus when the reference class is finite. But if the reference class is *infinite* the relevant fraction makes no sense. We can modify the relative frequency interpretation to handle (denumerably) infinite reference classes, but in order to do so we must first develop the notion of the *limit of an infinite sequence*. Consider the following sequence of X's and O's:

$$XOXOXOXOXOXOXOXOXOXOXOXOXOXOXOXOX \ldots$$

The dots indicate that the sequence is to be continued *ad infinitum* by alternating X's and O's. The sequence can be characterized precisely by the generating function: The kth term of the sequence is X if k is odd and O if k is even. Even though the sequence is infinite, it seems intuitively plausible to say that half of the members of the sequence are X's and half are O's. That is, we *want* to say that the relative frequency of X's within the class of all members of the sequence is $\frac{1}{2}$, as is the relative

---

[1] The frequency interpretation of the probability calculus may not be entirely adequate to account for the use of probability to formulate *laws of nature* as in quantum mechanics. If this is so it may be because laws of nature do not have solely a descriptive function. The status of laws of nature is a matter of intense current debate. The outcome of this debate may very well be that the use of "probability" in formulating laws of nature may be distinct from both its inductive use and its purely descriptive use. See sections VII.3 and IV.13.

frequency of O's. But we cannot say this, for these relative frequencies are not defined. We can, however, give our intuitive judgment currency in the following manner. For each finite initial segment of the sequence, there is a well defined relative frequency of X's:

Finite initial segments in order of increasing length	Relative frequency of X's
X	1
XO	$\frac{1}{2}$
XOX	$\frac{2}{3}$
$XOXO$	$\frac{1}{2}$
$XOXOX$	$\frac{3}{5}$
$XOXOXO$	$\frac{1}{2}$
$XOXOXOX$	$\frac{4}{7}$

This list of relative frequencies of X's in finite initial segments forms another sequence of numbers:

$$1 \quad \frac{1}{2} \quad \frac{2}{3} \quad \frac{1}{2} \quad \frac{3}{5} \quad \frac{1}{2} \quad \frac{4}{7} \; \ldots$$

(This sequence is generated by the function: The kth term of the sequence equals $\frac{1}{2}$ if k is even and $\frac{1}{2}(k + 1)/k$ if k is odd.) This sequence has a very important property. It can be shown that for any finite error tolerance e that is chosen, no matter how small, there is a member of the sequence such that *that member* is within e of $\frac{1}{2}$ and *every subsequent member* is also within e of $\frac{1}{2}$. For example, suppose e is chosen to be $\frac{1}{6}$. Then the difference between the third member of the sequence $\frac{2}{3}$ and $\frac{1}{2}$ is $\frac{1}{6}$, and the difference between any subsequent member of the sequence and $\frac{1}{2}$ is less than $\frac{1}{6}$. If e is chosen to be $\frac{1}{10}$ we would have to go out to the fifth member of the sequence $\frac{3}{5}$. The difference between this member and $\frac{1}{2}$ is $\frac{1}{10}$, and the difference between every subsequent member and $\frac{1}{2}$ is less than $\frac{1}{10}$. No matter how small a positive number is chosen for e, if we go out far enough along the sequence, we will find a member such that the difference between that member and $\frac{1}{2}$ is less than or equal to e and so is the difference between all subsequent members and $\frac{1}{2}$. This property of the sequence is expressed by saying that the limit of the sequence is $\frac{1}{2}$.[2]

---

[2] In general, the limit of an infinite sequence of numbers is a if and only if for every positive error tolerance, e, there is a member of the sequence such that that member differs from a by no more than e, and every subsequent member differs from a by no more than e.

We shall define the limiting relative frequency of the property, being an X, within our original sequence as the limit of the sequence of relative frequencies of X's within finite initial segments. Consequently the limiting relative frequency of X's in our original sequence is $\frac{1}{2}$. This is the cash value of the intuitive judgment that one-half of the members of the original sequence were X's.

Now we may define a relative frequency value for $\text{Pr}(A$ given $B)$ by arranging the individuals that have B (the members of the reference class) in a sequence and utilizing the limiting relative frequency of A within that sequence as the probability value. This suggests the following as an interpretation of the probability calculus for infinite reference classes:

> $\text{Pr}(A$ given $B) =$ The limiting relative frequency of A within a sequence composed of those individuals that have B

Unfortunately there are several reasons why this will not do as an interpretation of the probability calculus. The first reason is that it is possible that some of the relevant sequences do not approach *any* limit. Therefore some of the probabilities that should be defined would not have any value. Secondly the limit of a sequence may depend on the order in which its members are arranged. That is, it is possible for the members of an infinite reference class B to yield one limiting relative frequency of A when they are arranged in a certain sequence, and a different limiting relative frequency, or no limiting relative frequency at all, when they are arranged in a different sequence.[3] Thus the proffered definition might yield two different values for $\text{Pr}(A$ given $B)$, depending on the order in which the members of the reference class are arranged to form a sequence. If the probability calculus is developed in terms of properties, a legitimate interpretation of it must assign one and only one probability value to $\text{Pr}(A$ given $B)$ except in the case where B is null.

The problem can be circumvented by developing the probability calculus with respect to special kinds of infinite sequences and then supplying a limiting relative frequency interpretation. This is a difficult and delicate task, but it has been accomplished. We cannot go into the details here, but they are easily accessible.

---

[3] See Georg Henrik Von Wright, *A Treatise on Induction and Probability* (Paterson, N. J.: Littlefield, Adams & Co., 1960), p. 80.

Suggested readings

Rudolf Carnap, "The Two Concepts of Probability," in *Readings in Philo-sophical Analysis*, ed. Herbert Feigl and Wilfred Sellars (New York: Appleton-Century-Crofts, Inc., 1949), pp. 330–48.

Rudolf Carnap, *Logical Foundations of Probability*, 2nd ed. (Chicago: University of Chicago Press, 1962), chap. II and sec. 106C.

The following are recommended for the advanced student:

Hans Reichenbach, *The Theory of Probability* (Berkeley: University of California Press, 1949).

Richard von Mises, *Probability, Statistics and Truth*, 2nd ed. (New York: The Macmillan Company, 1957).

Reichenbach and von Mises present different solutions to the problem of giving a limiting relative frequency interpretation for infinite refer-ence classes. Von Mises' interpretation requires that the infinite sequences involved be "random" (von Mises, pp. 24–25). For clarification of this important and rather tricky concept of randomness see the following:

Alonzo Church, "On the Concept of a Random Sequence," *Bulletin of the American Mathematical Society*, vol. 44 (1938): 130–35.

Per Martin-Löf, "The Definition of Random Sequences," in *Information and Control* Vol. 9 (1966): 602–619.

VII.3 PROPENSITIES. The remark in footnote 1 of section VII.2, "the frequency interpretation of the probability calculus may not be entirely adequate to account for the use of probability to formulate *laws of nature* . . . " requires amplification. The reason is essentially the same as that which forced us to distinguish between accidental and lawlike sufficient conditions in section IV.13. A *law* to the effect that all A's are B's cannot be fairly represented simply as the factual claim that there happen to be no A's which are non-B's because in certain cases that sort of factual claim can be true *by accident*. (Remember "all coins in Nelson Goodman's pocket on VE day are silver.") Likewise a *prob-abilistic* law that asserts that the probability of a B being an A is $\frac{2}{3}$ cannot be fairly represented simply as the factual claim that the *relative frequency* of B's within the reference class of A's is $\frac{2}{3}$. Surely there can be accidental relative frequencies ($\frac{2}{3}$ of the coins now in my pocket are silver; 100% of the bodies composed of pure gold have a mass of 100,000 kilos). But more important, there can be cases where a law specifies a probability which disagrees with the actual relative fre-quency. Suppose a statistical law, a group of laws gives the result that in a certain special situation A, B will occur $\frac{2}{3}$ of the time. And suppose that this situation only occurs once in the history of the universe. Then the relative frequency must either have the value zero or one.

Why should you believe that such a situation could happen? (1) *Why couldn't it happen?* (2) The reference class, A, for a certain probability attributed by a physical law is specified by certain physical quantities taking on sharp values. Given such a stringent characterization of the reference class, it is quite possible that the reference class could be small. (3) In fact, we have cases where the reference class is *empty* (e.g., ideal gases). Here the relative frequency is undefined.

So probabilistic laws, like non-probabilistic laws, cannot be identified simply as factual statements that all, or some percentage of, A's are B's. Another similarity to non-probabilistic laws deserves mention. Such laws are intimately related to the ascription of *causal* or *dispositional* properties. When we say that a substance is soluble in water we mean that *if it were placed in water it would dissolve.* In ascribing this "iffy" dispositional property we are judging that being placed in water together with the microstructure of the substance in question is a *lawlike sufficient condition* for dissolving. An object may have a dispositional property at one time but not at another. A lump of iron may be magnetizable at one time, but if it is heated red hot it is no longer magnetizable. Likewise the elasticity of a piece of metal can change with temperature, metal fatigue, etc. Likewise, lawlike probabilities can come and go. The probability that an atom will emit a photon in a specified time interval will depend on the energy levels of its electrons, etc. Thus there are *probabilistic properties* that physical systems can come to exhibit and cease to exhibit. They are tendencies more or less strong in one direction or another. Or, to use the most common phrase, they are *propensities.* Most probabilistic scientific laws can be thought of as assigning propensities to states of physical systems.

Suggested readings

Arthur Pap, "Disposition Concepts and Extensional Logic," in *Minnesota Studies in the Philosophy of Science Vol. II*, ed. Feigl, Scriven, and Maxwell (Minneapolis: University of Minnesota, 1958), pp. 196–224.

Karl Popper, "The Propensity Interpretation of Probability," in *British Journal for the Philosophy of Science* 10 (1959): 25–42.

Ian Hacking, *Logic of Statistical Inference* (Cambridge: Basic Books, 1965).

VII.4. THE LOGICAL INTERPRETATION OF PROBABILITY.

The logical interpretation of probability is intended to account for the inductive use of "probability." Accordingly it takes the probability calculus to be formulated in terms of statements rather than properties. On the logical interpretation, conditional probabilities express *logical relations* between the statements involved (although these logical relations are different from the ones encountered in the study of deductive logic). Of course, in one sense it is obvious that, in the inductive use of "probability," $\Pr(q$ given $p)$ must express a logical relation between p and q. That is, it grades the inductive strength of that argument which has p as its premise and q as its conclusion.

However, something additional is meant by the claim that conditional probabilities express logical relations between the statements involved. What is meant is that probability ascription statements, that is, $\Pr(q$ given $p) = a$, are *analytic*; their truth or falsity does not depend on the facts. Under the logical interpretation, the value of $\Pr(q$ given $p)$ depends solely on the meaning of "probability" and the meanings of the statements "p" and "q" and is independent of the facts. Consequently no empirical investigation would be relevant to determining probability values, just as no empirical investigation would be relevant to determining the truth or falsity of the statement $p \vee \sim p$. To put the matter another way, under the logical interpretation, probability ascription statements, $\Pr(q$ given $p) = a$, make no factual claim. In contrast, under the relative frequency interpretation, such statements do make a factual claim about a relative frequency or limit of a relative frequency. Consequently under the relative frequency interpretation, empirical investigation would be relevant to determining probability values.

Those who maintain that a logical interpretation, rather than a frequency interpretation, is necessary to account for the inductive use of probability reason as follows: The inductive probability, $\Pr(q$ given $p)$, grades the evidential support that p gives to q. But if probability statements such as $\Pr(q$ given $p) = a$ are interpreted as making factual claims, then they must be evaluated inductively on the basis of the available evidence, e. To do this, we must use the inductive probability, $\Pr[\Pr(q$ given $p) = a$ given $e]$. But the ascription of a value to this inductive probability will also make a factual claim, and in order to evaluate this factual claim we must know another inductive probability, and so on *ad infinitum*. In order to know the value of an inductive probability, we would have to already know the value of an infinite number of other inductive probabilities. If this is the case, inductive logic could never get off the ground. Thus the proponent of the logical interpretation reasons that the choice of any other interpretation to account for the inductive use of probability leads to an infinite regress.

It should not be thought that, because probability ascriptions are analytic under the logical interpretation, the logical interpretation cannot take account of empirical data. The statement $\Pr(q$ given $p) = a$ will be analytic, but the statements p and q may make factual claims. (Indeed they may be statements about relative frequencies; thus the logical interpretation allows us to use inductive probability in order to evaluate the evidential support that a statement about relative frequency gives another statement, and vice versa.) To put the matter another way, under the logical interpretation, the epistemic probability of a statement, p, depends on just what empirical data is in our stock of knowledge. Thus while $\Pr_a(q$ given $p) = a$ would be analytic, $\Pr_e(q) = a$ would not.

As an illustration of a logical interpretation of probability, we shall use a simple version of an interpretation suggested by Carnap. Consider a simple language that has only two names, a and b, and two (logically independent) properties, F and G. The simple statements of this language are Fa; Fb; Ga; Gb. Complex statements are constructed out of simple statements by means of the logical connectives, as are complex properties. A *state description* is a conjunction containing as its conjuncts each atomic statement or its negation, but not both. The state descriptions for our language are:

1. $Fa\&Ga\&Fb\&Gb.$	9. $\sim Fa\&Ga\&Fb\&Gb.$
2. $Fa\&Ga\&Fb\&\sim Gb.$	10. $\sim Fa\&Ga\&Fb\&\sim Gb.$
3. $Fa\&Ga\&\sim Fb\&Gb.$	11. $\sim Fa\&Ga\&\sim Fb\&Gb.$
4. $Fa\&Ga\&\sim Fb\&Gb.$	12. $\sim Fa\&Ga\&\sim Fb\&\sim Gb.$
5. $Fa\&\sim Ga\&Fb\&Gb.$	13. $\sim Fa\&\sim Ga\&Fb\&Gb.$
6. $Fa\&\sim Ga\&Fb\&\sim Gb.$	14. $\sim Fa\&\sim Ga\&Fb\&\sim Gb.$
7. $Fa\&\sim Ga\&\sim Fb\&Gb.$	15. $\sim Fa\&\sim Ga\&\sim Fb\&Gb.$
8. $Fa\&\sim Ga\&\sim Fb\&\sim Gb.$	16. $\sim Fa\&\sim Ga\&\sim Fb\&\sim Gb.$

Each state description describes a possible state of affairs with respect to what properties are had by a and b. We will say that a statement holds in a given state description if and only if the argument with that state description as its only premise and that statement as its conclusion is deductively valid. For instance, Fa holds in state descriptions 1 through 8. A tautology, such as $Fav\sim Fa$, holds in all state descriptions. A contradiction, such as $Fa\&\sim Fa$, holds in no state descriptions. Now we could give a logical interpretation of the probability calculus as follows:

$$\text{Pr}_a(p) = \frac{\text{The number of state descriptions in which } p \text{ holds}}{\text{The total number of state descriptions}}$$

$$\text{Pr}_a(q \text{ given } p) = \frac{\text{Pr}_a(p \& q)}{\text{Pr}_a(p)}$$

At first glance, this interpretation seems quite plausible. It gives each of the state descriptions equal *a priori* probability. However, Carnap has shown that this interpretation has disastrous consequences for inductive logic. If we accept this interpretation then it will always be the case that $\text{Pr}_a(q) = \text{Pr}_a(q \text{ given } p)$.[4] Consequently the epistemic probability of q will always be equal to its *a priori* probability and will not be influenced by the stock of knowledge, *e*. Any interpretation of the probability calculus which leads to the result that the stock of knowledge is irrelevant to the epistemic probability of a statement cannot account for the inductive use of "probability." We must look elsewhere for a logical interpretation that can account for this inductive use.

Consider those complex properties that are conjunctions, containing as their conjuncts each simple property or its negation but not both. These are called Q properties. The Q properties in the language under consideration are:

Q_1: $F \& G$
Q_2: $\sim F \& G$
Q_3: $F \& \sim G$
Q_4: $\sim F \& G$

Note that in a presence table each Q property is present in exactly one case, and in each case exactly one Q property is present:

	F	G	Q_1	Q_2	Q_3	Q_4
Case 1:	P	P	P	A	A	A
Case 2:	A	P	A	P	A	A
Case 3:	P	A	A	A	P	A
Case 4:	A	A	A	A	A	P

The state descriptions can be easily reformulated in terms of Q properties. For instance, state description 1 becomes $Q_1 a \& Q_1 b$, state description 2 becomes $Q_1 a \& Q_3 b$, state description 3 becomes $Q_1 a \& Q_2 b$, etc.

---

[4] For simple (atomic) statements p and q.

We will call a statement that specifies how many individuals have each Q property a *structure description*. For instance, the following is a structure description: One individual has Q_1 and one individual has Q_4 and no individuals have Q_2 or Q_3. It is possible for more than one state description to correspond to a given structure description. For instance, state descriptions 4 and 13 correspond to the structure description given (since 4 can be reformulated as $Q_1a\&Q_4b$ and 13 can be reformulated as $Q_4a\&Q_1b$). State descriptions that correspond to the same structure description are said to be *isomorphic* to each other. On the other hand, some structure descriptions may have only one corresponding state description. For instance, only state description 1 corresponds to the structure description: Two individuals have Q_1 and no individuals have Q_2, Q_3, or Q_4. The 10 structure descriptions and the state descriptions that correspond to them are tabulated in Table 1.

Table 1

Structure description	Corresponding state description
Two Q_1	1
Two Q_2	11
Two Q_3	6
Two Q_4	16
One Q_1 and one Q_2	3, 9
One Q_1 and one Q_3	2, 5
One Q_1 and one Q_4	4, 13
One Q_2 and one Q_3	7, 10
One Q_2 and one Q_4	12, 15
One Q_3 and one Q_4	8, 14

Now instead of assigning *state descriptions* equal *a priori* probabilities, we shall assign *structure descriptions* equal *a priori* probabilities. In our illustration, we assign each structure description a value of $\frac{1}{10}$. When there is only one state description corresponding to a structure description, we assign it the probability value assigned to that structure description. Thus state descriptions 1, 11, 6, and 16 will each have an *a priori* probability of $\frac{1}{10}$. When more than one state description corresponds to a given structure description, we will divide the probability assigned to that structure description equally among the corresponding state descriptions. Therefore all the other state descriptions in our illustration will have an *a priori* probability $\frac{1}{20}$. Finally we will let the *a priori* probability of a statement be the sum of the *a priori* probabilities of all the state descriptions in which that statement holds. Along these lines we advance the following interpretation of the probability calculus in a given language, L:

> Let S be a state description in L. Let a be the number of structure descriptions in L and b be the number of state descriptions isomorphic to S. Then
>
> $$\Pr_a(S) = \frac{1}{a \times b}$$
>
> For any statement p in L, $\Pr_a(p) = $ the sum of the probabilities if the state descriptions in which p holds. (If p is a self-contradiction, and thus holds in no state description, $\Pr_a (p) = 0$.)

Conditional probabilities are defined in the usual way. This interpretation of the probability calculus avoids the difficulties of the earlier one. It allows our body of knowledge to influence epistemic probabilities in a reasonable manner. However, it is far from perfect, for reasons we will not go into here. The search for a plausible logical interpretation of probability has covered some interesting terrain. If you want to find out about it, try the following:

Suggested readings

Rudolf Carnap, *Logical Foundations of Probability*, 2nd ed. (Chicago: University of Chicago Press, 1962), chap. III and appendix.

Rudolf Carnap, *The Continuum of Inductive Methods* (Chicago: University of Chicago Press, 1952), pp. 1–55.

Jaako Hintikka, "A Two Dimensional Continuum of Inductive Methods," in *Aspects of Inductive Logic*, ed. Hintikka and Suppes (New York: Humanities Press, 1966).

VII.5 THE BAYESIAN INTERPRETATION. Bayesians view the probability calculus as a set of *rules of rationality* or *consistency conditions* for degrees of belief or for the betting behavior correlated with degrees of belief. The reason for calling these *consistency* conditions lies in the Dutch-Book theorems of Chapter VI. Let us call a set of betting quotients on a field of statements *coherent* if it admits of no

Dutch Book. Then Chapter VI showed that any coherent set of betting quotients for an appropriate field of propositions is an interpretation of the probability calculus.

The classical Bayesian position is that the rules of the probability calculus are the *only* such consistency conditions for degrees of belief. This position stands in sharp contrast to that which follows from the logical interpretation. According to the logical interpretation, there is one, analytically true, set of inductive probability statements. A rational set of epistemic probabilities would then be one generated by the true inductive probabilities operating on some stock of knowledge.

There is, however, a middle ground toward which many investigators have been moving. On the logical side it may be conceded that the meaning of inductive probability may not single out just one set of inductive probabilities (confirmation function), but rather a range of them. On the other hand, a Bayesian may admit that the rules of the probability calculus alone are not enough to fully account for the inductive aspects of degrees of belief. Remember Carnap's observation that the probability distribution which assigns each state description equal probability does not allow learning from experience in the following sense. If p is an atomic statement, and we move from the probability distribution in question to a new one by conditionalizing on an atomic sentence different from p, then $\Pr(p)$ will remain the same. Likewise for a long series of such conditionalizations. (A similar result holds for Jeffrey's rule.) This would mean the *only* way of changing our degree of belief in p would be to observe it. Such a set of epistemic probabilities is an inductive *trap* and might be considered irrational on just these grounds. Narrowing down the permissible epistemic probability distributions narrows down the possible inductive probabilities which could have generated them.

Thus, proponents of both the logical and Bayesian views may find themselves pursuing the same enterprise from different standpoints. Both regard the Dutch-Book theorem as showing that rational degrees of belief are probabilities. Both are interested in finding further constraints on rational degrees of belief and rational change of belief.

Exercise:

Speaking of applying the rule of conditionalization to the probability distribution which gives equal probability to each state description, I said that a similar result holds for Jeffrey's rule. What is that result?

Suggested readings

Kyburg and Smokler, eds., *Studies in Subjective Probability* (New York: John Wiley & Sons, Inc., 1963).

L. J. Savage, *The Foundations of Statistics* (New York: John Wiley & Sons, Inc., 1954).

Carnap and Jeffrey, eds., *Studies in Inductive Logic and Probability Vol. I* (Berkeley: University of California Press, 1971).

VII.6. INDUCTION AND THE FREQUENCY INTERPRETATION. Carnap maintains that the logical interpretation accounts for the inductive use of "probability," while the frequency interpretation accounts for the descriptive use. Other writers, notably Feigl and Reichenbach, have maintained that the frequency interpretation can account for both the descriptive and inductive uses of "probability."[5] The thesis that some form of the frequency interpretation can account for the descriptive use is reasonably uncontroversial. But in section VII.4 we presented an argument to the effect that an attempt to account for the inductive use on the basis of the relative frequency interpretation leads to a vicious infinite regress. In this section we shall examine a proposal by Reichenbach for avoiding this regress.

The inductive use of "probability" deals with statements, while the frequency interpretation deals with properties. If the frequency interpretation is to account for the inductive use, a bridge must be built between probability (relative frequency) values for pairs of properties and the values used to appraise the likelihood of statements on the basis of the evidence at hand. Reichenbach defines the *weight* or *predictional value* for a statement, *Fa*, as the limit of the relative frequency of the property, *F*, within a suitably chosen reference class.[6] The justification

---

[5] See Herbert Feigl, "The Logical Character of the Principle of Induction," in *Readings in Philosophical Analysis*, Herbert Feigl and Wilfred Sellars, ed. (New York: Appleton-Century-Crofts, Inc., 1949), pp. 297–304, and Hans Reichenbach, "The Logical Foundations of the Concept of Probability," in *Readings in Philosophical Analysis*, pp. 305–23.

[6] Just how the reference class should be chosen is an extremely difficult question. In many cases, a smaller reference class is to be preferred. The proportion of American males born in the twentieth century who live to age 60 is more relevant to the prediction that I will live to age 60 than the proportion of all people born in the twentieth century who live to age 60. Reichenbach recommends the smallest reference class for which there are reliable statistics. What

for this definition of weight, or predictional value, is that it can be shown, from the definition of the limit,[7] that if we consistently bet on statements having higher weight we shall be correct a greater proportion of times in the long run than if we bet on statements having lesser weight. Since a statement about the limit of a relative frequency makes a factual claim, a statement of the form Weight $(Fa) = k$ will also make a factual claim. In general, we will not know the value of Weight(Fa) since we will not have examined all the members of the reference class. How are we then to evaluate the claim that Weight(Fa) is equal to a certain value, k? In order to evaluate this claim, must we not know the value of Weight (Weight$(Fa) = k$)? And if this value is claimed to be m, how are we to evaluate the claim that Weight(Weight$(Fa) = k) = m$? In order to evaluate this claim, must we not know the value of Weight (Weight(Weight $(Fa) = k) = m$)? Thus we are faced with the threat of the infinite regress referred to in the last section. If we must know an infinite number of higher level weights, in order to rationally select a lower level weight, then the concept of weight could never be applied to the problem of prediction.

Reichenbach meets this challenge by introducing a rule for the rational selection of weights in the absence of knowledge of higher level weights. The rule requires us to take as our estimate of Weight(Fa) the relative frequency of the property F within the observed portion of the reference class. This rule of estimation is held to be rationally justified, in the absence of knowledge of higher level weights, by a version of the pragmatic justification of induction. If the relative frequency of F within the reference class does approach a limit, then our successive estimates based upon application of this rule, while more and more of the members of the reference class are observed, will approach that limit in the long run.[8] If the relative frequency of F within the reference class does not

---

statistics are reliable and thus which reference class is chosen depends on our stock of knowledge, e, in a way that is too complex to go into here. For Reichenbach's explanation of reliable statistics, see his *Theory of Probability*, p. 449. For a general discussion of the problem of the choice of the reference class, see Pap, *An Introduction to the Philosophy of Science*, pp. 186–88.

[7] The proof also requires certain assumptions about the betting situation. The assumption is that we bet on Fg, then Fh, then Fi, etc., where g, h, i, etc., are members of the reference class we chose, arranged in the order used to determine the limit of the relative frequency.

[8] This can be proved from the definition of the limit together with assumptions about the estimating situations similar to those mentioned for the betting situations.

approach a limit, then there is no value of Weight(Fa), and so no rule could find one. Thus Reichenbach takes his rule of estimation to be rationally justified since his rule will in the long run find a value of Weight(Fa) if there is a value for any rule to find.

Once we have estimated a number of weights by applying Reichenbach's rule, we can reapply his rule to these estimates in order to obtain estimates of higher level weights. When we have accumulated enough knowledge to estimate higher level weights, we have, in Reichenbach's terminology, passed from primitive knowledge to advanced knowledge. Once we reach the state of advanced knowledge, the estimates of higher level weights derived from Reichenbach's rule may conflict with the estimates it gives for lower level weights. For example, the rule may estimate Weight(Fa) as k. But on a higher level it may give a very low estimate of the weight of the statement Weight(Fa) $= k$ and a very high estimate of the weight of the statement Weight $(Fa) = z$. In such a case we would revise our initial estimate of Weight(Fa) from k to z. Thus in advanced knowledge our estimates of weights are to be determined by an interplay between various levels of induction.[9]

The estimates of the weights of statements are to be used as values for determining rational decisions. Thus in Reichenbach's system the concept of the estimate of the weight of a statement plays the same role as the concept of the epistemic probability of the statement in the logical interpretation of probability. Both depend on our stock of available knowledge, and both are to be used as values for determining rational decisions. A basic difference between the two approaches is that the logical interpretation provides a starting point for inductive logic by assigning *a priori* probabilities, while the frequency interpretation provides a starting point by relying on Reichenbach's rule of estimation. And the basic problems of induction can be resurrected to plague both approaches. The logical interpretation must answer the question "Why this assignment of *a priori* probabilities rather than another?" The frequency interpretation must answer the question "Why this rule of estimation rather than another?"

---

[9] Reichenbach gives plausible examples of this interplay in "The Logical Character of the Principle of Induction." However, the formulation of precise rules to govern this interplay is a difficult task. This is the problem of formulating an acceptable system of *concatenated induction*. Reichenbach attempts to solve this problem, without complete success, in *The Theory of Probability*.

Suggested readings

Hans Reichenbach, *Experience and Prediction* (Chicago: University of Chicago Press, 1938), sec. V.

Wesley C. Salmon, "Vindication of Induction," in *Current Issues in the Philosophy of Science*, Herbert Feigl and Grover Maxwell, eds. (New York: Holt, Rinehart and Winston, 1961), pp. 245–56. (In this same volume see the comments on Salmon's article by Barker and Rudner and Salmon's reply to Barker.)

Wesley C. Salmon, "Vindication of Induction," *Philosophy of Science*, Vol. 30, No. 3 (1963), 245–56.

Rudolf Carnap, *Logical Foundations of Probability* 2nd ed. (Chicago: University of Chicago Press, 1962), pp. 175–77. (Carnap here offers an informal comparison of his approach to inductive logic with that of Reichenbach.)

The following are recommended for the advanced student:

Rudolf Carnap, *Logical Foundations of Probability*, chap. 9.

Rudolf Carnap, *The Continuum of Inductive Methods* (Chicago: University of Chicago Press, 1952), especially secs. 1 through 7 and 14.

SUGGESTIONS FOR FURTHER STUDY

Too long a list of suggestions for further study is as useless as no list at all. If you have a philosophical interest in probability, the choice of a next book to read is so natural that I am tempted to limit my suggestions to this one:

> Richard Jeffrey, *The Logic of Decision* (New York: McGraw-Hill Book Company, 1965).

This excellent book is full of insight and should be read by any serious student of the subject.

Students interested in the special problems of lawlikeness and confirmation of laws should read the relevant sections of the following classics:

> Nelson Goodman, *Fact, Fiction, and Forecast* (Cambridge, Mass.: Harvard University Press, 1955).

> Carl Hempel, *Aspects of Scientific Explanation* (New York: The Free Press, 1965).

> Israel Scheffler, *The Anatomy of Inquiry* (New York: Alfred A. Knopf, Inc., 1963).

Students interested in the mathematical theory of probability can do no better than to start with:

> William Feller, *An Introduction to Probability Theory and Its Applications* (New York: John Wiley & Sons, Inc., 1966).

The foundations of modern probability theory lie in measure theory. The mathematically sophisticated student may consult the classic source:

> A. Kolmogorov, *Foundations of the Theory of Probability*, 2nd English ed. (New York: Chelsea Publishing Co., 1956).

or:

> Michel Loeve, *Probability Theory*, 3rd ed. (New York: D. Van Nostrand Co., Inc., 1963).

Students interested in statistics should read the book that started a revolution in the field:

Leonard Savage, *The Foundations of Statistics*, 2nd rev. ed. (New York: Dover Publications, Inc., 1972).

Students interested in inductive logic *à la* Carnap should read:

Carnap and Jeffrey, eds., *Studies in Inductive Logic and Probability* (Berkeley: University of California Press, 1971).

INDEX